MASS SHOOTINGS

Recent Titles in
Crime, Media, and Popular Culture

MASS SHOOTINGS

Media, Myths, and Realities

Jaclyn Schildkraut and H. Jaymi Elsass

Crime, Media, and Popular Culture
Frankie Y. Bailey and Steven Chermak,
Series Editors

PRAEGER™

An Imprint of ABC-CLIO, LLC
Santa Barbara, California • Denver, Colorado

Library of Congress Cataloging-in-Publication Data

Names: Schildkraut, Jaclyn, author. | Elsass, H. Jaymi.
Title: Mass shootings : media, myths, and realities / Jaclyn Schildkraut and H. Jaymi Elsass.
Description: Santa Barbara, California : Praeger, [2016] | Series: Crime, media, and
  popular culture | Includes bibliographical references and index.
Identifiers: LCCN 2015036730 | ISBN 9781440836527 (cloth : alk. paper) |
  ISBN 9781440836534 (ebook)
Subjects: LCSH: Mass murder. | Firearms. | Firearms and crime. | Violent crimes. |
  Murder in mass media. | Violence in mass media.
Classification: LCC HV6515 .S35 2016 | DDC 364.152/34—dc23
LC record available at http://lccn.loc.gov/2015036730

ISBN: 978–1–4408–3652–7
EISBN: 978–1–4408–3653–4

20 19 18 17 16   4 5

This book is also available on the World Wide Web as an eBook.
Visit www.abc-clio.com for details.

Praeger
An Imprint of ABC-CLIO, LLC

ABC-CLIO, LLC
130 Cremona Drive, P.O. Box 1911
Santa Barbara, California 93116-1911

This book is printed on acid-free paper ∞

Manufactured in the United States of America

To the victims of these senseless tragedies,
May your legacies live on and your losses inspire change.

Contents

Series Foreword

This volume is part of Praeger's interdisciplinary series on crime, media, and popular culture. Because of the pervasiveness of media in our lives and the salience of crime and criminal justice issues, we feel it is especially important to provide a home for scholars who are engaged in innovative and thoughtful research on crime and mass media issues. The books in the series touch on many broad themes in the study of crime and mass media, including process issues such as the social construction of crime and moral panics; presentation issues such as the images of victims, offenders, and criminal justice figures in the news and popular culture; and effects such as the influence of the media on criminal behavior and criminal justice administration.

One frequently used criminal justice model that illustrates the differences in specific types of criminal justice case processes is the criminal justice wedding cake (Walker, 1998). The wedding cake model describes four layers. At the bottom are misdemeanors: cases that are not serious and that are processed efficiently but that still account for a large percentage of criminal court personnel time because most cases fall within this layer. Another layer of cases that is processed quickly includes less-serious felonies. Although these cases are of more concern because they are serious crimes, court personnel still generally dispose of these with plea bargains and reduction of sentence because they fit common understandings of typical cases. The third layer identified includes serious felony cases. These events are of much higher priority, and court personnel exert considerably more time and effort to process these cases. Unlike the other layers, where cases are resolved amicably through plea bargaining, these cases often test the boundaries of the adversary court system with trials and hotly contested legal hearings. Although it is true that more time, effort, and concern are devoted to resolving cases that fall into this layer, ultimately, just like the misdemeanors and less-serious cases, these cases are quickly forgotten. Any of these cases might be covered in the news, but if any coverage occurs, it generally tends to be light and presented in areas that are not as frequently read or watched.

The final layer of wedding cake cases, however, is quite different. This layer refers to the celebrated cases of the criminal justice system. There are many examples of such cases, but for instance, consider the impacts of the terrorist attacks from September 11, 2001. This case was processed differently by criminal justice professionals, as every available resource was spent to manage the crisis and save evidence related to the attacks. It was the type of event that stops news workers in their tracks—once the first airplane struck the World Trade Center tower, it was clear that no other event that occurred would be important enough to be in the news that day. Newspapers devoted almost all of their space to coverage of the case, other television programming stopped, and the focus was on the events and the analysis of what was occurring. The Internet was overwhelmed by people trying to get any information or breaking news about what was occurring. The impacts on society have been tremendous: new government agencies have been formed, law enforcement priorities have changed, and legislation has been passed. The attacks quickly became part of the public's collective conscious influencing how people view terrorists and nonterrorists, creating fears and concerns about events that are not likely to ever occur again. It is thus important to better understand what events become celebrated cases, how the media describes and defines them, and how they change society.

In this book by Jaclyn Schildkraut and H. Jaymi Elsass, the reader is provided important insights into this phenomenon. It seems all too frequent that American society is punctuated by a mass shooting that brings to our attention extant threats of violence and concerns about safety. When mass shootings occur, there is often widespread concern and discussions among key stakeholders that try to not only explain what motivated an individual to do such a horrible act, but what can be done to prevent others from occurring. For example, although school shootings are statistically rare events, often they will be extensively covered and, as documented here, will result in widespread changes both within and external to schools focused on prevention of future attacks. The target of such discussions is often guns and gun control, opening up widespread debate about why there are so many guns in society, how they are used, and how we can better regulate them.

This is an exciting book for many reasons. First, it examines several public mass shootings that are probably familiar to the reader, but it also includes events that are not as well known but are of particular intrigue. Second, the book does a masterful job of sorting out the rather thorny problem of defining a mass shooting and describing why some events are not considered as such even though they are similar to other mass shootings. Third, it provides an outstanding account of the frequency of such events and thus gives us a better understanding of why some events are covered extensively and others are provided less coverage. That is, although such events are likely to at least get some coverage by news personnel, some events are much more likely to be remembered than others. Fourth, the book provides important insights into why such shootings occur, exploring the causes and explanations for these events. Finally, the book provides a comparative perspective by including mass shootings that have occurred in other countries. Although the United States accounts for a high percentage of the mass shootings that have occurred, it is quite interesting that other countries have experienced similar events, and the authors provide an insightful look at how these events are handled elsewhere.

In this book, Drs. Schildkraut and Elsass provide keen insights for a better understanding of mass shootings. They provide historical context, statistical information, and analysis of how the public has come to understand the nature of these events. Drawing on many of the most significant mass shootings that have occurred, Drs. Schildkraut and Elsass's book tells us what we need to know about the media and these celebrated cases. It is through this understanding and analysis that officials and stakeholders might consider innovative ways to more effectively respond to such terrible crimes.

Frankie Y. Bailey and Steven Chermak
Series Editors

Acknowledgments

We wish to thank our family and friends for their support both on and off this project. We also would like to thank our editor, Jessica Gribble, and Drs. Steve Chermak and Frankie Bailey, for the opportunity to make this project a reality. We also wish to thank Dr. Mark Stafford and Ms. Lauren Johnston for their assistance on this project.

Claims Making and Agenda Setting: How Myths Become Realities

Myth: "Guns don't kill people—Americans kill people."
—Michael Moore (in Chasmar, 2014)

On December 14, 2012, the peaceful town of Newtown, Connecticut, was changed forever when a 20-year-old gunman forcefully entered Sandy Hook Elementary School and opened fire. In his wake, 20 first-grade students and 6 faculty and staff members, including the school's principal, lay dead. The gunman committed suicide as authorities entered the school just five minutes after the first shot was fired. A later investigation of his residence revealed that prior to his rampage, he also had shot and killed his mother while she was asleep (Barron, 2012). Within minutes of the shooting, the story had taken hold of the nation's focus with little foreseeable chance of letting go.

The Sandy Hook shooting was not a new event by any means. Earlier that same week, a gunman opened fire in a Portland, Oregon, area mall, killing two patrons before committing suicide (Johnson & Kovaleski, 2012). In July 2012, a 24-year-old PhD student opened fire in an Aurora, Colorado, movie theater during a midnight screening of *The Dark Knight Rises* (Frosch & Johnson, 2012). A total of 12 people were killed and 58 others wounded before the shooter was apprehended outside the theater by police (Frosch & Johnson, 2012). In February 2012, a student killed three students and wounded several others when he opened fire at a Chardon, Ohio, high school (Tavernise & Preston, 2012). In other years, mass shootings have claimed the lives of victims at a number of different locations, including (but not limited to) during a political speaking engagement in Tucson, Arizona; on college campuses, including Virginia Tech, Northern Illinois University (NIU), Case Western Reserve University, and Florida State University; at the military base Fort Hood in Texas and the Navy Yard in Washington, D.C.; malls in Salt Lake City, Utah, and Omaha, Nebraska; places of worship in Oak Creek, Wisconsin; Colorado Springs, Colorado; and Charleston, South Carolina; and an immigration center in Binghamton, New York.

At varying levels, each of these events has become what Kellner (2003, 2008a, 2008b) calls a "media spectacle," whereby media outlets cover every facet of a particular story in an attempt to win the ratings war. These stories permeate television screens, especially on 24-hour news stations, including CNN, Fox News, and MSNBC, as well as through local and even international media. Headlines are splashed across daily newspapers, and the use of a digital format of these sources via the Internet allows even faster and more frequent story generation. These spectacles essentially take relatively uncommon events, sensationalize them, and make them appear far more commonplace than they actually are (Kellner, 2008a; Surette, 1992). Further, as Surette (1992) notes, the media use these events to "present a world of crime and justice that is not found in reality" (p. 246).

A number of outcomes result from the glorification of mass shootings beyond just ratings. News consumers may express greater fear of crime (see, for example, Chiricos, Padgett, & Gertz, 2000; Kaminski, Koons-Witt, Thompson, & Weiss, 2010; Kupchik & Bracy, 2009), even in response to relatively uncommon events. In some instances, when fear of crime is at its highest, the over-glorification of a particular issue in the media can incite what Cohen (1972) famously refers to as a "moral panic." A moral panic results when members of society believe that their personal values and interests are being threatened (Burns & Crawford, 1999; Goode & Ben-Yehuda, 1994; Springhall, 1999). Further, both the events and the subsequent responses to them have the ability to shape public opinion and drive policy change on a host of issues, including gun control, mental health, and violent media (Beale, 2006; Birkland & Lawrence, 2009; Schildkraut, Elsass, & Muschert, in press; Schildkraut & Hernandez, 2014; Schildkraut & Muschert, 2013; Soraghan, 2000).

SOME MYTHS (TURNED REALITIES) ABOUT MASS SHOOTINGS

In the rush to provide breaking coverage, news producers are faced with a challenge: do they get to the story first, or do they get there correctly? Most often, the former prevails, and as Robinson (2011) notes, accuracy of information is at times traded in exchange for winning the race to the air.

Gatekeepers who traditionally fact-checked information and determined which details were the most important (Gieber, 1964; Janowitz, 1975; Schudson, 1989; Shoemaker, 2006; Surette, 1992) now are bypassed in order to break the story first (Lipschultz & Hilt, 2011). In doing so, however, as Janowitz (1975) points out, personal opinions may override objectivity and facts, and O'Toole (2000) further notes that news reports may provide information that is "not necessarily complete, balanced, or accurate" (p. 3).

In trying to better understand live news coverage, Graber (2006) explains, "media personnel are often the first to try to fit breaking events into a coherent story" (p. 130). This process typically involves three distinct phases of news construction. First, news personnel rush to the scene, interrupt regular programming with breaking news coverage, and present "a flood of uncoordinated bulletins announcing the extraordinary event" (p. 130). As more details become available either from eyewitnesses or from responding law enforcement, the media then work to "correct past errors and put the situation into proper perspective" (p. 133). From there, the media work to place "the crisis into a larger, long-range perspective and to prepare people to cope with the aftermath" (p. 134; see also Shoemaker, 2006).

Even in those instances where the media works to correct their errors, the damage already may have been done. When news broke of the Sandy Hook shooting, for example, initial reports, starting with CNN, claimed that the gunman's brother, Ryan, was the perpetrator and even circulated his Facebook photo (Gilmer, 2012; Hack, 2012; Shontell, 2012; Soliwon & Nelson, 2012). Within five hours of the shooting, despite that he posted several messages on Facebook indicating that he had been at work in New York City at the time of the shooting (Gilmer, 2012; Shontell, 2012; Warren & Stebner, 2012), Ryan Lanza's picture had been splashed across television screens and re-shared on Facebook alone nearly 10,000 times (Soliwon & Nelson, 2012). In addition to the misidentification of Ryan Lanza, media outlets consistently reported that his mother, Nancy, had been a teacher at the school (Gilmer, 2012; Sargent, 2012; Warren & Stebner, 2012), which also was inaccurate (Sedensky, 2013). Early reports further suggested that there were multiple shooters, though this claim similarly was refuted a short time later (Gilmer, 2012; Jany, 2012; see also Colli, 2013; Fuchs, 2013; Sedensky, 2013).

Comparable inaccuracies plagued the Virginia Tech shootings more than five years earlier. Initial reports of the first shooting in the West Ambler Johnston dormitory identified victim Emily Hilscher's boyfriend, Karl Thornhill, as the killer (Kellner, 2008a). Having spent the weekend together, Thornhill had dropped her off less than 15 minutes before she was shot in her dorm room (Virginia Tech Review Panel [VTRP], 2007); he presumably was the last person to see her alive. Though he initially was a person of interest to law enforcement for the first attack, Thornhill later was cleared of any involvement just prior to the second shooting at Norris Hall (BBC News, 2007; VTRP, 2007). Other reports circulated in the wake of the shooting suggested that either the actual gunman and Emily Hilscher had been involved in a romantic relationship gone bad or he simply was infatuated with her (Coultan, Wright, & Gawenda, 2007; "Massacre gunman's deadly infatuation," 2007; Parker, 2012); neither of these claims ever was substantiated.

Such misreporting, however, is not solely associated with shootings occurring in schools. In a 2011 article, Lipschultz and Hilt examined local news television coverage of the 2007 Omaha, Nebraska, mall shooting over four different outlets for several hours after the story broke. Variation in the reporting of the incident was found across each of the news stations—some carried continuous coverage of the shooting while others opted only to break in when verified updates from law enforcement were available (Lipschultz & Hilt, 2011). The stations that elected to maintain continuous coverage relied on shaky, unedited footage and eyewitness accounts. They incorrectly reported the race of the shooter, leading the public to believe that a black male was still on the loose when the shooter, Robert Hawkins, a white male, was dead in the Von Maur department store. Eyewitnesses also named victims before law enforcement had a chance to provide an official release. Conversely, the news station that took the time to fact-check provided "more descriptive rather than interpretive [reporting] in the earliest moments of a breaking news story," which can help to ease the public's concern (Lipschultz & Hilt, 2011, p. 210). In a separate mall shooting, this one occurring in January 2014 in Columbia, Maryland, several news outlets reported that the shooting was domestic in nature (e.g., Almasy, 2014; Stebner, 2014), a claim that was not substantiated by law enforcement at the time (Zurawik, 2014).

These are just a few examples of the inaccuracies that have plagued the reporting of mass shootings. Yet erroneous reporting of "facts" has a considerably longer and more storied history. In one of the most famous examples, the *Chicago Daily Tribune* (now the *Chicago Tribune*) plastered the front page of their November 3, 1948, edition with the headline "Dewey Defeats Truman" (Cosgrove, 2014; Jones, n.d.). Despite pollster predictions that had provided the basis for the headline, Truman went on to win the election and become the 33rd president of the United States. Governor Thomas Dewey of New York, who had been predicted to be the victor, was instrumental in helping Dwight D. Eisenhower get elected four years later, having never been voted into the White House himself. So how do these myths come to be? To answer that question, we first must get to know the people who create them—the claims makers.

CLAIMS MAKERS: WHO THEY ARE AND WHAT THEY DO

Claims makers are those individuals who have the power to shape and spread their ideas about a particular social issue (Spector & Kitsuse, 1977), such as mass shootings. The claims that they make can be either in support of or objection to a particular social issue. Following mass shootings, for example, claims makers weigh in on purported causal factors, such as the availability of guns, lending support either for control measures or for the right to carry (which we discuss later in Chapter 5). Statements such as "if we had more gun control measures in place, then the shooting would not have happened" or "the presence of an armed guard could have stopped the gunman" represent attempts by the claims makers to validate their argument and push their respective agendas (Best, 1987, 1989).

Claims makers have the ability to influence public perception and policy in relation to social problems (Best, 1987). Spector and Kitsuse (1977) identify social problems as "the activities of individuals or groups making assertions of grievances or claims with respect to some putative conditions" (p. 75). More simply stated, these social problems are a product of those with the power or resources to define a particular issue as such. They typically also mirror the interests of the claims makers themselves. Once the claims makers have convinced others that an issue exists, they then can offer solutions to the problem or policies aimed at deriving such a result (Best, 1987). In the wake of mass shootings, for example, a host of different products aimed at preventing the next tragedy are offered, usually representing the financial interests of those companies pushing the devices (see Chapter 7).

There are three key steps to making claims about social problems (Best, 1987, 2006). The first is to identify a problem by offering a definition or, more generally, by giving it a name (Best, 1987, 2006). By defining the problem, claims makers can identify whether it is new or if it has been in existence but not present in the forefront (Best, 1987). In each case, this allows claims makers to create an appearance of originality that will entice citizens to be concerned about the matter at hand (Best, 1987). One technique that claims makers use in highlighting the issue is vagueness or, perhaps more accurately, the absence of a precise definition (Best, 1987). For example, the problem of "terrorism" has undergone many permutations of its definition, particularly after 9/11. In some instances, claims makers also have likened the 1999 Columbine High School shooting to an act of terrorism (Frymer, 2009), thereby creating added confusion in understanding the magnitude of the issue. Similarly, definitions of "mass shootings" also remain vague or problematic, as we discuss in Chapter 2.

The second component in the claims-making process is the use of examples (Best, 1987, 2006). Examples often may be incorporated throughout the discourse of the problem, but claims makers typically will rely on an extreme case or an initial example to underscore their own perceived seriousness of the problem (Best, 1987; see also Barak, 1994). Further, with the use of examples, the details imparted into the public consciousness serve as a general reference for all other events of a similar nature (Tuchman, 1978). For example, President George W. Bush heavily relied on 9/11 as his example for terrorism in his campaign to engage in war. Similarly, claims makers routinely have used Columbine as their main example when campaigning for safer schools and gun control following other incidents of shootings both in and out of schools. In fact, events at airports (the 2013 Los Angeles International Airport [LAX] shooting), malls (Columbia), and movie theaters (Aurora) each have been likened to a "Columbine at" that particular type of location in various news reports. In addition to furthering their view, these types of examples also easily are identified and related with by those people whom the claims makers are trying to convince of the social problem (Best, 1987).

Finally, claims makers similarly attempt to determine the magnitude of the social problem by discussing numeric estimates (Best, 1987, 2006; see also Barak, 1994; Sacco, 1995). By using these figures, claims makers essentially are able to offer some sort of context within which the social problem exists (Best, 1987). The larger the number, the greater the problem, and by extension, the more attention it will receive (Best, 1987). Following incidents of mass murder, regardless of the type (e.g., school shooting or terrorism), claims makers regularly include numeric figures to put the issue into context (see Chapter 4 for further discussion on the statistics associated with mass shootings). The 13 killed at Columbine often are highlighted by claims makers, being used as a point of reference for how horrific the shooting was. By comparison, the 1998 shooting at Westside Middle School in Jonesboro, Arkansas, claimed five lives, but the 2012 shooting at Sandy Hook Elementary School claimed 26 (excluding Nancy Lanza). Not only do these figures emphasize the importance of school shootings as a concern, they also offer a continuum upon which one can compare the events by the number of fatalities in the context of the broader issue (e.g., Sandy Hook is "worse" than Columbine as it was more lethal, and thereby a more severe indicator of the social problem). Regardless, the loss of even one life in these senseless tragedies is one too many.

One of the main complications with claims making is that often these problems are not put into context, but instead blown out of proportion (Best, 1987). Yet, given the reputation or stature of the claims maker, these assertions often are taken as accurate (Best, 2006). Claims making can make atypical problems seem typical, and typical problems seem atypical

(Best, 1987). Not only does this shape public perceptions of a given social problem, but the broader reach also extends to policy implementation, including those focused on increasing social control, prevention, and awareness (Barak, 1994; Best, 1987; Sacco, 1995). The inconsistencies between these myths and their realities are furthered through the language that is used by claims makers to spread their agendas, and ultimately affect the perceived importance of a particular social problem. As Jones, McFalls, and Gallagher (1989) have noted, claims makers have the ability to make "objective molehills" out of "subjective mountains" and vice versa (p. 341).

Claims makers conceptually have been subdivided into two groups—primary and secondary (Best, 1989). Primary claims makers are those who have some sort of exclusive or intimate knowledge about the problem (Best, 1989; Ogle, Eckman, & Leslie, 2003; O'Neal, 1997). This group may include victims, witnesses, or experts in a certain area who call attention to a particular issue and offer potential solutions or simply bring awareness to the problem (Best, 1989; Ogle et al., 2003). Secondary claims makers, on the other hand, are further removed from the issue and simply interpret or disseminate the claims made by the primary claims makers (Best, 1989; Ogle et al., 2003; O'Neal, 1997). Due to the consistent reinterpreting of claims made by the primary group, which also may include politicians and pundits, the media, according to Best (1989), are considered to be secondary claims makers (see also Ogle et al., 2003; O'Neal, 1997).

THE AGENDA-SETTING PROCESS AND HOW THINGS BECOME NEWS

In addition to reflecting what is taking place more generally in society, the media also play a critical role in helping to define social problems (Barak, 1994; Gans, 1979; Tuchman, 1978). Sacco (1995), for example, notes that

> The ways in which the news media collect, sort, and contextualize crime reports help to shape public consciousness regarding which conditions need to be seen as urgent problems, what kinds of problems they represent, and, by implication, how they should be resolved. (p. 141)

This process, known as agenda setting, enables the mass media to highlight particular attributes of a story that call attention to and lend support for claims made by members of the primary group (Entman, 2007; McCombs, 1997; McCombs & Shaw, 1972; Weaver, 2007).

According to McCombs (1997), one of the main goals of agenda setting is to achieve consensus among the public about the importance of a particular topic or issue, and the news media are instrumental in generating this consensus. By highlighting certain stories or issues as important (or perhaps, more accurately, as more important than others), news producers call attention to issues that either directly or indirectly may affect a particular individual or community (Barak, 1994; Entman, 2007; McCombs, 1997; Reese, 2007). Over time, as more coverage is allocated to a particular issue, the importance of that issue for the public is likely to increase, and eventually becomes a priority for the public's agenda (Entman, 2007; McCombs, 1997; Reese, 2007). As this saliency increases, policies aimed at addressing the issue also can be pushed as part of the agenda (Entman, 2007).

As Cohen (1963) summarizes, the media "may not be successful much of the time in telling people what to think, but it is stunningly successful in telling people what to think *about*" (p. 13). By consciously deciding which aspects of a story to highlight or what sources to incorporate, the media play an active role in constructing a certain narrative about a specific topic (Barak, 1994; Gans, 1979; Tuchman, 1978; Weaver & Elliott, 1985). Even still, the shaping of the public agenda may not always be so deliberate but rather an unintended outcome of reporting the news (McCombs, 1997). Given the media's heavy reliance on "official sources," including law enforcement and politicians, the information that news consumers receive largely is shaped by primary claims makers, with the media serving as secondary claims makers (Berkowitz, 1987).

Rarely, however, does the news or public agenda focus on more than a few key issues at a time (McCombs, 1997). This limited focus stems from the fact that very few issues (or even specific events) are able to command the consensus needed to maintain their presence in the forefront (McCombs, 1997). Most often, the media focus on those issues that are the most serious or atypical in nature (Barak, 1994; Sacco, 1995) or those that threaten society's perceived stability (Gans, 1979). At the same time, the limited focus on only a few key issues allows for a more complete, full-bodied discussion to take place in both public and media discourses. When an issue is of perceived importance, the media agenda is impacted as the demand for more information increases (Scheufele & Tewksbury, 2007). Accordingly, how the mass media portray such issues also impacts the way in which the public perceives and understands them (Barak, 1994; Scheufele & Tewksbury, 2007).

In a broader sense, crime news is one way in which the process of agenda setting can be observed. Pick up a newspaper or turn on an evening news broadcast and you will find the same thing that many researchers have observed—up to 50 percent of the coverage will be dedicated to stories about crime (Chermak, 1995; Graber, 1980; Maguire, Sandage, & Weatherby, 1999; Maguire, Weatherby, & Mathers, 2002; Paulsen, 2003; Surette, 1992). Most commonly, the media focus a disproportionate amount of attention on the most serious and violent crimes, even though property crimes are considerably more common (Chermak, 1994, 1995; Graber, 1980; Gruenewald, Pizarro, & Chermak, 2009; Jewkes, 2004; Maguire et al., 1999; Mayr & Machin, 2012; Paulsen, 2003). Due to time and space constraints, however, even the most serious of crimes, such as homicide, will not always garner coverage (Chermak, 1995, 1998; Johnstone, Hawkins, & Michener, 1994; Pritchard & Hughes, 1997; Weiss & Chermak, 1998), and of those that do, the amount varies based on the perceived seriousness of the event (Chermak, 1998; Gruenewald et al., 2009). Schildkraut and Donley (2012), for example, found that of the 223 homicides that occurred in Baltimore in 2010, 60 cases (or nearly 27 percent of the year's homicides) received no coverage in the local newspaper, and considerable variability in the amount and placement of the stories also existed. Other studies exploring newspaper reporting of homicides (e.g., Gruenewald et al., 2009; Johnstone et al., 1994; Paulsen, 2003) have found similar patterns in coverage variability. Ultimately, by focusing on only the most severe or extreme cases, the media give audiences a distorted understanding of crime (Barak, 1994; Maguire et al., 2002; Robinson, 2011).

The process of agenda setting also is evident in the coverage of mass shootings, an even rarer phenomenon than homicide itself. Duwe (2005) examined 909 cases of mass murder more broadly that spanned the twentieth century. His findings indicate that the media disproportionately focus on high-profile cases—those with larger body counts, public locations, assault weapons, and often suicidal offenders—that are indicative of a counterfactual presentation of mass murder. These *event* traits, along with stranger victims, public locations, use of a firearm, and older and/or white offenders, also provide a model of "newsworthiness" through which to examine these events. A more recent examination focused solely on mass shootings reports similar findings (Schildkraut, Elsass, & Meredith, 2015).

The disjointed coverage patterns, coupled with the manner in which the stories are presented, have a number of consequences for the public's understanding of mass shootings, particularly as researchers (e.g., Graber, 1980; Surette, 1992) have found that up to 95 percent of the general public receives most of its information about crime directly from the media. As Duwe (2005) appropriately summarizes,

> The overemphasis placed on the most sensational and least representative mass killings, though hardly surprising, has significant implications for the social construction of mass murder. Because claims makers have uncritically and almost exclusively used news coverage (or more specifically, national news coverage) as the main source of information on mass killings, they have made a number of questionable assertions, not only about long-term trends in the prevalence of mass murder but also about the characteristics of the typical mass killing. (p. 60)

The media's focus on high-profile cases creates an opportunity for claims makers to use these celebrated cases as examples for why these events are social problems, but it also provides an entertainment product for the media to sell (Duwe, 2005). Perhaps, however, the greatest complication to stem from the coverage of mass shootings in the media is that they contribute to a considerable misunderstanding about both individual events and a collective phenomenon.

A PREVIEW OF COMING ATTRACTIONS

So with all of the pull and exposure that the media has, why does this book matter? The answer to that is simple—because not everything that the media tells us as members of society is accurate. News and information about mass shootings are no exception to this, as we have illustrated throughout this chapter. In the quest for answers, especially in the first minutes and hours after an attack, a number of myths are introduced into the public discourse, most often through the media. Some of these will be corrected; others remain unchanged. Most will be in the moment with a limited shelf life, yet a select few myths will resurface repetitively with each new event that occurs.

The goal of this book is to address some of these more common myths that persist in the wake of mass shootings. Each chapter begins with a common myth that is told through the media, either in their portrayal of the event or as offered by other claims makers. These quotes also are representative of the common discourse that we as a nation are exposed to and take part in following a mass shooting, often regardless of its location (e.g., school, mall, movie theater, church, or airport). By combining information from media accounts, governmental reports, and academic research, we are able to paint a more complete and robust understanding of these events and address the myths associated with them.

We start where any story should—at the beginning. In order to understand a problem, we first must know what that problem is. Chapter 2 addresses the challenge of defining mass shootings, which, while seemingly easy, is a complex issue that makes understanding these tragedies even more difficult. Chapter 3 then provides a historical overview of public mass shootings, from the 1800s through more modern events. In Chapter 4, we explore the numbers associated with mass shootings—how often these events occur, where they take place, and who is involved. We also consider how the prevalence (or lack thereof) of mass shootings fits within the larger crime picture in the United States.

Once the stage has been set with a solid understanding of the background of this phenomenon, we then turn our attention to exploring some of the more complex myths associated with mass shootings. Chapter 5 examines causal factors often associated with these events, with particular attention paid to the three main "usual suspects"—guns, mental health, and violent media (Schildkraut et al., in press; Schildkraut & Muschert, 2013). Chapter 6 considers mass shootings in other countries and whether this phenomenon simply is a problem in the United States or a more complex issue around the world. Chapter 7 provides a detailed analysis of the prevention strategies and solutions often offered in the wake of a shooting to deter future attacks.

In the remaining two chapters, we consider the bigger picture of mass shootings and their place within our mediatized society. Chapter 8 examines how the shooters themselves have utilized the media as a tool for spreading their intentions and propaganda. It also considers how members of society reciprocate such communication with the shooters, even after their death. In Chapter 9, our final act, we explore the legacy of mass shootings in our modern society, and consider how these events and their related myths may evolve in years to come.

2

What Is a
"Mass Shooting"?

Myth: "In the two years since the mass shooting in Newtown, Connecticut, there have been at least 94 school shootings including fatal and nonfatal assaults, suicides, and unintentional shootings—an average of nearly one a week."

—Everytown for Gun Safety (2014)

Mass shootings. Rampage shootings. School shootings. Mall shootings. Movie theater shootings. Active shooter events. Over the years, a variety of terms have been introduced in the media discourse to identify acts of mass shootings. These labels, often employed interchangeably, are utilized to put a particular event into context for news consumers, under the presumption that responses to such tragedies will vary based on the number or age of the victims, where the shooting takes place, and who perpetrated the act. In reality, despite that there may be variation in these characteristics as they relate to an event more generally, mass shootings share many more similarities than differences. Still, the idea of "what is a mass shooting," while seemingly easy to answer, has yet to be decided.

News stories, even when live from the scene, often fit into neat packages of reporting, video clips, sound bites, and occasional interviews. The attempt to label mass shootings into separate subcategories allows for easier packaging of information to present to audiences. It simultaneously creates an opportunity for news producers and others in an agenda-setting capacity to target a specific group of consumers. For example, emphasizing that a shooting happened at a school may be skewed toward parents with children in the same demographic or others who work at or attend classes at a similar institution. Repeatedly highlighting that a shooting took place at a mall, a movie theater, or an airport may resonate more strongly with viewers who patronize these types of establishments. Just as beer and car advertisements are more commonly aired during football games as compared to marketing on women's networks, such as *WE* or *Oxygen*, news producers may package their stories about mass shootings with specific audiences in mind to attract the most viewers (and boost ratings).

The question arises, however, whether breaking apart an already rare phenomenon into smaller, more distinct categories achieves this end or instead confuses the issue. Additionally, what happens when that definition is vague, poorly constructed, or crafted in a way that it actually inflates the statistics? The absence of a consistent, generally accepted definition can lead to a host of different issues, the most important of which is an understanding of just how many events are (or are not) occurring each year, which is further discussed in Chapter 4.

In this chapter, we explore various definitions that have been used to explain or identify these events, and how these descriptions have evolved, particularly in the last 16 years following the 1999 Columbine High School shooting. We also consider how these definitions serve to include or exclude certain events, thereby increasing confusion regarding the number of events that actually occur annually. Finally, we offer a proposed working definition for how to categorize these events that will serve as the basis for the remainder of the book.

A "TEXTBOOK" DEFINITION

Throughout the years, a variety of definitions have been offered to categorize mass shootings. This practice first was seen with school shootings, particularly after Columbine catapulted this phenomenon into the national spotlight. Researchers, government agencies, and politicians alike struggled to explain the apparent outbreak of lethal school shootings, both before and after Columbine, which gave way to the appearance that such events were occurring more frequently than they actually were (Schildkraut, Elsass, & Stafford, 2015; see also Rocque, 2012). A number of the definitions proposed, however, have created even greater challenges in putting these events into context due to issues in their construction.

Take, for example, the Centers for Disease Control's (CDC) criteria for case inclusion from their School-Associated Violent Death Study, which has been published annually since 1992 in conjunction with the U.S. Department of Education and the U.S. Department of Justice:

A case is defined as a fatal injury (e.g., homicide, suicide, or legal intervention) that occurs on school property, on the way to/from school, or during or on the way to/from a school-sponsored event. Only violent deaths associated with U.S. elementary and secondary schools, both public and private, are included. (CDC, 2014; see also Anderson et al., 2001, p. 2695)

Individuals relying on the CDC definition often report related statistics as total incidents, despite that the report differentiates between types of events. Furthermore, the parameters for inclusion consider events that occur not only at the institution itself but also at school-related functions or in transit to either location. As such, an incident in which an individual commits suicide at a bus stop using a firearm would be considered a school shooting under the CDC's definition, as would a gang shooting outside of a school (Weiner, 2013) or a shooting during an argument at a high school football game (Stevens, 2014).

In a joint report between the U.S. Department of Education and the Secret Service, researchers focused on what they labeled as "incidents of targeted school violence":

[a]ny incident where (i) a current student or recent former student attacked someone at his or her school with lethal means (e.g., a gun or knife); and, (ii) where the student attacker purposefully chose his or her school as the location of the attack. (Vossekuil, Fein, Reddy, Borum, & Modzeleski, 2002, p. 7; see also U.S. Secret Service, 2002; Warnick, Johnson, & Rocha, 2010)

While Vossekuil and colleagues' (2002) definition is more narrow in scope compared to that of the CDC, there still are several challenges with employing such a description to understanding the rate of mass shootings in schools. First, the definition includes incidents that were carried out with a knife, despite that the majority of perpetrators used firearms (Vossekuil et al., 2002). Additionally, the definition limits the categorizing of the perpetrators to just students, thereby failing to consider other members of the school community or even outsiders assuming the role of the shooter (e.g., Thompson, 2005, which discusses a Texas father found guilty of shooting his son's football coach in the school's field house).

It was not until 2004 that a generally accepted definition of school shootings was formed. In their book *Rampage: The Social Roots of School Shootings*, Newman, Fox, Harding, Mehta, and Roth (2004) defined rampage school shootings as those events that

[t]ake place on a school-related *public stage* before an *audience*; involve multiple victims, some of whom are shot simply for their symbolic significance or

at random; and involve one or more shooters who are students or former students of the school. (p. 50, emphasis added)

Newman and colleagues' (2004) definition has served as the basis for categorizing acts of school shootings since its publication, particularly among researchers in the academic community. In fact, a number of other studies (e.g., Fox & Harding, 2005; Kalish & Kimmel, 2010; Langman, 2009; Levin & Madfis, 2009; Muschert, 2007a, 2007b; Muschert & Ragnedda, 2010; Newman & Fox, 2009; Tonso, 2009; Wike & Fraser, 2009) have relied on this definition. Both Langman (2009) and Muschert (2007a) have used Newman and colleagues' definition to refine our understanding about school shootings as a phenomenon. Muschert (2007a), for example, utilized the definition to differentiate these events from other types of incidents, including mass murders, terrorist attacks, targeted shootings, and government shootings. Langman (2009) proposed a typology to differentiate between school shootings based on the perpetrators themselves, focusing on three different categories—the traumatized, the psychotic, and the psychopathic. For most researchers examining school shootings, the definition presented in *Rampage* remains the uncontested description of the phenomenon.

Although many utilize Newman and colleagues' (2004) definition, new interpretations continue to be forwarded and each is problematic in its own right. Consider the quote from Everytown for Gun Safety (2014) from the beginning of this chapter (see also Feinblatt, 2014). The organization's statistics about school shootings in the two years after Sandy Hook were based on the following criteria:

> Incidents were classified as school shootings when a firearm was discharged inside a school building or on school or campus grounds, as documented by the press or confirmed through further inquiries with law enforcement. Incidents in which guns were brought into schools but not fired, or were fired off school grounds after having been possessed in schools, were not included. (Everytown for Gun Safety, 2014)

Aside from the fact that the statistics were primarily gathered from media accounts rather than official sources, such as police reports (most of which are available through an inquiry under the Freedom of Information Act), a bigger issue lies in the requirement that a gun need only discharge at a school—it does not specifically need to be aimed at a person.

The American Academy of Child and Adolescent Psychiatry (2008) has estimated that over 1 million children, on average, bring a gun into schools each year. It is not unreasonable to presume, based on an inherent margin of error with people, that there would be accidental discharges or unintentional shootings without the motivation typically aligned with school shootings. In fact, in its report, Everytown for Gun Safety (2014) notes that of the 94 shootings in schools following Sandy Hook, 19 (approximately 20 percent) were incidents where a gun was discharged on school property without a single injury or fatality. Six of these discharges were classified as accidental.

Furthermore, the organization's definition is overly broad in that it does not consider motivation or the link of the perpetrators to the school; in its present form, it is the location alone that is the key determinant of whether or not an event is classified as a school shooting. One shooting listed in 2013, which occurred at West Orange High School in Winter Garden, Florida, later was suspected to be gang affiliated (Weiner, 2013; see also Stableford, 2014), though because of its location, it was included in the statistics, thereby inflating the actual number of "school shootings" since Sandy Hook. Still, when such a statistic is put forward by a national organization, such as Everytown for Gun Safety, it can take on a life of its own as it is continually looped through the media discourse (e.g., Carroll & O'Connor, 2014; Stableford, 2014), giving the public an inconsistent understanding of these events' prevalence.

BROADENING THE SCOPE

While society was fixated on the label of "school shootings," other mass shootings taking place at a public location, such as malls, workplaces, restaurants, or even commuter trains, was considered just that—a mass shooting. No special name or definition was used to explain the shooting. It simply was thought of as a single event in which a number of individuals were killed. Further, since the victims typically were older than those involved in school shootings, as were the perpetrators, these events usually failed to garner the same attention in the media (e.g., Schildkraut, Elsass, & Meredith, 2015), though they were more likely to be covered as compared to other homicides.

In more recent years, there has been a call to define mass shootings more broadly. This initiative was particularly common among federal law enforcement agencies, such as the Department of Homeland Security (DHS) and the Federal Bureau of Investigation (FBI). Rather than classifying mass shootings in such vague terminology, however, DHS introduced a new term, "active shooter," which commonly is referenced in more recent media coverage of mass shooting events. According to DHS (2008), an active shooter is

> [a]n individual actively engaged in killing or attempting to kill people in a confined and populated area; in most cases, active shooters use firearm(s) and there is no pattern or method to the selection of their victims. (p. 2)

The definition proposed by DHS has been widely accepted among other government agencies, including the FBI (Blair & Schweit, 2014), the Federal Emergency Management Agency (FEMA, 2013), and the U.S. Department of Education (2013), as well as organizations tasked with response protocols, such as the ALICE Training Institute (n.d.a). The FBI later broadened the scope of the definition slightly to acknowledge situations involving multiple shooters and removed the word "confined" to address events occurring outside of physical structures (Blair & Schweit, 2014).

Most commonly, the term "active shooter" is utilized by law enforcement to describe an event in progress and related response protocols (e.g., the New York City Police Department's 2010 report on risk mitigation). Its use by the media to explain mass shooting events, however, has made the terminology more commonplace in the general discourse. In fact, despite that a number of events may not even fit the description (such as gang shootings), the term "active shooter" has become the latest catchphrase, much in the way that bullying consistently was used as a motivating factor (and buzzword) for Columbine and subsequent school shootings. In many instances, when live coverage breaks or stories are written as a shooting occurs, the media will categorize the event as an "active shooter" scene. If it is later determined that the shooting does not fit this definition and story corrections are not issued, this also can impact the public's understanding of the actual prevalence of events.

Aside from the terminology used in the media discourse, the use of the phrase "active shooter" also has been contested among academics, a debate that even has taken place through the media itself (see Lott, 2014; Sanburn, 2014). One of the main criticisms upon which the debate hinges is the interchanging of terminology between active shooter events and mass shootings. While there has yet to be a universal definition for mass *shootings*, one congressional report identifies such events (specifically those occurring publicly) as

> [i]ncidents occurring in relatively public places, involving four or more deaths—not including the shooter(s)—and gunmen who select victims somewhat indiscriminately. The violence in these cases is not a means to an end—the gunmen do not pursue criminal profit or kill in the name of terrorist ideologies, for example. (Bjelopera, Bagalman, Caldwell, Finklea, & McCallion, 2013, p. 1)

More common, however, is the reliance on the FBI's definition of mass *killings*, which is similar to the description proposed by Bjelopera and colleagues (2013). Specifically, the FBI identifies mass killings as "[a] number of murders (four or more) occurring in the same incident, with *no distinctive time period between the murders*" (Morton & Hilts, 2006, p. 8, emphasis added).

The latter part of the definition is especially important, as it is how the FBI has come to differentiate such events from serial murders, which often involve a cooling-off period between killings. While mass killings usually occur at a single location, spree killings typically take place over a series of locations. Spree killings also do not involve a cooling-off period, which sets them apart from serial murders (Morton & Hilts, 2006).

At the same time, however, the definition of mass killings (mass murder) is itself problematic. In order to qualify as a mass murder under both of these proposed definitions (Bjelopera et al., 2013; Morton & Hilts, 2006), a minimum of four people must be *killed*. If we consider events such as the 1998 shooting at Thurston High School in Springfield, Oregon, in which a 15-year-old killed two classmates and wounded 27 others, or the 2012 shooting at a Chardon, Ohio, high school, where a 17-year-old student killed three and wounded two others, they would not be considered a mass murder or mass shooting. Similarly, the definition excludes events in which the motivations and actions are consistent with deadlier shootings, yet there are no fatalities, such as with the 2007 shooting at a Cleveland, Ohio, alternative high school by a 14-year-old, in which two teachers and two students were wounded but no one was killed. Excluding such events, particularly when motivations and actions are in line with other killings, including Columbine, Virginia Tech, and Sandy Hook, leads to a misunderstanding of the numbers associated with the phenomenon (related to both school shootings and mass shootings more generally).

Critics of the phrase "active shooter" further argue that statistics may be skewed because the terminology is so new (James Alan Fox, as quoted in Sanburn, 2014). Since many studies rely on media accounts, at least in part, to identify shooting incidents, the recentness of the term as a search keyword can limit the results, especially in older years before the phrase was routine in the media vocabulary (Sanburn, 2014). This can translate into missing data as well as the figures being skewed toward more recent years, creating a sense of overinflated statistics and the perception that there is an extreme increase in events when, in reality, the rate may be nearly constant (Lott, 2014; Sanburn, 2014).

That is not to say that an active shooter case cannot evolve into a mass shooting (J. Pete Blair, as quoted in Sanburn, 2014). Some events will; others may not. In order to accurately determine these statistics, however, there has to be an agreed-upon set of criteria for assessment. This often is absent from mass shootings because of the additional terminology, such as "active shooter" or "rampage shooting," that is intermingled into the discourse, both by the media and through the general public. Accordingly, we turn our attention to some considerations related to these criteria to help formulate a new working definition for the phenomenon to help us better understand the prevalence of these events.

WHERE DOES IT FIT?

As noted earlier, not all mass shooting events easily are categorized into carefully constructed parameters of a particular type of event. What do we do when a shooting transcends these classifications? How do we define or label the shooting? What message should be attached when the story is told? Where does the event fit?

In the absence of a precise definition to explain the broader phenomenon of mass shootings, news audiences may be left pondering such questions. Take, for example, the February 12, 2010, shooting at the University of Alabama at Huntsville, in which three people were killed and three others were wounded. At first glance, this event could fit under the umbrella of school shootings, as it occurred at a college campus. Closer examination of the shooting's circumstances, however, casts doubt as to whether this would be the appropriate classification.

School shootings, according to researchers (e.g., Langman, 2009; Muschert, 2007a; Newman et al., 2004), typically are perpetrated by students who either are currently enrolled or formerly attended the school. The perpetrator of the University of Alabama at Huntsville shooting, however, was a professor. Shooter Amy Bishop, who recently had been denied tenure and advised that her teaching contract would not be renewed, opened fire at a department meeting, killing the department chair and two other professors. She attempted to commit suicide, but the handgun she was using malfunctioned. Bishop was arrested outside of the building and later charged with one count of capital murder and three counts of attempted murder. She was convicted in 2012 and sentenced to life in prison without the possibility of parole.

In a similar incident, occurring nearly a month after the University of Alabama at Huntsville shooting, custodian Nathaniel Brown opened fire at Ohio State University. He killed his supervisor and wounded another individual in the shooting before committing suicide. Since, in each case, the university was the place of employment rather than where the perpetrators attended to get an education (what schools typically are considered in purpose), it is plausible that these shootings could better be categorized as incidents of workplace violence.

It also is important to consider those events that involve perpetrators who have no direct ties to the school itself. Consider the following examples.

In 2006, a Vermont man enters an elementary school after murdering his ex-girlfriend's mother and opens fire, killing a teacher and wounding two students. In 2010, a Littleton, Colorado, man opened fire in a middle school after being denied a tour of the campus, wounding two students. That same year, a Tennessee man opened fire and wounded a school's principal and assistant principal, while in California, a man fired shots on a school playground, wounding two students.

Perhaps one of the most notorious examples of "school shootings" being perpetrated by outsiders is the 2006 Amish Schoolhouse shooting in Nickel Mines, Pennsylvania. A milk delivery driver, Charles Carl Roberts, entered the one-room schoolhouse on the morning of October 2. He first ordered all of the boys to leave, as well as several others who were present. The school's teacher was able to escape to a nearby farm, where she called the authorities. After barricading the entrances to the schoolhouse shut, the shooter bound the remaining 10 girls and lined them up along the blackboard. He began firing, killing five of the girls and wounding the others. As Pennsylvania State Troopers closed in on the scene, the shooter committed suicide.

So does each of these events constitute a school shooting? That depends on who you ask. If you asked the U.S. Department of Education or the Secret Service, the answer would be no. In each of these events, the shooter was not a current or former student of the school. Conversely, the CDC and even Newman and colleagues (2004) would be inclined to describe these events as school shootings because of the location. If location is the determinant, however, then gang shootings or those that occur in conjunction with a domestic dispute, for example, theoretically should count as a school shooting if they occur on the grounds of the institution—yet, the *motivation* is different, which is why many, particularly academics, consider these events to be fundamentally different. This consideration is just one of many we will take into account as we continue to work toward a definition of mass shootings.

WHAT ABOUT SPREE SHOOTINGS?

Before we can consider a new definition, however, there is a more recent trend within mass shootings that must be considered—the idea of spree shooting. As noted earlier, the FBI has differentiated between mass murders and spree killings, suggesting that the difference between these two types of events is the number of locations the killing occurs within (Morton & Hilts, 2006). This brings up an important question to consider when crafting our definition. If active shooting events can turn into mass shootings (J. Pete Blair, in Sanburn, 2014), can mass shootings also be spree killings?

Traditionally, when we think about mass shootings, this was not a question that ever needed to be posed. Most events, such as Columbine, or more recent shootings, such as the 2011 shooting at a Tucson, Arizona, political rally or the 2012 shootings at an Aurora, Colorado, movie theater and a Clackamas, Oregon, mall, occur at a single location. In other events, such as those shootings at the University of Texas (1966), Thurston High School (1998), a pair of Atlanta, Georgia, investment firms (1999), and Sandy Hook Elementary School (2012), the perpetrators committed other homicides prior to their rampage. In each of these episodes, the shooters killed their immediate family members—spouses, children, parents, and in-laws living in the home. When classifying the overall event, however, these shootings often are categorized based on the mass killing, with the offender's loved ones considered collateral damage secondary to the main event. Additionally, events such as the 2007 Virginia Tech shooting are considered single incidents, despite that there were multiple active crime scenes (though not at the same time).

But if we think about the idea of spree shootings as those occurring over multiple locations, should these events not be considered as such in addition to being labeled school or mass shootings? This is an important question to consider, particularly as mass shooters are becoming more mobile. On May 23, 2014, for example, 22-year-old Elliot Rodger engaged on a spree of shootings throughout the Santa Barbara, California, community of Isla Vista (CBS News, 2014; Santa Barbara County Sheriff's Office, 2015). After stabbing three people to death in his apartment, he drove to a nearby sorority house near the University of California, Santa Barbara, and shot three female students outside, two of whom died. He next proceeded to a nearby market, where he shot and killed a patron who was standing outside of the establishment. He then drove through the community, shooting several pedestrians and hitting others with his car. During the rampage, Rodger exchanged gunfire with law enforcement on two separate occasions, being hit once by police. The shootings ended when he, after crashing his vehicle into a parked car, committed suicide. A total of 6 people were killed and an additional 14 were wounded.

As word of the Isla Vista shootings broke, the media were quick to label it an active shooter incident, particularly as coverage began airing while the rampage was in progress. Once the event was over, it quickly was relabeled as a mass shooting, consistent with other incidents before it, despite the fact that the shootings occurred over several locations (thereby, in part, excluding it as a mass shooting, which is said by Bjelopera and colleagues, 2013, to occur in a single location). If we consider the earlier definition used by the FBI (Morton & Hilts, 2006), then the event fits the description of a spree shooting—it occurred over multiple locations with no cooling-off period. At the same time, it also meets some (but not all) of the criteria for multiple explanations of mass murder—there were more than four people killed in public places and the victims were chosen indiscriminately (Bjelopera et al., 2013; Morton & Hilts, 2006). Yet regardless of this overlap, the media and the public alike refuse to consider the existence of a gray area, instead opting for a black-and-white, one-or-the-other approach to classifying these events.

In the same vein, another question arises—if a spree shooting also can be considered a mass shooting, as we have demonstrated with the Isla Vista shootings, then why are other events of spree homicide, such as the DC sniper case, not considered a mass shooting? Over a nearly three-week period in 2002, 41-year-old John Allen Muhammad and 17-year-old Lee Boyd Malvo killed 10 and critically wounded 3 others in a series of shootings in the Washington, DC, metropolitan area, including incidents in both Maryland and Virginia (CNN Library, 2014). After their arrest, the shooters were linked to 10 additional incidents in 6 states, resulting in the deaths of 5 people and injuries to 5 others (CNN Library, 2014). Both were convicted of the shootings; Muhammad was executed by lethal injection in 2009 (CNN Library, 2014), while Malvo was sentenced to life in prison without the possibility of parole (Associated Press, 2006d).

At first glance, we can notice several similarities between the Isla Vista shootings and the DC sniper case. Both events meet the criteria of mass murder, as more than four people were killed. The two incidents also were spread across multiple locations. Yet while the Isla Vista shooting is labeled a mass murder, most people consider the DC sniper killings to be a spree shooting incident. So why, when there are more similarities than differences, are these events categorically different?

There are two consistent explanations that arise in the discourse. The first deals with the issue of time—the Isla Vista shooting occurred in a single day;[1] the DC snipers were active for 20 days.[2] Yet the definitions we explored earlier do not help us to clarify this time component. Spree shootings often have no cooling-off period (Morton & Hilts, 2006). Similarly, mass shootings are said to have no "distinctive" time period. But what is a "distinctive" time period? How is this defined? How do we quantify the "cooling-off period" associated with serial killers (see Morton & Hilts, 2006) to know whether or not the DC sniper shootings qualify? Such vague language is endemic in the criminology and criminal justice disciplines, yet without these hard-and-fast rules, it makes it all but impossible to definitively argue that one is a spree killing while the other is a mass shooting.

The second consideration that arises when trying to differentiate is motivation. The DC sniper case often is regarded as a terrorist incident, which would exclude it from Bjelopera and colleagues' (2013) description of mass shootings. According to the U.S. Code (18 U.S.C. § 2331), domestic terrorism in particular is defined as activities with three key characteristics:

- Involve acts dangerous to human life that violate federal or state law;
- Appear intended (i) to intimidate or coerce a civilian population; (ii) to influence the policy of a government by intimidation or coercion; or (iii) to affect the conduct of a government by mass destruction, assassination, or kidnapping; and
- Occur primarily within the territorial jurisdiction of the U.S.

While the overall motivation for the DC sniper killings remains contested, elements of the attacks—particularly the shooters' ransom demand from the government for millions of dollars, which was to be used to train children as a jihad against citizens (Associated Press, 2006d)—clearly fall in line with the U.S. Code's definition of terrorism.

Consider, however, mass shootings such as Isla Vista, Columbine, or Aurora. Each event involves a number of murders, which are illegal. All occur within the United States. It also could be argued that these shootings were intended, in one way or another, to intimidate a particular population (the Santa Barbara community, the entire high school, or patrons at the movie theater or neighboring mall). With this in mind, could it not then be argued that each of these shooters had terroristic motivations, which thereby also would exclude them (and virtually every other mass shooter) from Bjelopera and colleagues' (2013) definition?

THE NEED FOR RECONCEPTUALIZATION

While it may appear that after this review we are left with more questions than answers, the reality is that we actually have the opportunity to clarify some of this confusion through the creation of a more unified, robust definition. Beyond the absence of a precise definition of "mass shooting," any attempts to understand this phenomenon have been plagued by two key problems. First, most terminology and subsequent definitions either are vague or are overly narrow in their construction. Even when certain events share similarities with other episodes, they may be excluded from these categorizations over semantics (e.g., not enough people were *killed*, despite that the total victim counts exceed the threshold of four). This ties in with the second issue—overdiversification. As a result of there not being one generally accepted definition for these events, the media, and the public by extension, consistently classify these events into smaller, more fragmented categories—school shootings, mall shootings, workplace shootings.

These issues form the basis of the need for a reconceptualization of mass shootings. In a recent commentary, Harris and Harris (2012) called for a broadening of Newman and colleagues' widely accepted definition of school shootings and a new exploration of rampage violence, and mass shootings more specifically. As we noted earlier, school shootings have become their own distinct phenomenon, both in the media and even among academic researchers (e.g., Muschert, 2007a). Yet events such as the 2011 Tucson, Arizona, shooting of Congresswoman Giffords, as well as earlier attacks (e.g., the 1984 San Ysidro, California, McDonald's massacre and the 1991 shooting at a Luby's Cafeteria in Killeen, Texas), do not vastly differ from those episodes occurring in schools. The motivations often are quite similar, as is the manner in which victims are selected (at random).

The main differences between these events and Columbine, for example, are the location of the event and the age of the perpetrators as well as the victims. James Huberty, the perpetrator of the San Ysidro McDonald's shooting, was 41 years old at the time of the incident. George Hennard was 35 years old when he opened fire in a Killeen, Texas, restaurant (Brennan, 2012). More recent shooters, such as Jacob Roberts (Clackamas, Oregon, 2012) and James Holmes (Aurora, Colorado, 2012), however, are younger on average, thereby minimizing the importance of the perpetrator's age as a defining characteristic, particularly as the focus broadens beyond school shootings. Similarly, the locations of these shootings often are more of a function of convenience and ease of access, rather than specifically being chosen for some symbolic value.

There are several benefits to broadening Newman and colleagues' (2004) definition of mass shootings as discussed in Harris and Harris's (2012) commentary. First, many of the responses filling the discourse following these events remain the same—gun control, right-to-carry laws, mental health, and violent media (Harris & Harris, 2012; Schildkraut & Muschert, 2013). Uniting different types of events (e.g., school shootings, workplace shootings, and other mass shootings) under a single definition will enable researchers to conduct more focused, and ultimately robust, studies (Harris & Harris, 2012). This joining also may yield more transdisciplinary research—including the social science, public health, and mental health disciplines—which can in turn lead to more productive and effective legislation (Harris & Harris, 2012). Additionally, Harris and Harris (2012) note that because Newman and colleagues' (2004) definition focuses on systems failure rather than individual causality, such transdisciplinary research would lead to a better understanding of rampage violence, which itself is a "multidimensional social problem" (p. 1055). Finally, expanding Newman and colleagues' (2004) definition to encompass all acts of mass shootings is beneficial in that it unites episodic violent crime events, which differ significantly from those that are more common, such as gang violence or even general school violence or homicide (Harris & Harris, 2012).

FORGING A NEW IDENTITY

Now that we have identified the deficiencies in previous descriptions used to explain or identify mass shootings, we are better equipped to craft a definition that offers a more uniform understanding of the phenomenon. It is important to acknowledge that no matter how well crafted a definition may seem, there is no "one size fits all" explanation for a particular phenomenon, such as mass shootings. Inherently, there always will be cases that do not fit the mold. Subsequently, every event is unlikely to be captured, and there is an inherent margin of error that consistently is present. The goal, however, is to be as inclusive and uniform as possible.

Previous explanations highlight four key areas that should be the focus of our new definition. The first of these addresses the number of *victims*, which is critical to understanding the "mass" in mass shootings. Most dictionary definitions of the term qualify "mass" as a large quantity. What these explanations fail to do, however, is clarify the number of victims required for consideration as a "large quantity." The definitions of various terms used to identify mass shootings typically have quantified this term at four or more. As we highlighted earlier, however, these explanations contextualize events as mass shootings only if there are four or more *fatalities*.

We suggest that this needs to be reconsidered in terms of all victims, rather than just those who are deceased. There are a number of reasons why some victims will survive and others do not, including the type or location of their wounds, emergency response time, and distance to the hospital. Additionally, advances in medical technologies mean that more people likely are able to be saved, thereby reducing the number of fatalities and, by extension, minimizing the number of shootings that meet the four death criteria. That aside, the shooter still intended for each to die, regardless of the outcome. The case of the 1998 Thurston High School shooting discussed earlier is a perfect example—why would we not consider an event in which 29 people either were killed or were wounded a mass shooting? Such a question highlights the need to reconsider the concept of "mass" as it is applied to these definitions.

It also is important to consider that victims are not only those who are struck by bullets. Individuals who are present at a specific location when a shooting erupts still are potential targets for a shooter and should not immediately be discredited simply because they were not wounded or killed. Take, for example, shootings that have occurred in malls. At the time of the shootings, there are thousands of patrons at the mall. Theoretically then, the injury and death tolls conceivably could have been much higher. Further, the presence of so many potential targets is qualitatively different from a shooting that may occur in a domestic violence incident, when only the shooter and the victim are present. Accordingly, it may be beneficial to consider victims in a more abstract sense rather than fixating on a specific number or a hard, definitive line when carving out a definition of mass shootings.

The next aspect we must consider is the *location* of the shooting. As we have discerned, it is insufficient to suggest that mass shootings occur at a single location. Instead, we must acknowledge that these events can extend over several different geographical points. More importantly to the definition, these locations must be public, chosen either at random or for their symbolic value. Most often, these sites are chosen out of opportunity and the presence of available targets.

In conjunction with the idea of multiple locations, we must acknowledge that there is a particular *time* component associated with mass shootings. While there may be one or more collateral incidents in the days leading up to the mass shooting, in which other homicides, including those of relatives and friends, can transpire, the main attack typically occurs within a single 24-hour period. This qualification will help us to differentiate attacks, such as the Isla Vista shootings of 2014, from earlier incidents like the DC snipers, despite that we have shown these two assaults do share some similarities.

The final component to consider is the *motivation* of the perpetrators. In many instances, this remains unknown. Few shooters leave clues behind (e.g., Santa Barbara County Sheriff's Office, 2015; Schildkraut, 2012b; Serazio, 2010), but the driving forces behind these acts still could be hazy. A potential motivation for these perpetrators is revenge, though if their victims are a function of opportunity rather than being specifically targeted, it is unclear who the driving force behind the retaliation is. Instead, it may be best to exclude those motivations, such as gang shootings and targeted militant or terroristic activities, which are not characteristic of such events.

Each of these concepts, in a sense, is interrelated. The number of victims is tied to the location, as there will be more victims, both potential and actual, in a public setting. In a public, rather than private, setting, the perpetrators' motivations of symbolism and widespread shock or fear is more clearly realized. This assemblage of motivations links back to the victims and how they are indiscriminately selected. The culmination of these elements ties into the timing of the attack, which, when appearing to occur instantaneously, further highlights the perceived randomness of the shooting.

Together, these four elements form the basis of our definition of mass shootings, which serves as the foundation for the remainder of this book:

A mass shooting is an incident of targeted violence carried out by one or more shooters at one or more public or populated locations. Multiple victims (both injuries and fatalities) are associated with the attack, and both the victims and location(s) are chosen either at random or for their symbolic value. The event occurs within a single 24-hour period, though most attacks typically last only a few minutes. The motivation of the shooting must not correlate with gang violence or targeted militant or terroristic activity.

Our definition seeks to unite various definitions used to explain this phenomenon, extracting those portions that are beneficial to understanding these events while excluding those fragments that are at odds with each other or the general idea of mass shootings. We further base our definition on Newman and colleagues' (2004) widely regarded work, while at the same time expanding it in accordance with Harris and Harris's (2012) call for reconceptualization of how these events are examined.

NOTES

1. Even other shootings that we noted earlier could be thought of as spree shootings (e.g., Thurston High School, the All-Tech Investment Group/Momentum Securities shootings, Virginia Tech, Sandy Hook); these shooters also were at large for a short period of time between killings, often just hours or a few days.

2. Although the shooters were at large for 20 days within the DC metropolitan area (excluding the shootings in other states they were linked to after their arrests), these murders occurred on only 10 of those days (CNN Library, 2014).

3

A History of Public
Mass Shootings

Myth: "Gun rampages have become a staple of modern American life."
—Beauchamp (2013)

Mass murder more generally has been characterized as occurring in the United States in two waves (Duwe, 2004). The first occurred in the 1920s and 1930s, and mainly included acts of familicide. The second wave began in the 1960s, and was on a considerably larger scale than the first. As Duwe (2004) points out, however, the second wave also was characterized by more public mass shootings, beginning with the 1966 Tower shooting at the University of Texas. In the years following, and growing more apparent after 1980, public mass shootings have captured the attention of news consumers across the nation. These events often are considered to be more newsworthy than general homicide or even mass murder more broadly, despite only accounting for less than 1 percent and 15 percent of each, respectively (Duwe, 2000, 2004).

Due to the increasing media coverage of the second wave of mass killings, people often associate this period with the beginning of the mass shootings "epidemic." Yet in reality, public mass shootings as we know them had been occurring for nearly 150 years prior. While the quote above insists that these events are a part of our modern, mainstream culture, the reality is that they have a far more storied history than many people are aware. In this chapter, we explore the evolution of public mass shootings, beginning in the era before the 1900s and advancing through more modern shootings. We also discuss important historical events within the country that helped to shape the newsworthiness of these events as they occurred.

SHOOTINGS PRIOR TO THE 1900s

While there were episodes of mass violence prior to the start of the 1900s, the majority of these incidents did not involve firearms. On July 26, 1764, for example, in what today is known as Greencastle, Pennsylvania, four Native Americans from the Lenape tribe entered the local schoolhouse as part of Pontiac's Rebellion, a response to a broken promise by the British to turn over land to the group (Strait, 2010; Yates, 2013). Inside the schoolhouse were teacher Enoch Brown and 11 students who had just begun their day. The tribesmen clubbed and scalped all who were inside; Brown and 10 of the students died as a result of their injuries. One student, who also had been scalped, survived his injuries and was able to escape after hiding in a fireplace in the school.

Still, there were some incidents that would constitute a mass shooting by more modern standards, particularly in the late 1800s. Like in the latter part of the twentieth century, many of these events appeared to occur more frequently in schools or school-like settings. On July 25, 1880, Charles Berhues approached a Baton Rouge, Louisiana, Sunday school where his cousin, Morris, was an attendant ("General summary," 1880). Upset that Morris had married a girl he liked, Berhues opened fire, killing one and wounding four others, including his cousin. On February 14, 1883, Lem Harbaugh fired shots from a needle gun toward a group of schoolchildren at the Ponca Creek schoolhouse just outside of Florence, Nebraska, killing three ("Criminally careless," 1883). On March 30, 1891, an unknown assailant opened fire, wounding 14 audience members, at a performance at a Liberty, Mississippi, church ("Fourteen persons wounded," 1891). Less than two weeks later, on April 9, James Ferguson fired shots at a group of schoolchildren playing outside in Newburgh, New York ("Fired into a group," 1891). None of the children were killed, though five suffered gunshot wounds. Two years later, gunfire erupted at a high school dance in Plaindealing, Louisiana, on March 26, 1893 ("Shot to death," 1893). Two people were killed and an additional three, including one of the school's teachers, were wounded. On December 12, 1898, five people were shot and killed and two others wounded at a school exhibition in Charleston, West Virginia, after a teacher attempted to calm a disturbance ("Virginia hoodlums," 1898).

The media coverage of these events was nowhere near the barrage of stories we see today when a shooting erupts, primarily since television and the accompanying 24-hour news stations had yet to be invented. Most of the coverage of these events were no more than a paragraph in length, often buried later in the newspaper sections surrounded by advertisements. Even when stories made the front page, they still were minimal in terms of coverage prominence (including length of the story and its placement on the page; see Chermak, 1998; Paulsen, 2003). The majority of the events also were not covered in major national newspapers, though their stories were found in publications outside of the shooting location.

THE TURN OF THE CENTURY AND THE FIRST WAVE OF MASS SHOOTINGS

Following the turn of the century, the United States quickly found itself in a period of turmoil. Though a prosperous time for the country generally, the late 1920s and 1930s brought financial strife for a growing section of the population. By October 1929, the catastrophic collapse of the New York Stock Exchange thrust the country into an economic depression (McElvaine, 2009). This event, coupled with agricultural complications resulting from World War I, including overproduction issues and an inability to export crops to Europe (McElvaine, 2009), made it increasingly difficult for individual farmers to support their families (Duwe, 2004). This coincided with the first wave of mass murder in the twentieth century, which largely consisted of familicides, often occurring on rural farms (Duwe, 2004). Increased stress brought on by economic hardship plaguing the country resulted in fathers who, due to their inability to provide financial security, murdered their families in an effort to protect them from starvation and embarrassment (Shelley, 1981). Though the Great Depression subsided by 1939, the chaos continued as the United States found itself embroiled in World War II (McElvaine, 2009). Even after the end of the conflict, the country would spend decades rebuilding not only its military and economy, but also its culture, in an effort to regain some sense of normality. These events had an impact not only on crime in general in the United States (Shelley, 1981) but also on episodes of mass violence—including mass shootings.

Those events occurring outside of the home often were the result of arguments and involved only the offender and a single victim (e.g., "Boy kills teacher," 1919; "Boy shot by teacher," 1903; "School teacher's crime," 1902; "2 dead in school tragedy," 1908). The most commonly associated event during this time, often confused as a shooting, was the 1927 Bath, Michigan, schoolhouse attack (Ellsworth, 1991). On May 18, farmer Andrew Kehoe, treasurer of the local school board, was in the midst of a foreclosure on his land and also recently had been defeated for a town clerk position. After the loss, he decided to get revenge. On the morning of the attack,

Kehoe first killed his wife. He then detonated bombs at the farm, destroying the house and other buildings. Nearly simultaneously, a series of bombs made from dynamite and pyrotol (an explosive used in combination with the dynamite to create an incendiary blast) detonated under the elementary school in town. Six adults and 38 children were killed at the school; Kehoe committed suicide by detonating a bomb in his truck. The Bath school disaster remains the deadliest act of mass *murder* at an educational institution to date.

Despite that the 1920s and 1930s were a quieter and more peaceful era in the United States, there still were several incidents of public mass shootings, albeit fewer than in later decades. On March 14, 1912, gunfire erupted at the Carroll County courthouse in Hillsville, Virginia ("Outlaws slay," 1912). Family members of Floyd Allen, who was on trial and had just been convicted of interfering with an investigation of another case, proceeded to shoot and kill the judge, prosecutor, and sheriff. Two others, including a witness who had testified in the most recent hearing, also were killed, and seven others, including Allen, were wounded. After several days, some of the shooters were captured ("Allens in Roanoke jail," 1912); others would be taken into custody over the following weeks ("Young Allen bandit," 1912). Floyd Allen ultimately was tried and convicted of the murder of the judge and sentenced to death ("Floyd Allen must pay," 1912).

Like other small business owners during the 1910s, Monroe Phillips suffered from real estate losses during the Great Depression ("Kills five," 1915). On March 6, 1915, after a deal fell through, Phillips killed 5 and wounded 20 others. He was shot and killed by a local lawyer as he continued to try and fire at citizens nearby. Nearly 35 years later, on September 6, 1949, 28-year-old veteran Howard Unruh opened fire on his Camden, New Jersey, block (Berger, 1949). Angered over derogatory comments directed toward him, Unruh killed 13 and wounded others before being apprehended by police.

As with those events occurring in the 1800s, public mass shootings in schools were more likely to be covered than those occurring in other areas, due in part to the aforementioned link to familicide. On January 17, 1913, Manuel Fernandez opened fire at a Honolulu, Hawaii, school, killing one and wounding seven others ("Jealousy causes crime," 1913). John Glover shot and killed two students at a Valdosta, Georgia, schoolhouse before being killed by a retaliating mob that had hunted him down ("Flashes," 1922). On May 6, 1940, junior high school principal Verling Spencer opened fire at a school board meeting in South Pasadena, California, killing four and wounding two others, as well as himself ("Angry principal kills 4," 1940). In one of the first mass shootings in schools carried out by a student, 15-year-old Billy Prevatte opened fire at his Washington, DC–area junior high school on May 4, 1956 (Associated Press, 1956). He killed one teacher and wounded two others before fleeing the school, at which time he was apprehended by two nearby construction workers.

Primary and secondary schools, however, were not the only locations in which mass shootings took place. On August 8, 1919, Roger Sprague, an assistant at the University of California's Chemistry Department, opened fire ("Insane chemist," 1919). Upset about being unable to secure a permanent position, the gunman wounded two professors and attempted to shoot the university's vice president before being subdued and ultimately arrested. On December 12, 1935, Victor Koussow, a former employee of a New York City hospital and medical school, opened fire ("2 doctors slain," 1935). Disgruntled over his termination, he killed the associate dean of the dental school and another associate professor. A third professor was wounded in the shooting. Koussow then committed suicide.

The coverage patterns of these events varied in part from those shootings taking place in the 1800s. Shootings in the new millennium were more likely to get front page coverage. This prominent coverage, however, was contingent upon the story containing some type of sensational element, such as the outlaw backdrop of the Carroll County courthouse shooting or a high-profile medical center in a bustling metropolis. Even still, sensational characteristics were not a guarantee for front page coverage. Stories in the early part of the 1900s also, by and large, tended to be longer than their earlier counterparts. While a few were only a paragraph in length, many of them took full columns with some even continuing on to subsequent pages.

THE 1960s AND THE START OF THE SECOND WAVE

On August 1, 1966, 25-year-old Charles Whitman climbed the Tower at the University of Texas (United Press International, 1966). Armed with a foot locker full of guns, ammunition, and other supplies, he began firing at people who were walking across the university's open quad. Over the next 80 minutes, the shooter killed 15 people and wounded 32 others. Police responding to the incident exchanged gunfire with Whitman from the ground, creating a diversion so that other officers could ascend the Tower and engage the suspect. Ultimately, he was shot and killed by police officer Houston McCoy. The subsequent investigation revealed that prior to his rampage, Whitman had shot and killed his wife and mother in their homes. The shooter also left a suicide note, calling for his body to be autopsied to determine if he had a mental disorder that caused the shooting (Associated Press, 1966a); a malignant tumor found during the examination was believed to have contributed to the attack (Waldron, 1966), though this later was refuted in the final investigative report ("Governor's Committee," 1966).

Unlike other events that had occurred prior, the Tower shooting was unprecedented in its media coverage. For one of the first times, reporters covered the shooting live from the scene ("45 years later," 2011; McDowall, 2012); viewers were able to look on as a frenzied crowd tried to find safety and police officers engaged the gunman. The story was covered across the nation, and the reporting itself departed from that of prior shootings. The *New York Times*, for example, published 17 articles over the first 30 days after the shooting, three of which were front page. They also published multiple articles about the story on a single day, which had not occurred before, as well as referenced back to earlier shootings as a point of comparison (see "Killings recall Unruh rampage," 1966). The story also was big state news—the *Dallas Morning News*, for example, published 68 articles in the same time frame.

The Tower shooting kicked off what many criminologists (e.g., Chester, 1993; Duwe, 2004; Falk, 1990; "The age of mass murder," 1991) categorize as a wave of mass murder. While the majority of these researchers labeled the onset as unprecedented, it has been shown (see Duwe, 2004) that, as discussed in the prior section, the 1920s and 1930s also had uncharacteristically high levels of mass murder, thus negating this label. Regardless, the dynamic patterns of media coverage, coupled with the changing crime landscape in the United States, brought renewed attention to the phenomenon of public mass shootings. The Tower shooting, just two weeks after serial murderer Richard Speck's killing spree, also solidified interest in these types of heinous and sensational crimes ("The age of mass murder," 1991).

The 1960s saw the beginning of an uptick of crime in the United States, for both homicide and other forms of crime. Homicide, for example, was at an all-time low rate of 4.0 murders per 100,000 people in 1957. Between the mid-1960s and the end of the following decade (1979), the homicide rate had more than doubled to 9.7 homicides per 100,000 people—and continued to grow, peaking at 10.2 murders per 100,000 people the following year. Despite a period of slight decline beginning in 1982, the rates again increased starting in the late 1980s, peaking in 1991 before starting to decrease over the remainder of the decade (Fox & Zawitz, 2007).

The changing crime landscape was attributable, at least in part, to a shift in the dynamics of society more broadly (see Cohen & Felson, 1979). More and more people, including women who traditionally had been homemakers, were entering the workforce. As a result, interactions between individuals became more distant and superficial—people were more likely to look out for themselves and less inclined to watch out for others, particularly people they did not know. The change in the workforce dynamics also increased the number of targets (or potential victims) that were available to would-be offenders. Further, changing consumer products created additional opportunities to commit crimes.

Other public mass shootings captured the media spotlight during the 1960s. Just weeks after the University of Texas shooting, 26-year-old Arthur Davis opened fire at a New Haven, Connecticut, apartment on the morning of August 26, 1966 (Borders, 1966). He shot seven people inside, killing five. Just two months later, on November 12, 1966, 18-year-old Robert Smith forced five women and two children to lie face down on the floor of a Mesa, Arizona, beauty school (Associated Press, 1966b). He opened fire, killing four of the women and one of the children; the remaining two people were injured.

During the 1960s, the United States' involvement in the war in Vietnam also escalated, with troop levels increasing each year (U.S. Department of State, n.d.). As the nation's participation in the war continued into the 1970s, public support for such involvement quickly waned (U.S. Department of State, n.d.). Across the nation, protests against the war erupted. One such demonstration took place on May 4, 1970, on the Kent State University campus in Ohio (Kifner, 1970). Believing that a sniper was nearby, the National Guard attempted to break up the crowd of around 1,000 people by gunfire. Four students of the university were killed; eight others were wounded.

While the Kent State event was not a mass shooting as we have defined it here (as the "perpetrators" were not individuals on a mission but rather military personnel exhibiting crowd control), it did pave the way for heightened attention to other public attacks. On November 11, 1971, 21-year-old Larry Harmon opened fire at a Spokane, Washington, church, killing one and wounding four others before being shot to death 30 minutes later by police ("Father blames LSD," 1971). Three years later, on December 30, 1974, 17-year-old Anthony Barbaro killed three and wounded nine others at his Olean, New York, area high school (McFadden, 1974). He was arrested and later convicted; he committed suicide on November 1, 1975 ("Upstate youth," 1975). Less than two months before Barbaro's suicide, on September 11, 1975, 15-year-old James Briggs opened fire at his Oklahoma City high school, killing one and wounding five others (Associated Press, 1975b). On July 12, 1976, 37-year-old janitor Edward Alloway entered the library at California State University-Fullerton (Lindsey, 1976) and opened fire, killing five and wounding two others; he was arrested a short time later at a nearby hotel. Brenda Spencer, a 16-year-old, opened fire at the elementary school across the street from her home on January 29, 1979, killing two and wounding nine others, including a responding police officer ("San Diego girl slays 2," 1979). After a six-hour standoff with police, she was taken into custody.

The 1980s began with a new president—Ronald Reagan—and a new vision—getting tough on crime. Despite strategies aimed at reducing the increasing rates of crime, including mandatory sentencing, habitual offender laws, reduced judicial discretion, and longer prison terms (Mauer, 2001), public mass shootings, like other types of offenses, persisted. On August 20, 1982, 51-year-old Carl Brown opened fire at a garage that had recently serviced his lawn mower (Volsky, 1982). He murdered eight and wounded three others before fleeing the scene; he subsequently was killed after being run over by civilians who had chased him. Abdelkrim Belachheb, an unemployed waiter, killed six and wounded one other at a Dallas, Texas, nightclub on June 29, 1984 (Associated Press, 1984). He later was apprehended after police chased him through the city. Less than one month later, on July 18, 1984, James Huberty opened fire at a San Ysidro, California, McDonald's restaurant (Wright, Levine, & Herron, 1984). The gunman, a recently fired security guard, killed 21 people and injured 19 others in an attack that lasted 90 minutes; the rampage ended when he was shot by a police sniper. William Cruse killed 6 people and wounded 10 others at two Palm Bay, Florida, shopping centers on April 24, 1987, before being apprehended by police (Barron, 1987). On January 17, 1989, 24-year-old Patrick Purdy killed 5 students and wounded 30 other people when he opened fire on students at recess at a Stockton, California, school (Reinhold, 1989).

The 1980s also saw a number of workplace shootings, leading some (e.g., Kelleher, 1997) to classify such events as a "new strain" of mass murders, despite that they were occurring at a similar frequency to earlier decades (Duwe, 2004). Patrick Sherrill, a mail carrier who recently had experienced issues at work, opened fire at an Edmond, Oklahoma, post office on August 20, 1986. He killed 14 people and wounded 7 others; the shooter then committed suicide after police tried to negotiate with him (Applebome, 1986). It was this shooting from which the term "going postal" was coined (Bovsun, 2010). On February 17, 1988, Richard Farley shot and killed seven people and wounded four others at a Sunnyvale, California, military plant before surrendering to police following a standoff (Lindsey, 1988). On September 14, 1989, Joseph Wesbecker, a factory worker in Louisville, Kentucky, who was on disability leave, returned to his employer and opened fire, killing 7 and wounding 13 before committing suicide (Associated Press, 1989a).

THE "EPIDEMIC" OF VIOLENCE IN THE 1990s

As the nation entered the 1990s, so too did its changing landscape of crime. Due in part to President Reagan's "get tough on crime" campaign of the 1980s (Gest, 2001), rates of crime—both violent and property—began to decline. Similarly, the level of violence in schools also began to decrease (Best, 2006; Burns & Crawford, 1999; Wike & Fraser, 2009). This perception was shattered at the end of the decade with a string of high-profile shootings in schools, underscored by the 1999 shooting at Columbine High School.

Columbine was not a new event. In the latter half of the 1990s, other shootings in public schools had occurred in cities across the country, including (but not limited to) Moses Lake, Washington (1996); Bethel, Alaska (1997); Pearl, Mississippi (1997); West Paducah, Kentucky (1997); Jonesboro, Arkansas (1998); and Springfield, Oregon (1998). With each passing event, the public became increasingly aware of random episodes of lethal violence in schools, but still acknowledged that these institutions were among the safest places for children to be. These and similar stories were picked up in the national media, though the coverage (compared to what we know today—e.g., Schildkraut, 2014, or Schildkraut & Muschert, 2014) was sparse (Muschert & Carr, 2006).

On April 20, 1999, everything changed. Columbine High School seniors Eric Harris and Dylan Klebold arrived at their school like every other morning. That day, however, their intention was not to attend classes, but rather to destroy their school and everyone in it. After nearly two years of meticulous planning, the shooters arrived armed with two 20-pound propane tank bombs, nearly 100 other improvised explosive devices (IEDs), such as pipe bombs and Molotov cocktails, and four guns (Columbine Review Commission, 2001). The propane tank bombs, carefully concealed in large duffle bags, were left in the cafeteria with their timers set to detonate at 11:17 a.m.—the time that the shooters had observed the cafeteria was at capacity (roughly 500 students). They then planned to use the firearms—a 9-mm carbine rifle, an IntraTec TEC DC-9 semi-automatic pistol, and two sawed-off shotguns—to shoot any survivors fleeing the blasts.

Despite their preparations, the propane tank bombs failed to detonate. Realizing this, Harris and Klebold approached the school, shooting at everyone they encountered. Several students were killed and others wounded outside of the school. Once inside, the shooting continued, interrupted only by pauses to launch IEDs throughout the building or reload their guns. The shooters methodically wove through the school, with the majority of their time spent in the cafeteria and the library. While in the cafeteria, they fired a number of rounds at the propane tank bombs in an attempt to detonate them (though they were unsuccessful) and discharged additional IEDs. In the library, the pair shot at numerous students who had taken refuge under the tables. Within a matter of minutes, 10 students had been killed in the library, while a number of others were seriously wounded. The shooters also exchanged gunfire with law enforcement that had arrived on scene and were providing cover to paramedics tending to the injured. After the scene had been active for a total of 47 minutes, the shooters committed suicide in the library. In their wake, a total of 12 students and 1 teacher lay dead.

The tragedy at Columbine was a watershed event (Larkin, 2009; Muschert, 2002), and went on to become the archetypal mass shooting to which all other similar events, later including those outside of schools, would be compared (Altheide, 2009; Kalish & Kimmel, 2010; Larkin, 2007, 2009; Muschert, 2007b; Muschert & Larkin, 2007). In a time marred by war in the Middle East (emphasized by the Gulf War at the beginning of the decade); several high-profile incidents of domestic terrorism (including the 1995 Oklahoma City bombing and the 1996 attacks at the Olympics in Atlanta, Georgia); the Heaven's Gate cult mass suicide; the Branch Davidian standoff in Waco, Texas; the 1993 bombing at the World Trade Center in New York City; and the President Clinton-Monica Lewinsky scandal, the Columbine High School shooting was the third most closely followed news story (Pew Research Center for the People & the Press, 1999). The shooting was eclipsed only by the 1992 Rodney King verdict and the 1996 crash of TWA flight 800. Columbine also attracted the most interest of any news story in 1999, with 68 percent of Americans saying they very closely followed accounts of the event. Interestingly, while the 1998 shootings at Westside Middle School in Jonesboro, Arkansas, and Thurston High School in Springfield, Oregon, were the first and second most closely followed stories of their year, respectively, they still were followed by approximately 20 percent less people than Columbine.

While the cultural importance of the event is highly noteworthy, Columbine also represents an important shift in journalistic practices, particularly with respect to how (and how much) such events are covered. When the story first broke, CNN aired over six hours of uninterrupted coverage of the shootings live from Littleton, including footage of SWAT officers rescuing terrified students from the school (Muschert, 2002). The shooting also went on to become the top crime story of evening news broadcasts (Robinson, 2011). In the year following the event, over 319 stories were aired. For the first month alone, the three major news networks—ABC, CBS, and NBC—devoted no less than half of their nightly news airtime to stories about Columbine (Robinson, 2011). This translated to 53 individual stories accounting for nearly four hours of total airtime in just one week (Maguire, Weatherby, & Mathers, 2002). Compared to 13 additional school shootings occurring around the same time as Columbine, the latter garnered nearly equitable coverage as the others combined (Maguire et al., 2002). Such disproportional coverage of school shootings was not limited solely to television news. Newman (2006) found that in the year following the shooting, approximately 10,000 articles were published about Columbine in the nation's 50 largest newspapers.

The Columbine shooting also became a catalyst for a national discourse about a number of issues, from violence in schools to gun control. Apprehension grew over "alienated youth gone horribly wrong," or those who shared traits with the shooters, such as wearing black trench coats or listening to "Goth rock," including Marilyn Manson, Rammstein, and KMFDM (Frymer, 2009, p. 1387; see also Larkin, 2007; Ogle, Eckman, & Leslie, 2003; Springhall, 1999). Schools began implementing zero tolerance policies, requiring students to wear uniforms and carry identification cards, and installing metal detectors (Schildkraut & Hernandez, 2014; Schildkraut & Muschert, 2014). Across the nation, over 800 pieces of gun control legislation were introduced, though only 10 percent passed and were enacted into law (Schildkraut & Hernandez, 2014; Soraghan, 2000). Many of these concerns were exacerbated through sensationalized media coverage, particularly as politicians also took to the press to push their respective agendas. In sum, Columbine changed the way school shootings were perceived, and the discourse transcended Littleton to encompass all suburban high schools (Altheide, 2009; Fox & DeLateur, 2014; Muschert, 2009). These events no longer were perceived as isolated acts of violence, but instead became a cause of national concern (Muschert, 2009).

Despite the attention school shootings received from both the media and the public, they were not the only high-profile mass shootings to occur during the decade. On October 16, 1991, George Hennard drove his truck through the front plate-glass windows of a Luby's Cafeteria in Killeen, Texas. As patrons inside the restaurant approached the vehicle to help the driver, he opened fire with a pair of guns. By the end of his rampage, 23 people had been killed, 10 of whom died from a single gunshot wound to the head (Associated Press, 1991b; Chin, 1991; Hayes, 1991). An additional 20 patrons and employees were wounded in the attack. During the shooting, Hennard exchanged gunfire with law enforcement and was struck twice by police bullets (Associated Press, 1991b). He then retreated to the restaurant's bathroom and committed suicide (Hayes, 1991). The Luby's Cafeteria massacre, as the event has come to be known, remains the deadliest mass shooting in the United States outside of an academic institution. It also is the third most lethal attack in the nation behind the Virginia Tech (2007) and Sandy Hook Elementary School (2012) shootings.

A separate mass shooting occurred on a New York commuter train on December 7, 1993. Just after 5:30 p.m., Colin Ferguson boarded the Long Island Rail Road, which was traveling from Pennsylvania (Penn) Station in New York City to Mineola, at the Jamaica Station in Queens. As the train approached a stop in Garden City, Ferguson rose to his feet and began walking through the car, methodically shooting passengers as he moved (Faison, 1993).

The shooter was tackled as he went to reload his firearm for a third time; passengers held him down until law enforcement arrived to take him into custody. In his wake, 6 people had been killed and an additional 19 were wounded. The shooter later was convicted on a number of counts and was sentenced to six consecutive life sentences, plus additional time for the attempted murders and weapons charges (Associated Press, 2013b). He currently is incarcerated in a New York state penitentiary.

This pair of shootings led two women into a crusade against gun violence, each, however, on opposite sides of the fight. Suzanna Gratia Hupp had been dining with her parents, Al and Ursula, at the Killeen, Texas, Luby's restaurant when the shooting erupted. Al was killed as he charged the shooter in an attempt to end the event; Ursula was killed as she stayed behind with her husband's body (Jankowski, 2011). Carolyn McCarthy's husband, Dennis, and son, Kevin, were on the Long Island Rail Road when that shooting began. Dennis was killed, and Kevin was wounded severely by a gunshot to the head, though he would go on to make a significant (yet incomplete) recovery (Wilson, 2012).

On the day of the Luby's Cafeteria massacre, Hupp had left her firearm locked in her vehicle to comply with Texas's concealed weapons law (Jankowski, 2011). She went on to testify at several key hearings across the country for concealed carry laws, noting that if she had her weapon on her during the shooting, she would have been able to save lives. Hupp later ran for and won a seat in the Texas House of Representatives on this platform, and was one of the state's leading Second Amendment supporters during her 10 years in office. McCarthy, on the other hand, went on to become one of the nation's leading gun control advocates. Following the Long Island Rail Road shooting, she won a seat in the U.S. House of Representatives in 1996, representing New York's 4th District (Associated Press, 2013b; O'Keefe, 2014). She sponsored a number of key pieces of gun control legislation, including the NICS Improvement Amendments Act of 2007, which was signed into law by President Bush in 2008 (H.R. 2640), and several versions of the Gun Show Loophole Closing Act (2011, H.R. 591; 2013, H.R. 141) and Assault Weapons Ban of 2013 (H.R. 437, 2013), which were less successful. Citing failing health, McCarthy retired at the end of the 2014 Congressional session (Associated Press, 2013b; O'Keefe, 2014).

On July 29, 1999, several months after the Columbine shootings, Mark Barton, a fledgling day trader, walked into the office of Momentum Securities in the exclusive Buckhead neighborhood of Atlanta, Georgia (Sack, 1999). Disgruntled over significant financial losses he had incurred through his stock market dealings, Barton opened fire, killing four people. He then crossed the street to All-Tech Investment Group, a company with whom he had previously traded but was cut off from several months earlier, and killed five people before fleeing. An additional 12 people were wounded in the pair of shootings. The shooter was spotted approximately five hours later driving north on Interstate 75 and was cornered by police ("Georgia killer's note," 1999). He committed suicide with a pair of handguns as they closed in. A later search of his home revealed that prior to his rampage, Barton had killed his wife, Leanne, and his two children.

Barton's rampage was one of the first major mass shootings following Columbine, and the first to take place outside of a school, though another school shooting in neighboring Conyers, Georgia, had occurred one month to the day after the shooting in Littleton. Within approximately 50 minutes of the start of the shootings, major cable news networks—beginning with MSNBC—had broken into coverage of the story ("Shootings in Atlanta," 1999). Following the precedent that had been set earlier with Columbine, the reporting lasted for hours. Increased attention was not limited solely to television broadcasts, however. The *New York Times* published 17 stories, excluding letters to the editor, in the first 30 days after the shootings. Four of those stories cross-referenced the Columbine shootings.

MASS SHOOTINGS IN THE NEW MILLENNIUM

As the country entered the 2000s, the lasting effects of the Columbine shooting seemingly followed. Still reeling from the tragedy, it appeared that both national and media focuses were on episodes of lethal violence in schools. In 2001, a pair of school shootings in the San Diego, California, school district seemed to rivet the country. On March 5, 2001, 15-year-old Charles "Andy" Williams entered Santana High School in Santee and opened fire (Purdum, 2001a). He killed 2 students and wounded 13 others before being apprehended by police. Just over two weeks later, on March 22, 18-year-old Jason Hoffman entered Granite Hills High School in nearby El Cajon, where he had been a student. He wounded five people before being taken into police custody (Purdum, 2001b).

Each time a new shooting occurred, the media took to the airwaves with live, uninterrupted coverage. In 2003, a freshman at Ricori High School in Cold Spring, Minnesota, killed one student and wounded a second before being taken into police custody ("Student shoots two," 2003). In 2005, a student at Red Lake High School in northern Minnesota opened fire on his school, killing seven and wounding five others. Prior to his rampage, the shooter also had killed his grandfather and his companion (Wilgoren, 2005b). Later that same year, a student at Campbell County High School in Jacksboro, Tennessee, killed the school's assistant principal and wounded two other administrators before being apprehended by the police (Goodman, 2005). An eighth grader opened fire in his Reno, Nevada, middle school in 2006, wounding two before being arrested (Associated Press, 2006b). In October 2006, a milk delivery driver entered the one-room Amish school-house in Nickel Mines, Pennsylvania, and lined all of the female students against the blackboard after releasing the males and adults (Holusha, 2006). He shot each of the 10 girls execution style, killing five and wounding the others, before committing suicide as law enforcement prepared to enter the building. Despite the number of incidents of school shootings after Colum-bine, no single event had garnered close to the same amount of attention, even when compared to the former shooting.

In 2007, as Fox and Savage (2009) note, mass murder graduated to college in what remains, to date, the deadliest mass shooting, both in a school and in the nation more generally. On April 16, Virginia Tech senior Seung-Hui Cho entered the West Ambler Johnston (WAJ) Hall dormitory, where he shot and killed freshman Emily Hilscher and senior Ryan Clark (Virginia Tech Review Panel [VTRP], 2007). After two hours, he entered Norris Hall on the oppo-site side of the campus, a building that housed the university's Engineering Department, and chained the doors shut. He made his way to the second floor of the building and opened fire, killing 25 students and 5 faculty mem-bers in a 10-minute span. An additional 23 were wounded. As law enforce-ment entered the building, the shooter committed suicide.

Despite being likened to a "Columbine at a college," the shootings at Vir-ginia Tech identified a number of key issues, particularly for institutions of higher education across the country (Glum, 2015). One of the most criti-cized areas after the event was the use of the campus's emergency notification system (Schildkraut, McKenna, & Elsass, 2015; VTRP, 2007). On the day of the shooting, text message notifications were not yet available; Virginia Tech relied primarily on email communications to warn campus community members of the attacks. Other methods, such as sirens, also were operational on the day of the shootings, though they later were deemed to be ineffective.

Another point of contention stemming from the shootings was the delay in notifying the campus about the shootings (Schildkraut, McKenna, & Elsass, 2015). Despite that the WAJ shootings occurred at 7:15 a.m., the first notifi-cation was not transmitted to faculty, staff, and students until 9:26 a.m.—the same time that the shooter was chaining the doors shut. This delay was the result of university police believing the first incident to be an isolated act of domestic violence. The Virginia Tech Policy Group, which is the organiza-tion charged with approving the dissemination of emergency notifications, also was delayed in being convened because of this belief. The second emer-gency notification alerting the campus of an active shooter was not transmitted until 9:50 a.m., one minute before the shooter killed himself. Therefore, it has been argued that had notifications about the first incident been transmitted earlier, it may have eliminated or, at the very least, reduced the fatalities in the second shooting.

As a result of the lessons learned from Virginia Tech, colleges and universities across the nation began installing new emergency response systems or overhauling their existing technology (see, generally, Foster, 2007; Gulum & Murray, 2009; Hamblen, 2008; Mark, 2008; Mastrodicasa, 2008; Seo, Torabi, Sa, & Blair, 2012). Such protocols were put to the test at Northern Illinois University (NIU) only 10 months later. Just after 3:00 p.m. on February 14, 2008, graduate student Steven Kazmierczak entered an introductory oceanography class in Cole Hall and opened fire (NIU, 2008; Vann, 2013). He killed 5 and wounded 21 others before committing suicide. The entire shooting lasted less than six minutes. After receiving a call from a local reporter who was monitoring the police scanners, the vice president of public affairs contacted the president of the university for authorization to transmit emergency notifications (NIU, 2008). The approval was provided just eight minutes later (at 3:20 p.m.) and emergency alerts immediately were transmitted to students, faculty, and staff. Though the campus was notified of the shootings quicker than the Virginia Tech community had been, the NIU incident still offered opportunities to improve crisis communications.

Despite that other shootings, at both colleges and universities as well as primary and secondary schools, occurred after Virginia Tech and NIU, they failed to become more than a blip on the media radar. In 2012, however, the nation was once again riveted by a significant act of school violence. On December 14, 2012, 20-year-old Adam Lanza forcefully entered Sandy Hook Elementary School in Newtown, Connecticut, and opened fire (Barron, 2012; Sedensky, 2013). During the rampage, which lasted less than five minutes, the shooter killed 20 first-grade students and 6 of their educators. As law enforcement closed in, he committed suicide. A later search of his home revealed that prior to the shooting, he also had shot and killed his mother as she was sleeping.

If the discourse on school safety had cooled the more distant Columbine became, the shooting at Sandy Hook was the gasoline that rekindled an inferno. While a considerable amount of discussion focused in on the usual suspects of guns, mental health, and violent media (see Chapter 5), safety in primary and secondary schools also was high on the agenda. Sandy Hook Elementary School was a model for doing everything right. The school routinely practiced safety drills, including those involving active shooter situations. Upon her appointment in 2010, Principal Dawn Hochsprung had installed a new security system at the school that required the entrances to automatically lock at 9:30 a.m. when classes began (Martinez, 2012). Visitors after that time would have to be buzzed in by the main office and would be identified by video before being granted access to the school (Sedensky, 2013). On the day of the shooting, the quick thinking of educators throughout the school who immediately locked down their classrooms after hearing gunshots across the intercom saved countless other lives (Sedensky, 2013). The actions of Principal Hochsprung and school psychologist Mary Sherlach also may have saved lives that day. Upon hearing the breaking glass and gunfire, they engaged the shooter in the school's main hallway, potentially buying time for others nearby to shelter in place. Both women were among those killed in the attack.

At the same time, however, the shooting revealed vulnerabilities that plagued not just their school but also other institutions across the nation. While the school was locked down daily at 9:30 a.m., the main entrance into the school where the shooter had penetrated was made of glass and easily broke with a few gunshots (Sedensky, 2013). This led other schools nationwide to reconsider the structure and design of their entrances and how they could be improved to deter or stop a potential attacker (e.g., Tammen, 2015). The 9-1-1 calls made on the day of the shooting, released nearly one year after the event, also highlighted concerns. In two of the recordings, teachers identified that their classrooms were unlocked and that they were unable to secure the entrances (Stoller & Strauss, 2013). At the time of the shooting, classroom doors locked from outside the room in the hallway and also required a key to be secured. This revelation led a number of schools to consider the implementation of panic lockdown buttons (see Chapter 7). Other familiar responses, such as metal detectors and ID cards, also entered the discussion. Yet as the Sandy Hook Advisory Commission warned in their final report, published March 6, 2015:

> The initial, and entirely natural, reaction to a tragedy like the shootings at Sandy Hook Elementary School is to consider steps that would make it virtually impossible for such a violent event to occur at a school ever again. . . . Some countries have transformed their schools into what might at best be described as gated communities, but which might more accurately be described as akin to minimum security prisons in terms of their design. Such facilities may, in fact, effectively eliminate some of the risk of an event like Sandy Hook. But they achieve that objective at great cost, not just financial, but mental, emotional and developmental as well. That is not the direction the Commission believes the American educational system should follow. (p. 14)

The Sandy Hook shooting also was a catalyst for a number of grassroots movements, particularly by the parents of the children lost on December 14.

Michele Gay, whose seven-year-old daughter Josephine was killed, collaborated with Alyssa Parker, who lost her six-year-old daughter Emilie in the shooting, to form Safe and Sound: A Sandy Hook Initiative (http://www.safeandsoundschools.org). Safe and Sound focuses on smart, commonsense preventative measures and strategies that schools can employ to increase security. Jeremy Richman and Jennifer Hensel, who lost their six-year-old daughter Avielle in the shooting, started The Avielle Foundation (http://www.aviellefoundation.org), an organization aimed at researching brain development and function and its relationship with violence. Nicole Hockley, who lost her six-year-old son Dylan, and Mark Barden, whose seven-year-old son Daniel also was killed in the shooting, founded Sandy Hook Promise (http://www.sandyhookpromise.org), a group aimed at reducing gun violence toward children.

Both Virginia Tech and Sandy Hook garnered exceptional amounts of coverage and high levels of viewership. On the day of Virginia Tech, for example, 60 percent of network news airtime and 76 percent of cable news airtime were dedicated to coverage of the shootings (Pew Research Center for the People & the Press, 2007). Fox News attracted 1.8 million viewers to their coverage, while CNN drew in 1.4 million viewers (Garofoli, 2007). In the year prior to Virginia Tech, these same networks brought in an average of 900,000 and 450,000 daily viewers, respectively (Pew Research Center's Project for Excellence in Journalism, 2006). MSNBC's website also experienced a surge in traffic, jumping from 400,000 daily page views (TheWebStats.com, 2011) to 108.8 million visits on the day of the shooting (Garofoli, 2007). In the 30 days following the shootings, the *New York Times* published 63 articles about Virginia Tech; there was similar coverage in the *New York Post* (Schildkraut, 2012a, 2014).

The Sandy Hook shootings were covered even more extensively by the media, due in part to the convergence of factors of newsworthiness surrounding the case. Sorenson, Manz, and Berk (1998) have found that those incidents involving at least one factor—"white, in the youngest and oldest age groups, women, of high socioeconomic status, killed by strangers"—are more newsworthy; Sandy Hook had each of these and more (p. 1514). A total of 130 articles published in the *New York Times* in the month following the shooting (Schildkraut, 2014; Schildkraut & Muschert, 2014). For over three days (72 hours) after the shooting, nearly every broadcast on cable news networks, including CNN and Fox News, was live from Newtown (Applebome & Stetler, 2012; Askar, 2012). This translated to big ratings. On CNN, for example, shows broadcast in their late afternoon and evening news slots (from 3:00 p.m. to 9:00 p.m.), including Wolf Blitzer's *The Situation Room*, *Anderson Cooper 360*, *CNN Newsroom*, *Erin Burnett Outfront*, and *Piers Morgan*

Tonight, attracted between 2 and 3 million viewers each (Kondolojy, 2012). In fact, according to the Nielsen ratings, *The Situation Room* was the second highest rated cable show among adults 18 to 49 (Kondolojy, 2012).

The pervasive coverage of Virginia Tech and Sandy Hook had far-reaching outcomes beyond just the ratings they garnered. Following Virginia Tech, and subsequently NIU 10 months later, fear of crime among college students increased (Fallahi, Austad, Fallon, & Leishman, 2009; Kaminski, Koons-Witt, Thompson, & Weiss, 2010). One poll indicated that respondents believed the 2012 Sandy Hook shooting to be reflective of broader social problems in the nation, despite perceiving similar acts occurring at the same time as isolated incidents ("Washington Post-ABC News poll," n.d.). Still, irrespective of their high death tolls and relative amounts of media coverage, both Virginia Tech and Sandy Hook failed to garner the same amount of attention as Columbine, though they are important markers in a longer narrative about mass shootings in schools (Schildkraut & Muschert, 2014).

Aside from mass shootings in schools, events in other locations also seemed to capture national media attention as they occurred. One such venue was shopping malls. On February 2, 2007, 18-year-old Sulejman Talović opened fire at Trolley Square Mall in Salt Lake City, Utah (Salt Lake City Police Department, 2008). The shooter first fired at a father and son in the parking garage; the father was wounded but able to escape while the son was killed. After entering the mall, the shooter continued to fire his weapon as he went in and out of stores, even after being engaged by an off-duty officer, Ken Hammond, who was at the mall with his wife, as well as other responding police officers. After six minutes, Talović was shot and killed by officers who were able to approach from behind through a different mall entrance. In total, five patrons were killed, and another four were wounded.

Just over eight months later, gunfire erupted in the Von Maur department store at the Westroads Mall in Omaha, Nebraska (Lipschultz & Hilt, 2011). On December 5, 2007, 19-year-old Robert Hawkins entered the store and took the elevator up to the third floor. When the doors opened, he began firing. Over the next six minutes, he shot and killed eight individuals and wounded another four. He then committed suicide as law enforcement entered the store. To date, the Von Maur attack is the deadliest shooting in a U.S. mall.

In subsequent years, additional mall shootings took place. In 2012, just three days before the Sandy Hook shooting, 22-year-old Jacob Tyler Roberts opened fire in a Clackamas, Oregon, mall, killing two and injuring one before taking his own life (Schwirtz, 2012). On January 25, 2014, 19-year-old Darion Aguilar shot and killed two employees at a Columbia, Maryland, mall before committing suicide (Smith & Fitzsimmons, 2014). As with school shootings, those attacks occurring in malls also identified potential concerns for patron safety and overall security. Unlike schools, however, these complexes pose different challenges, including the presence of many more people (and potential targets), as well as more entrances in need of securing (Smith, Q., 2013). Such challenges make regularly offered preventative measures, such as metal detectors, unrealistic. Instead, malls most commonly increase the presence of security officers to combat a perceived threat.

One place that many would not consider to be a potential target of mass shooters would be places of worship, such as churches or temples, yet there have been a number of violent attacks in these venues. On March 12, 2005, Terry Ratzmann entered his church in Brookfield, Wisconsin, and opened fire (Wilgoren, 2005a). He killed six members of the congregation, including the church's pastor, before committing suicide. Four others were injured in the attack. Though a motive remained elusive, church members who knew the shooter noted that he suffered from depression, previously had lost his job, and was upset over a sermon from a few weeks earlier, leading to speculation that the shootings were motivated by religion. Brookfield also later was home to another mass shooting on October 21, 2012, when gunman Radcliffe Haughton opened fire at a day spa, killing three and wounding four others before committing suicide (Yaccino & Davey, 2012).

On December 9, 2007, 24-year-old Matthew Murray opened fire at the New Life Church in Colorado Springs, Colorado (McFadden, 2007). In the parking lot, he killed sisters Stephanie and Rachel Works and wounded their father, David (Johnson & Frosch, 2007). Once inside, he shot and injured two additional people before he was wounded by multiple bullets fired by Jeanne Assam, a former police officer and member of the church, who was carrying her concealed weapon. After the exchange with Assam, the shooter committed suicide. It later was determined that approximately 12 hours earlier, Murray had opened fire at an Arvada, Colorado, youth mission center, located about 70 miles north of Colorado Springs. There he had killed two of the center's members and wounded an additional two.

Just over seven months after the Colorado shootings, on July 27, 2008, Jim David Adkisson started shooting in a Knoxville, Tennessee, church during a theatrical performance (Dewan, 2008). He killed two people and wounded six others before being tackled by other members of the church. The shooter then was taken into police custody, later pleading guilty and being sentenced to life in prison (Satterfield, 2009). The manifesto he left behind showed that the attack had been motivated by hate for liberals and homosexuality, and criticized the church for being a cult that supported these.

In a year marked by a number of high-profile mass shootings, 2012 also included a shooting at a place of worship. On August 5, Wade Michael Page entered a Sikh temple in Oak Creek, Wisconsin, and opened fire

(Yaccino, Schwirtz, & Santora, 2012). He killed three and wounded four others before being shot to death by a responding law enforcement officer. Occurring just two weeks after another high-profile mass shooting at an Aurora, Colorado, movie theater, the Sikh temple shooting received relatively modest coverage in the media. In fact, the *New York Times* published just five articles on the shooting (Schildkraut, 2014). Writers for a political magazine, *The Week*, proposed four theories as to why the Oak Creek shooting received less coverage: (1) victims of the Sikh shooting were being treated as second-class victims because their religion is not mainstream; (2) people can relate more with being in a movie theater than in a Sikh temple; (3) the Sikh temple had less drama—meaning that there were less victims, the shooter was killed rather than being taken alive, and the event wasn't dubbed "The Batman murders" complete with a killer who allegedly claimed to be the Joker; and (4) media fatigue ("Why the Sikh temple shooting," 2012, para. 2).

Workplace shootings also appeared to be more prevalent during the first 15 years of the new millennium. On December 26, 2000, software tester Michael McDermott opened fire at the Internet consulting firm in Wakefield, Massachusetts, where he was employed, killing seven before being arrested (Goldberg, 2000). On July 8, 2003, Douglas Williams killed six employees and wounded eight others at a Lockheed Martin plant in Meridian, Mississippi, before committing suicide (Halbfinger, 2003; Halbfinger & Hart, 2003). The following month, on August 7, 2003, Salvador Tapia, a former employee of a Chicago-area auto supply warehouse, returned to the company and began shooting, killing six people before taking his own life (Wilgoren, 2003). On June 25, 2008, Wesley Higdon opened fire at a Henderson, Kentucky, plastics company where he was employed, killing five and wounding one before committing suicide (Driehaus, 2008). Missouri factory worker Timothy Hendron killed three and wounded five others before taking his own life at a St. Louis-area plant on January 7, 2010 (Robbins, 2010). Seven months later, truck driver Omar Thornton opened fire at Hartford Beer Distributors in Manchester, Connecticut, killing eight and wounding two; he then killed himself (Rivera & Robbins, 2010). On September 27, 2012, recently terminated Andrew Engeldinger returned to Accent Signage Systems in Minneapolis, Minnesota, and opened fire, killing five and wounding two before committing suicide (Associated Press, 2012).

One particular strand of workplace shootings that gained prominent media attention was those occurring at military installations within the United States. On November 5, 2009, Major Nidal Hasan opened fire at Fort Hood, a military base just outside of Killeen, Texas (McFadden, 2009). The shooter, an army psychiatrist who was facing deployment, killed 13 and wounded 32 others. The gunman was shot four times by Sergeant Kim

Munley, who had responded to the call for shots fired (McKinley, 2009). He survived his wounds and later was convicted and sentenced to death (Kenber, 2013). Sergeant Munley also was injured but survived (Simon & Spellman, 2009).

On September 16, 2013, former military man and civilian contractor Aaron Alexis entered Washington, DC's Navy Yard (Botelho & Sterling, 2013; Leger, Welch, & Bacon, 2013). He opened fire, killing 12 and wounding 2 others. The shooter engaged with police, and was killed in the gunfight; an additional person was injured in the shootout. A later investigation revealed that as a reservist, coupled with his contractor status, the shooter faced no problems accessing the military facility. The investigation also turned up surveillance camera footage of the attacks, which later was broadcast through numerous media outlets (Botelho & Sterling, 2013).

Less than eight months after the Navy Yard attack, Fort Hood was once again rocked by a mass shooting. On April 2, 2014, Specialist Ivan Lopez opened fire on the Texas military base, killing 3 and wounding 16 others (Associated Press, 2014b; Montgomery, Fernandez, & Southall, 2014). As he was confronted by police, the shooter, an Iraq War veteran who was being treated for mental illness and post-traumatic stress disorder (PTSD), committed suicide. Motives for the shootings by Alexis and Lopez were unclear, though early speculation suggested mental illness was a contributing factor (Botelho & Sterling, 2013; Fernandez & Blinder, 2014). Still, the fact that these three shootings took place on military installations did not stop the media from, at least initially, speculating that the motivation may have been terrorism (Morello, Hermann, & Williams, 2013; Stern, 2015).

Two other high-profile mass shootings also stand out in the new millennium, but for different reasons than many of these other shootings. The first, occurring on January 8, 2011, involved a high-profile victim, the likes of which had not been seen in previous mass shootings. On the day of the shooting, Congresswoman Gabrielle Giffords of Tucson, Arizona, was holding a meeting at a local shopping center to give her constituents a chance to discuss issues in their community (Lacey & Herszenhorn, 2011). During the event, 22-year-old Jared Loughner opened fire, critically wounding Giffords and 12 others. He also killed six people, including John Roll, a federal judge, and nine-year-old Christina Taylor Green, who had come to listen to the Congresswoman speak because she was interested in politics (Berger, 2011).

After being subdued by bystanders, he was taken into police custody (Barry, 2011). He later was charged with and indicted on 49 different counts, including murder and attempted murder (Cratty, 2011). Though the shooter pled not guilty to all charges (Goldman, 2011), he quickly was deemed incompetent to stand trial and was remanded to a federal psychiatric facility for prisoners (Lacey, 2011a). After nearly a year and a half of treatment, which included forced medication, the shooter pled guilty in exchange for a sentence of life in prison (Santos, 2012). Congresswoman Giffords continues to recover from the shooting (Page, 2014).

Just over a year and a half after the Tucson shooting, another high-profile mass shooting captured the national media spotlight, this time with a Hollywood twist. In the early morning hours of July 20, 2012, as movie-goers had gathered to watch the midnight premiere of the latest *Batman* movie, 24-year-old James Holmes entered Theater 9 at the Century 21 movie plaza from a door near the screen (Frosch & Johnson, 2012). Dressed in head-to-toe ballistics gear, he first threw several canisters of irritant into the crowd, then began shooting as patrons reacted. He killed 12 people and wounded 58 others before being taken into custody by police just outside of the theater.

When police later went to search the shooter's apartment nearby, they found that he had booby-trapped it with a number of incendiary devices to explode on entry (Frosch & Johnson, 2012). Much of the media coverage of the day showed first responders trying to safely breach the apartment and secure the devices, interchanged with footage from the earlier scene at the theater. Further investigation into the shooting revealed that all of the weapons present at the theater (an assault rifle, a shotgun, and two handguns), as well as more than 6,000 rounds of ammunition, were purchased by Holmes in the 60 days leading up to the attack. This discovery, coupled with Aurora's proximity to Littleton—less than 17 miles between the two sites—rekindled the memories of the earlier Columbine shootings and dialogue about gun control and the right to carry.

Also fueling the media madness was the first pictures of the shooter from his initial appearance in court, which showed him with hair dyed orange. Despite that the Joker's hair was green in the *Batman* comics and movies, the media still constantly likened the shooter to the movie villain. Commercial advertisements for the movie were pulled for the day of the shooting, with international premieres also delayed. Members of the cast and production crew met with victims of the shooting, all of which was highly covered through the media. Despite the intense media focus on the case, many of the pretrial proceedings were not been publicized through the forum. In June 2013, Holmes's defense team entered a plea of not guilty by reason of insanity in an attempt to spare the shooter from the possibility of a death sentence (Sandell, McKinley, & Ng, 2013). His trial began on April 27, 2015 (Associated Press, 2015). A live streaming broadcast of the proceedings was permitted by the district court judge, with a number of limitations (Parker, 2014). The guilty verdict, handed down on July 16, 2015 (Johnson & Rascon, 2015), and subsequent sentencing phases, also were broadcast live.

While these and other shootings occurred in what has been dubbed a "post-Columbine era" (see Schildkraut, 2014), they also occurred during a time when anxiety over extreme acts of violence in the United States was at an all-time high. Just after the start of the millennium, the nation's worst act of terrorism on its soil took place. On September 11, 2001, members of the al Qaeda terrorist organization from Afghanistan hijacked four commercial airliners flying out of Boston, Washington, DC, and Newark, New Jersey (Zelikow, 2005). At 8:46 a.m., the first of the planes, American Airlines Flight 11, crashed into the North Tower of the World Trade Center. The South Tower of the Trade Center was struck at 9:03 a.m. by United Airlines Flight 175.

As soon as the first plane had hit, news stations everywhere broke with live coverage from the scene, the iconic picture of the North Tower billowing with smoke from a large gaping hole near its top. Images of firefighters and police cars racing through the streets of Manhattan toward the tower, and of people fleeing from the building, filled screens in households worldwide. It was during this live coverage that viewers saw Flight 175 strike the South Tower. With both towers ablaze, it was clear that the Unites States was under attack.

Approximately a half hour later, transmissions indicated that another aircraft, later determined to be American Airlines Flight 77, was headed toward the nation's capital, specifically targeting the White House. At 9:37 a.m., Flight 77 slammed into the Pentagon building at over 500 miles per hour. After burning for 55 minutes, the South Tower of the World Trade Center collapsed at 9:58 a.m. Minutes later, around 10:03 a.m., a fourth plane— United Airlines Flight 93, heading from Newark to San Francisco—crashed into an open field in Shanksville, Pennsylvania, as passengers attempted to regain control from the hijackers. Its intended target was never clarified, though the plane had been heading toward Washington, DC, when it was taken down. At 10:28 a.m., the North Tower of the World Trade Center gave way and collapsed as millions of viewers looked on.

A total of 2,977 people (excluding the hijackers) lost their lives on September 11, 2001, in what has become the deadliest attack in the United States (CNN Library, 2015a), including at least 11 unborn children (Ngo, 2011). Further, this death toll continues to rise due to issues such as various forms of cancer contracted as a result of exposure to the debris field and complications from injuries suffered in the attacks (Prince, 2014). In the hours after the towers' collapses, recovery efforts were broadcast as rescuers searched for survivors in the rubble. By that evening, President George W. Bush (2001) had vowed to exact revenge against those responsible for the attacks. In the weeks, months, and years thereafter, he would keep that promise, as the

United States became embroiled in a war with Iraq and Afghanistan and a search for Osama bin Laden, the mastermind of the attacks. On May 1, 2011, President Barack Obama announced that bin Laden had been killed during a raid on his Pakistani compound (Baker, Cooper, & Mazzetti, 2011).

The September 11 terrorist attacks had a profound impact on everyday life in the United States, and ultimately changed the landscape of how violence was perceived in the nation. Law enforcement presence across the country increased. Security at airports tightened, which may have helped mitigate the loss of life with a pair of shootings (2002 and 2013) at Los Angeles International Airport (Lyman, 2002; Medina & Lovett, 2013). Extreme acts of violence quickly were labeled terrorism, as discussed in Chapter 2 (see also Stern, 2015). Fear and anxieties were heightened with other events of terrorism, such as the 2013 Boston Marathon bombing, in which a pair of pressure cooker bombs detonated almost simultaneously near the race's finish line, killing 3 and wounding 264 others (Reuters, 2013). A fourth person, MIT police officer Sean Collier, later was killed as he engaged with the suspects, who were attempting to flee (Allen, Levenson, & Ryan, 2015). Tamerlan Tsarnaev was killed in a shootout with law enforcement (Sullivan, Barr, & Zezima, 2013); his brother, Dzohkar, later was captured alive and ultimately tried and convicted for the attacks (O'Neill, 2015) and sentenced to death (Valencia, 2015).

Another critical ingredient to the perceptions of mass shootings in the new millennium is the explosion of social media. Though MySpace often is credited with being the first social media platform, it quickly became antiquated once Facebook hit the Internet in 2004. Founded by Harvard undergraduate student Mark Zuckerberg, Facebook originally was designed as an online community for Harvard students (McCracken, 2014). Zuckerberg strategically opened the site to other schools in the following years, eventually opening it up to the public in 2006 (McCracken, 2014). Facebook's popularity increased, eventually attracting over 1 billion active users each month (Tam, 2013). Aside from its popularity for information sharing among friends, Facebook also is a powerful tool in responses to mass shootings. Following the 2007 Virginia Tech shootings, students used the platform to reach out and let others know they were okay, as well as to comment on the victims (Haddow & Haddow, 2014). Reporters also use Facebook to determine who had been impacted by the attacks in order to connect for information for their stories, allowing users to take the role of information subsidies (Thompson, 2011; Wigley & Fontenot, 2009).

In 2006, a new social media site hit the market and became an instant success. Unlike Facebook, this new site, called Twitter, functioned less as an online community and more as a microblogging platform, similar to RSS feeds

(Kwak, Lee, Park, & Moon, 2010). Users post brief messages of 140 characters or less, called "tweets," which other users can read and reshare, a process known as "retweeting" (Elsass, Schildkraut, & Stafford, 2014; Kwak et al., 2010). These messages need not be intended for a specific user, and do not require the same reciprocal communication as Facebook (Elsass et al., 2014). Regardless of the number of followers (or subscribers) for the original source, research has shown that retweeting allows a single message to reach an average of 1,000 users (Kwak et al., 2010).

The Twitter platform has become increasingly important in breaking news in real time (Braun & Gillespie, 2011; Hermida, 2010). Though prior to the start of the movie, users were posting about their excitement for the premiere, within minutes of the Aurora, Colorado, shooting, movie goers were tweeting what had happened inside the theater as the gunman opened fire (Haddow & Haddow, 2014; Sutter, 2012). Tweets included information from the scene, as well as real-time pictures and videos that had not even been captured by news organizations. Even as the investigation continued to unfold in the hours and days after the shooting, the Aurora Police Department continually advised the media and viewers during press conferences to check their Twitter feed for more frequent updates.

Several months later, the Sandy Hook Elementary School shooting story also unfolded on social media outlets, including Twitter. Both celebrities (DeNinno, 2102) and politicians (Trifunov, 2012) took to the platform to express their sympathy and condolences for those lost in the tragedy. Posts made by Sandy Hook principal Dawn Hochsprung, who had been active on the site, continuously were retweeted or replied to. Members of the victims' families, such as teacher Victoria Soto's sister, Carlee, also took to the site to express their grief over their losses. Messages with the hashtag, a signifier for a topic on Twitter, related to the shooting, including #PrayForNewtown, #SandyHook, and #Newtown, were among the top trends within a few hours of the shooting (Bell, M., 2012). According to Topsy (www.topsy.com), a Twitter analytics company, in the first 24 hours after the shooting, over 1.5 million tweets with #SandyHook were shared or reshared.

Real-time tweeting of events also has occurred in the context of political campaigns and natural disasters (Hughes & Palen, 2009). This practice is not limited to events in the United States. In 2011, the raid that killed Osama bin Laden was live tweeted by a Pakistani man (Sutter, 2012). Twitter also took a prominent role in the Boston Marathon bombings (Fry, 2014). The first reports about the attack were posted through Twitter, then continuously retweeted (Haddow & Haddow, 2014). In just under an hour and a half after the bombs had exploded, 300,000 tweets had been posted about the event (Stern, 2013). Twenty minutes later, the number of mentions about the bombing had increased to 700,000 (Stern, 2013). The popularity of Twitter as a news source was particularly prevalent among users 18 to 29 (Pew Research Center for the People & the Press, 2013). Not only was the platform used to tweet general news and condolences about the attack, but it also became a source of strength and camaraderie. The identifier #BostonStrong became a symbol of solidarity after the attacks or, as Zimmer (2013) notes, "the phrase that rallied a city." Additionally, the Boston Police Department and the FBI utilized the platform to both quickly and widely disseminate information about the suspects during the manhunt (Haddow & Haddow, 2014). Twitter, along with Facebook and other various Internet sites, was credited with the quick identification and apprehension of the suspects (Presuitti, 2013).

THE REST IS, WELL, HISTORY

Over the past 250 years, the phenomenon of public mass shootings has undergone a continual evolution. These events no longer are thought of mainly in the context of schools, but rather acknowledgment has been made that other locations are equally as vulnerable to such attacks. The amount of media attention, due in part to changing technologies, also has made these shootings appear to be more commonplace, despite that, in fact, they are not, as we discuss in the next chapter. Such considerations, coupled with the definitional issues discussed in Chapter 2, present a significant misunderstanding as to just how many events are (or are not) occurring in the United States. We next turn our attention to remedying this complexity.

4

Mass Shootings by
the Numbers

Myth: "[Shootings are] unfortunately not all that rare an occurrence anymore in this country"
—Tapper, December 13, 2013

In the wake of a mass shooting, it is common for a wide variety of fallacies to be vigorously proclaimed. Among these, misconceptions concerning their frequency, historical trends, the risk of becoming a victim, stereotypes about shooters, and the dangerousness of America seem to dominate the airwaves. This chapter seeks to debunk those myths as well as others heavily touted after news of a mass shooting breaks. We work to contextualize mass shootings in statistics in order to provide a realistic understanding of the trends with regard to frequency of these types of events and a person's likelihood of victimization, while also couching these events in a discussion of homicide and violent crime more generally in the United States. Additionally, we provide examples that discredit the stereotype of mass shooters typically portrayed by the media and politicians.

MASS SHOOTING EVENT STATISTICS

Most people learn about criminality through the media, as almost 95 percent of the population relies on it for crime news (Graber, 1980; Surette, 1992). More than 50 percent of the stories typically are dedicated to crime (Maguire, Weatherby, & Mathers, 2002; Pollak & Kubrin, 2007; Surette, 1992). Usually, the most serious and violent incidents receive the vast majority of attention because of constraints on time and space (Chermak, 1995; Graber, 1980; Gruenewald, Pizarro, & Chermak, 2009; Krajicek, 1998; Mayr & Machin, 2012). Furthermore, only a small fraction of crime events actually are covered by the media and those selected often garner unequal amounts of attention (Chermak, 1995; Gruenewald et al., 2009; Schildkraut, Elsass, & Meredith, 2015). This is problematic because by focusing on only the most severe, extreme, and therefore newsworthy cases, the media distort the general public's understanding of crime in the United States as well as a person's actual likelihood of victimization (Barak, 1994; Krajicek, 1998; Maguire et al., 2002; Robinson, 2011).

When considering mass murder generally, previous studies have found that events in which firearms are used receive significantly more media coverage than those committed by other means (Duwe, 2000; see also Dietz, 1986; Fox & Levin, 1994a, 1998; Petee, Padgett, & York, 1997). With regard to mass shootings specifically, the public's chief source of information is the media because few individuals ever will directly experience an event of this type (Graber, 1980; Surette, 1992). Additionally, mass shootings usually are deemed more newsworthy, compared to other types of crime and, therefore, tend to garner a substantial amount of media attention (Chyi & McCombs, 2004; Elsass, Schildkraut, & Stafford, 2014; Muschert & Carr, 2006; Schildkraut, 2012a; Schildkraut & Muschert, 2014), though there are differences between the coverage that individual events receive (Duwe, 2000; Schildkraut, 2014; Schildkraut, Elsass, & Meredith, 2015). The media, in effect, have the ability to shape the public's perception of the problem (Duwe, 2000; see also Best, 1987, 1990), and this abundance of coverage results in people believing that mass shooting events happen more often than they actually do (Schildkraut, Elsass, & Stafford, 2015). Furthermore, people tend to believe that these events have become more commonplace over time (see, generally, Ehrenfreund & Goldfarb, 2015; Healy, 2015; Lutz, 2012; Plumer, 2012; Wing & Stein, 2014).

There has been much debate over how to define mass shootings for the purpose of classifying events (see Chapter 2 for an in-depth discussion of definitional issues). After much consideration, we define a mass shooting as

[a]n incident of targeted violence carried out by one or more shooters at one or more public or populated locations. Multiple victims (both injuries and fatalities) are associated with the attack, and both the victims and location(s) are chosen either at random or for their symbolic value. The event occurs within a single 24-hour period, though most attacks typically last only a few minutes. The motivation of the shooting must not correlate with gang violence or targeted militant or terroristic activity.

As we commonly must rely on news reports to compile information about different crimes, using the details about each event released by the media to decide whether the rampage fits the definition, it is very likely that some events have been overlooked or incorrectly omitted. Moreover, as technological advances have made identifying possible mass shootings easier today, we have the news media at our fingertips. This was not the case for times past, and therefore, it is likely that crimes committed in earlier decades may inadvertently have been excluded.

An additional issue involves the existence of false positive or false negative new media search results. When a search term has multiple meanings, false positives may occur, thereby returning results that do not necessarily meet the definition (Deacon, 2007; Schildkraut, 2014; Soothill & Grover, 1997). Conversely, false negatives occur when a search term is so narrow that news articles, and therefore mass shooting events, are excluded because they do not meet the criteria as entered. The possibility of false positives and false negatives increases the likelihood that the list of events that meet our definition of a mass shooting that has been compiled is not fully exhaustive.

As per this definition, through 2014 there have been 306 mass shootings in the United States. The first mass shooting occurred at a school in Baton Rouge, Louisiana, on July 25, 1880, and since that day, these types of mass murders have taken place in all but five states (Maine, New Hampshire, Rhode Island, North Dakota, and South Dakota). With respect to the region of the country, they have occurred most frequently in the western United States (95 events), followed by the Southeast (88 events), the Midwest (59 events), the Northeast (38 events), and the Southwest (26 events) regions.

Though often touted as being on the rise (e.g., Ehrenfreund & Goldfarb, 2015; Healy, 2015; Lutz, 2012; Plumer, 2012; Wing & Stein, 2014), mass shootings are not becoming more commonplace, nor have they increased in overall death toll over the last several decades (Fox & DeLateur, 2014). According to Fox and DeLateur (2014), there have been nearly 20 attacks per year on average in the United States over the past few decades. The researchers go on to point out that "without minimizing the pain and suffering of hundreds of those who have been victimized in recent attacks, the facts clearly say that there has been no increase in mass shootings and certainly no epidemic" (Fox & DeLateur, 2014, p. 130; see also, Duwe, 2004). Even school shootings, though briefly spiking in the mid-1990s, have occurred throughout the history of formal education in the United States (Rocque, 2012). Despite the clear findings that mass shootings are not on the rise, but in fact have remained relatively stable over time, the general public still has a tendency to believe that these types of events are becoming more commonplace (Schildkraut, Elsass, & Stafford, 2015). This erroneous belief undoubtedly is due in large part to the news media's coverage of mass shooting events and the greater availability of news in today's society with the advent of new technology (Heath & Gilbert, 1996), such as the Internet and smartphones (see Chapter 8).

The amount and framing of news coverage can affect how likely people think they are to become a victim of a mass shooting and their fear of crime, which may in turn lead to broader reactions in the form of individual responses to a possible moral panic (Schildkraut & Elsass, in press; see also Baldassare, Bonner, Petek, & Shrestha, 2013). While it is true that almost all of the research conducted in this area focuses specifically on school shootings, given the similarities between these events and mass shootings more generally, findings may be able to be extended to the public at large, as has been demonstrated in opinion polls. It has been found that mass shootings may influence individuals to believe that they are more likely to be a victim of these types of events than is actually the case. Following Columbine, for example, Gallup found that 66 to 68 percent of people agreed that there was some likelihood a similar event could happen in their own community (Gillespie, 2000; Saad, 2012b). After the 2005 shooting at Red Lake High School, this agreement increased to 73 percent (Saad, 2012a, 2012b). This trend continued after the 2007 Virginia Tech shootings, with college students found to be likely to believe that similar attacks could happen again (Fallahi, Austad, Fallon, & Leishman, 2009).

The problem with these perceptions of risk is that they are greatly disproportionate to a person's actual statistical likelihood of becoming a victim of a mass shooting. Mass shootings, and school shootings in particular, are statistically rare events. In the six school years preceding Columbine, for example, there were 226 deaths attributable to school shootings (Bernard, 1999; Donohue, Schiraldi, & Ziedenberg, 1998). In the same time frame, over 50 million students were enrolled in more than 80,000 schools in the United States (Sanchez, 1998). Therefore, the likelihood of any of those students falling victim to a school shooting was less than 0.00005 percent, which makes the same students significantly more likely to be struck by lightning than to be killed by an active shooter at their school (Bernard, 1999; Donohue et al., 1998). The statistical odds of an individual in the general public becoming the victim of a mass shooting, regardless of location, are even smaller. Yet people still remain fearful of becoming the victim of a mass shooter, despite the statistical unlikelihood of such a possibility. As Duwe (2000) points out, prior research has suggested that it is the media's coverage of mass murder that increases the public's fear of crime (see also Fox & Levin, 1994a; Levin & Fox, 1996). This may occur through the inflation of perceived risk, which has been found to impact this fear (Warr, 2000; Warr & Stafford, 1983).

Not all reactions specifically are related to a particular event, however. Instead, such perceptions may be attributable to the phenomenon of mass shootings more generally. Schildkraut, Elsass, and Stafford (2015) examined reactions to school shootings in the context of moral panics and found that college students who were more fearful had an increased likelihood of perceiving that these events occur more frequently than they actually do. They also were more likely to believe in the existence of a moral panic over school shootings (Schildkraut, Elsass, & Stafford, 2015). In a separate study, Elsass and colleagues (2014) examined the role of media consumption's effect on attitudes about school shootings, finding that social media usage, and Twitter in particular, led to greater beliefs that school shootings were a major problem in the United States (see Chapter 8 for a thorough discussion of the role of social media).

Misconceptions about mass shootings do not end with discussions of their frequency or a person's likelihood of victimization, as there exists a number of nonfactual generalizations about the locations of the events themselves that are problematic. One such falsehood is that mass shootings happen more often in rural and suburban areas (see, e.g., Kass, 2012; "School shootings," 1999). While it is true that some high-profile mass shootings, such as the rampages at Columbine, Virginia Tech, Aurora, and Sandy Hook, have occurred in suburban areas, this does not mean that these types of events happen with more frequency in suburbia.

It is difficult to characterize past mass shooting locales into urban, suburban, and rural categories, as cities and towns change over time; therefore, a place that was rural when an attack took place in the early 1900s may be suburban or urban today. What is clear, however, is that mass shootings do occur in urban environments. Through 2014, there have been attacks in major cities in nearly every state, including Chicago, Kansas City, New York, Los Angeles, Denver, Philadelphia, New Orleans, Columbus, Little Rock, Atlanta, Las Vegas, Seattle, Fort Worth, Omaha, Austin, Tucson, and Honolulu. On the surface, there appears to be little discernible difference in the numbers of mass shootings that occur in urban versus suburban/rural locations.

Within major cities, attacks have happened in a wide variety of places. These include a Salt Lake City mall; military base in Washington, DC; nightclub in Dallas; airport in Los Angeles; school in Chicago; law office in San Francisco; tourist attraction in New York City; convenience store in Houston; bar in Columbus; café in Seattle; and investment firm in Philadelphia. Further still, with regard to school shootings specifically, it is not true that "mass shootings at schools tend to occur in suburbs and small towns" (Kass, 2012, para. 17), as at least 50 of the 117 school rampages that occurred between 1880 and 2014 took place in a major city. This number likely would increase if minor cities were able to be more readily identified.

Another misconception is that mass shootings almost always occur in schools. This fallacy is likely due to the disproportionate amount of media coverage that school shootings typically garner. There have been 117 school shootings in the United States through 2014. Thus, just over 37 percent of the mass shootings that have occurred in the United States between 1880 and 2014 took place in schools. The remaining attacks have taken place in a variety of locales including (but not limited to) malls, law offices, movie theaters, political rallies, workplaces, museums, salons, airports, restaurants, courthouses, churches, grocery stores, government buildings, hospitals, post offices, gyms, and private residences. While mass shootings in schools have happened with the highest frequency, they are not far ahead of those that take place in workplaces, which characterizes 88 rampages between 1880 and 2014. Together, school and workplace attacks make up over 65 percent of all mass shooting events that have occurred in the United States. As individuals spend a large amount of their time per week in these locations, future research should investigate how these kinds of events compare to one another in order to gain more insight into these most common types of mass shooting locations.

MASS SHOOTER STATISTICS

One of the most significant areas within the discussion of mass shootings to suffer from inaccurate stereotypes centers on the perpetrators themselves. While stereotypes appear to be a necessary and ever-present part of the human thought process, the quick coding of infinite detail in the world around us results in a "*selective* simplification in which information is lost, and misinformation may be added" (Simmons, 1965, p. 225). Thus, when stereotypes based on fallacies for a phenomenon that most people will never directly experience, such as a mass shooting, are used to inform the public and direct public policy, there are likely to be serious repercussions. Politicians, media, and the general public seem to have adopted a profile for mass shooters: young white males brandishing assault rifles who commit suicide after their attacks (Petee et al., 1997; see also Healy, 2015; Hesse, 2015; Kluger, 2014; Mingus & Zopf, 2010; Wise, 2001; Xie, 2014). This, however, is not necessarily rooted in reality as many shooters have portrayed characteristics out of line with the widely accepted stereotype. Additionally, some aspects of the depiction are features that describe a minority of shooters, rather than the majority.

One of the most common assumptions made with regard to mass shooters is that they are all male (e.g., Hesse, 2015; Kalish & Kimmel, 2010; Kluger, 2014); yet, there have been a number of female perpetrators in the United

States. In fact, between 1880 and 2014, there have been 11 attacks committed solely by females, and an additional event in which a woman perpetrated a mass shooting with her husband. Brenda Spencer was only 16 years old when she became the first woman to commit a mass shooting in the United States. On January 29, 1979, in San Diego, California, Spencer took aim at students awaiting access to the grounds of Grover Cleveland Elementary School, which was located across the street from her home (Associated Press, 1979). The attack killed the school's principal and custodian, and left eight children and a police officer wounded. Though she may have been the first female school shooter, Spencer would not be the last. Others include Heather Smith, Laurie Dann, and Latina Williams, who killed a total of six people and wounded eight others in three separate attacks at schools.

Just as mass shootings do not occur solely at schools, female perpetrators do not target only educational campuses. The second most common location for mass shooting events is workplaces, and female shooters have chosen those locales for their attacks as well. Perhaps the most well-known attack in a workplace occurred on February 12, 2010, perpetrated by 44-year-old Amy Bishop at the University of Alabama in Huntsville, where she was an assistant professor of biology (Abcarian & Fausset, 2010). After having been denied tenure status at the university, Bishop opened fire during a routine Biology Department faculty meeting, leaving three dead—including one member of her tenure decision committee—and three others wounded. Other female mass shooters who targeted their workplaces include De-Kieu Duy, Jennifer San Marco, and Yvonne Hiller, who left 10 dead and 2 wounded in the wake of three separate attacks.

The remaining female mass shooters have chosen other types of locations at which to open fire. Included in this group is 43-year-old Shelia W. Chaney Wilson. On October 5, 2003, Wilson killed her pastor and her mother at Turner Monumental A. M. E. Church located in Atlanta, Georgia. Another example is 22-year-old Amanda Miller, who, with her husband as an accomplice, killed three people during a spree shooting that left victims across multiple locations in Las Vegas, Nevada, on June 8, 2014.

Lovett (2012), though talking specifically about school attacker Brenda Spencer, makes clear why the fallacy of constantly equating mass shooters with masculinity is problematic:

> Our biases about gender and violence make us want to make Spencer an outlier. While it is true that most school shooters have been male and that our cultural association of masculinity and violence may contribute to a shooter's profile, this association also leads our society to de-emphasize what we might learn from women like Spencer. (para. 6–7)

Clearly, ignoring attacks perpetrated by females not only is disrespectful and insensitive to the victims of their rampages but also creates a missed opportunity to gain important insight into mass shooters beyond the widely accepted masculine stereotype (e.g., Consalvo, 2003; Kalish & Kimmel, 2010; Kimmel & Mahler, 2003; Muschert & Ragnedda, 2010; Tonso, 2009). As Lovett (2012) points out, Brenda Spencer's attack "come[s] the closest to offering a potentially illuminating precedent to the Newtown [Sandy Hook] shootings," as both perpetrators targeted elementary school children. Comparisons between similar events, regardless of the sex of the perpetrator, undoubtedly would be fruitful for the overall discourse on mass shootings. Moreover, female mass shooters may have much to teach us not only about mass shooters in particular but also about women who commit violent crime and about female criminality in general.

Another widely accepted fallacy about mass shooters is that they all are white (see Hesse, 2015; Kimmel & Leek, 2012; Mingus & Zopf, 2010; Wise, 2001; Xie, 2014). Through 2014, there have been 314 perpetrators in 306 events in the United States that meet our definition of a mass shooting. Of the 249 shooters whose races are known, 135 were white, with the remaining 114 being members of racial minority groups (64 blacks, 25 Hispanics, 14 Asians, and 11 members of other races including Native Americans and biracial or multiracial individuals). While it appears that whites dominate the field, it is important to note that, especially in a country as racially diverse as the United States, it is more appropriate to compare rates than raw numbers. Rates take into account each racial group's prevalence in the general population. When the racial breakdown of the country is considered in these measures, the dominance by whites is much less drastic.

According to the most recent populations from the U.S. Census Bureau (2011), non-Hispanic whites make up approximately 69.1 percent of the U.S. population, followed by Hispanics (12.5 percent), non-Hispanic blacks (12.3 percent), and Asians (3.6 percent). Other races, including Native Americans, Pacific Islanders, and those identifying as biracial or multiracial, make up 8.9 percent of the U.S. population. Therefore, though whites make up over 69 percent of the general population, they are responsible for only just over 54 percent of the mass shootings that occur in the United States. Blacks and Asians both are overrepresented among mass shooters, with more than 25 percent and almost 6 percent, respectively. Hispanics and other racial groups (including Native Americans and those identifying as biracial or multiracial) are underrepresented, with 10 percent and over 4 percent of mass shooters coming from those groups, respectively. These comparable figures clearly highlight the fallacy in the stereotype that mass shooters disproportionately are white.

Undoubtedly, the stereotype that mass shooters are white is a misleading notion, as the deadliest shooting rampage to date in U.S. history was perpetrated by an Asian man. Seung-Hui Cho killed 32 and left 23 wounded in his rampage at Virginia Tech, and this is just one example of a mass shooting being perpetrated by a racial minority. Between 2000 and 2014, examining attackers whose races are known, there have been fewer white mass shooters (80) than individuals from racial minority groups (91). Examples of mass shooters from racial minority groups since the twenty-first century include Aaron Alexis, a black man who killed 12 and wounded 8 at a Washington, DC, Navy Yard (U.S. Department of Defense, 2013); Salvador Tapia, a Hispanic man who killed 6 when he opened fire at an auto parts company where he once worked in Chicago (Roberts, 2003); Jeffrey Weise, a Native American teenager who murdered his grandfather and another person at his home before killing 7 and wounding 5 others at Red Lake High School in Minnesota ("School gunman," 2005); and Nidal Hasan, a man of Palestinian descent who killed 13 and injured 32 others at Fort Hood (McFadden, 2009).

There also is little difference between white and minority mass shooters in terms of number of victims. Between 1880 and 2014, white mass shooters killed 533 people and wounded 680 others. By comparison, mass shooters from racial minority groups killed 402 individuals and left 368 wounded over the same time period. Yet the differences become less stark when examining mass shootings that have occurred in the twenty-first century alone. Both white mass shooters and attackers from racial minority groups each have killed a total of 279 people between 2000 and 2014, though whites have left more injured (314 people versus 265 people, respectively).

This evaluation further diminishes the legitimacy of the often touted stereotype that mass shooters are white as not only have there been a large percentage of perpetrators from a wide variety of racial groups, but there have been approximately equal numbers of victims created by white and minority mass shooters since the start of the twenty-first century. Additionally, it has been found that though some of the most deadly mass shootings are perpetrated by racial minorities, these events tend to receive less media coverage (Schildkraut, Elsass, & Meredith, 2015). The forwarding of this generalization is particularly disturbing as it may lead people to overlook warning signs in others who do not fit the flawed stereotype as reported in the news media and portrayed in pop culture.

Another aspect of the erroneous profile of mass shooters that has been depicted is that they typically are young. Of the 300 mass shooters in the United States since 1880 whose ages are known, more than half were over age 30 at the time of their attack. While it often is the case that young people come to mind when the term "mass shooter" is used, that is not necessarily synonymous with reality, as the average age of these perpetrators is 33 years. This inconsistency is even more problematic when one considers that violent video games commonly are vilified as a cause of mass shootings (see Chapter 5), though rarely are such games attributed to older individuals (Ferguson, 2011), age groups from which over half of the mass shooters in the United States come.

In the United States, there have been 74 mass shooters in their teens, 62 in their twenties, 62 in their thirties, 56 in their forties, 29 in their fifties, 12 in their sixties, 4 in their seventies, and 1 in his eighties. Examples of older mass shooters include 35-year-old George Jo Hennard, who killed 35 and wounded 23 at a restaurant in Killeen, Texas (Fox & Levin, 1994a); 44-year-old postal worker Patrick Henry Sherrill, who killed 14 and wounded 7 at a post office in Edmond, Oklahoma (Fox & Levin, 1994b); 55-year-old Gian Luigi Ferri, who killed 8 and wounded 6 at a law office in San Francisco (Dwyer & Hochmuth, 2013); 60-year-old William Cruse, who killed 6 and wounded 10 in a spree killing across Palm Bay, Florida (Bearak, 1987); 71-year-old Walter K. Shell, who killed 2 at a law office in Johnson City, Tennessee (Campbell, 2012); and 88-year-old James Wenneker von Brunn, who killed 1 and injured 1 at the U.S. Holocaust Memorial Museum in Washington, DC (Associated Press, 2009).

Though the frequency of mass shooters decreases by age group across the life course, this is unsurprising as this trend is in line with findings concerning criminality more generally. Research on age and offending has exposed what has been referred to as the "age-crime curve" (Dean, Brame, & Piquero, 1996; Farrington, 1986; Stolzenberg & D'Alessio, 2008; Sweeten, Piquero, & Steinberg, 2013), with criminal offending peaking in middle to late adolescence before dropping sharply and remaining low throughout adulthood. Further, the majority of individuals naturally age out of crime (Farrington, 1986; Hirschi & Gottfredson, 1983; Sampson & Laub, 2003; Sweeten et al., 2013). Given the negative correlation between criminality and age for the population in general, it is not surprising to find fewer mass shooters as age increases.

Yet, though just under half of the shooters come from the teens and twenties groups, they dominate the profile of mass shooters in the media (see Friedman, 2014; Hesse, 2015; Kluger, 2014; Schulman, 2013; Xie, 2014), with little to no attention being paid to the existence of older perpetrators. This is likely to have given rise to, or at least have strengthened, the stereotype that mass shooters are overwhelmingly young. Again, when the inaccurate stereotype is reinforced, it runs the risk of becoming ingrained in the minds of the general public. This can lead to people overlooking warning signs in others because the individual in question does not fit the incorrect profile of a mass shooter that has been accepted.

Very often after news of a mass shooting breaks, the conversation quickly turns to firearms as the gun control versus gun rights debate almost inevitably reignites (see Chapter 5 for details on this debate). Arguably the most scrutinized type of firearm during this commentary is the assault rifle, what is commonly, and incorrectly, referred to by politicians, pundits, and the general public as an "AR." The acronym AR, as in AR-15 rifle, does not stand for "assault rifle," but actually is the abbreviation for a specific weapon made by the company ArmaLite, which originally developed the weapon in the 1950s, according to the National Shooting Sports Foundation ("Modern sporting," n.d.). A true assault rifle is fully automatic, thereby continuing to shoot bullets as long as the trigger is engaged, resulting in multiple rounds per trigger pull. This type of weapon has been heavily restricted from civilian ownership since 1934. What most commentators actually are referring to are semiautomatic rifles styled to resemble military weapons; however, these firearms shoot only one round per trigger pull, though they reload automatically as long as bullets are available in the gun's magazine.

A very common misconception is that mass shooters prefer these types of weapons—semiautomatic, military-style rifles. Yet a study done by Fox and DeLateur (2014) clearly shows that mass shooters' weapons of choice overwhelmingly are semiautomatic handguns. In the 142 shootings examined, 68 were committed with semiautomatic handguns; 35 with semiautomatic, military-style rifles; 20 with revolvers; and 19 with shotguns (Fox & DeLateur, 2014; see also Follman, Pan, & Aronsen, 2013). The deadliest mass shooting in American history—the rampage at Virginia Tech—was carried out using two semiautomatic handguns: a Glock 19 and a Walther P22 (Virginia Tech Review Panel [VTRP], 2007). Based on these findings, we must question the motivation of focusing so much attention on restricting ownership of semiautomatic, military-style rifles while generally giving less policy attention to semiautomatic handguns, as they are used much more often in mass shooting events.

The last piece of the stereotype that requires debunking is the belief that mass shooters usually commit suicide (see Rogers, 2012). Actually, over half of the mass shooters in the United States through 2014 did not die during the commission of their attacks. Of the 312 known perpetrators (two shooters' identities, and therefore whereabouts, are unknown), 166 lived through their rampages. Examples of attackers who survived their mass shootings include Colin Ferguson, who killed 11 and wounded 37 on a train car on Long Island, New York, in 1993 (Kuby & Kunstler, 1995); Howard Unruh, who killed 13 and wounded 3 in a spree killing in Camden, New Jersey, in 1953 (Franscell, 2011); James Holmes, who killed 12 and wounded 58 in a movie theater in Aurora, Colorado, in 2012 (Fox & Levin, 2014); and Luther

Casteel, who killed 2 and wounded 16 in a bar in Elgin, Illinois, in 2001 (Ciokajlo, 2002). This trend does not hold, however, when focusing on mass shootings that have occurred since the turn of the twenty-first century, as 91 mass shooters have died during their rampages, with only 81 having lived through their attacks in the last 15 years.

Still, between 1880 and 2014, there have been 146 mass shooters who died during their attacks. While there does not appear to be a pattern to which types of shooters commit suicide or die during the commission of their attacks with regard to sex, race, or geographical region, Lankford (2015) found that there do exist some fundamental differences between mass shooters who commit suicide and those who live through their rampages. Mass shooters were found to be more likely to die as a result of their attack if they carried greater numbers of weapons to the scene and if they killed more victims. Additionally, perpetrators who targeted factories or warehouses and open commercial locations were significantly more likely to commit suicide (Lankford, 2015). These findings support previous research that there are differences between individuals who commit murder and those who engage in murder-suicide (see, generally, Eliason, 2009; Lankford, 2015; Malphurs & Cohen, 2002).

Yet, there remains a complicating issue involving the cause of death for shooters. It is uncertain exactly how many attackers commit suicide, as some shooters are killed either by law enforcement or others on the scene. Charles Whitman, for example, was killed by law enforcement who overtook him on the observation deck of the Tower, thereby ending his 1966 attack (Lavergne, 1997). Whitman murdered his wife and mother before ascending to the top of the Tower on the University of Texas campus and shooting people as they walked below. In other cases, it is less clear whether a shooter died of a self-inflicted wound, or at the hands of another person, such as a law enforcement officer. Additionally, it is unknown how shooters who commit suicide upon being confronted by law enforcement compare to those who choose to kill themselves without coming into contact with officers. It is possible that these two groups are qualitatively distinct. Future studies should investigate the differences between different types of attackers with regard to shooter deaths as findings may be valuable to law enforcement training.

As previously noted, there are mass shooters who do commit suicide, with the most famous examples arguably being the perpetrators of the 1999 Columbine massacre. Eric Harris and Dylan Klebold committed suicide in the library of Columbine High School after killing 13 people and wounding 24 others (Columbine Review Commission, 2001). This event may have been a major catalyst for the suicide stereotype as not only has it become an "archetypal case" (Schildkraut, 2012a, para. 44; see also Schildkraut, 2012b; Schildkraut & Muschert, 2013), therefore having the details of the attack including the shooters' deaths constantly reiterated in the media, but also a picture of the deceased perpetrators in the library has been widely circulated on the Internet. While it is clear that a majority of shooters (over 52 percent) have committed suicide after their attacks since this 1999 rampage, which was not the case prior, it is unclear whether the suicides at Columbine are the cause for the shift in the trend. Other well-known mass shooters who committed suicide in the post–Columbine era include Seung-Hui Cho at Virginia Tech (VTRP, 2007), Adam Lanza at Sandy Hook (Sandy Hook Advisory Commission, 2015), Aaron Alexis at a Washington, DC, Navy Yard (U.S. Department of Defense, 2013), and Elliot Rodger in Santa Barbara ("California mass shooter," 2014).

While stereotypes can be useful shortcuts to understanding and quickly processing the world around us, they can create pitfalls when they are incorrect. This is especially true if inaccurate generalizations are being used to inform public policy, as is the case with the stereotype of mass shooters—young white males wielding assault rifles who commit suicide after their rampages. Public policy, especially laws constructed with the purpose of reducing crimes as devastating as mass shootings, should be based on empirical research rather than widely touted fallacies rooted in emotion. Relying on stereotypes to guide the drafting of our policies and laws only will be detrimental to American society and, in the case of mass shootings, may cost us lives.

MASS SHOOTINGS VERSUS GENERAL HOMICIDE

It is not uncommon to hear others condemn the future of America to ruin by claiming that increasing crime and violence is making the United States infinitely more dangerous, and often, it is these same people who proclaim that mass shootings are an epidemic in this country. Such claims, however, are inaccurate and baseless. There are lower rates of violent crime in the United States today than there ever have been (Federal Bureau of Investigation [FBI], 2014; Friedson & Sharkey, 2015), homicide rates are historically low (FBI, 2014), and the frequency of mass shootings per year has remained relatively stable over time (Fox & DeLateur, 2014). Further, while 69 percent of homicides in the United States in 2013 were committed with a firearm (FBI, 2014), murder in a mass shooting is extremely rare. Still, "the public's fear, anxiety, and widely held belief that the problem is getting worse" (Fox & DeLateur, 2014, p. 130) persists.

According to the FBI's (2014) Uniform Crime Reports (UCR), there was a 4.4 percent reduction in the number of homicides in 2013 from the previous year. In 2013, there was a decline of 5.1 percent in the murder rate from 2012, thereby continuing the downward trend that long has been in effect

(FBI, 2014). With regard to the homicide rate, which takes into account population size, there has been a steady decrease in the United States from 9 murders per 100,000 inhabitants in 1994 to 4.5 murders per 100,000 inhabitants in 2013, the most recent year for which data are available. Since homicide data typically are considered to be the most reliable of all crime data (Pridemore, 2005), these figures clearly demonstrate that murder is becoming less common in the United States. While it is true that all official crime data fail to measure law violations that go unreported to law enforcement—termed "the dark figure of crime" (Skogan, 1977)—homicide generally is believed to suffer from this limitation to a lesser degree (Pridemore, 2005).

Like homicide specifically, violent crime more generally has been on the decline in the United States for decades. In 2013, the estimated number of violent criminal offenses decreased by 4.4 percent from the previous year, making the violent crime rate 367.9 per 100,000 inhabitants (FBI, 2014). This rate highlights a dramatic decrease from 713.6 violent crimes per 100,000 inhabitants, which was the rate in the United States in 1994 (FBI, 2014). In reality, homicide, when compared to violent crime more generally, is a rare occurrence (Dobrin, 2001; Piquero, MacDonald, Dobrin, Daigle, & Cullen, 2005; Pridemore, 2005). In 2013, it accounted for just over 1 percent of all violent crimes in the United States recorded in the UCR (FBI, 2014).

Beyond that, homicide is just one type of violent crime, which makes up only a small part of law violations in the United States each year. In 2013, violent crime accounted for only approximately 12.1 percent of criminal acts in the United States; the remaining 87.9 percent were classified as property crimes (FBI, 2014). Of the four types of violent crime for which the FBI (2014) collects data (homicide, rape, robbery, and aggravated assault), homicide occurs with the lowest frequency by far. This trend holds when comparing these violent crimes across years through the examination of each type of crime's rate per 100,000 inhabitants (FBI, 2014). While it should be noted that there are limitations to the UCR beyond issues surrounding the dark figure of crime, including voluntary reporting on the part of law enforcement jurisdictions and a limited number of offense types for which data are collected, it remains clear that violent crime is unusual. Homicide is the most uncommon of the violent crimes, and murder by a mass shooter, a single type of homicide, is extraordinarily rare.

WHAT DOES IT ALL MEAN?

Human nature is unpredictable, making it impossible to completely prevent mass shootings, and therefore, the risk never can be totally eliminated. This does not mean, however, that nothing should be done to discourage potential mass shooters and decrease lethality of rampages when they do occur. Doing something, as Fox and DeLateur (2014) point out, is better than doing nothing, though this is the case only if tactics are designed based on research rather than sensation, and "taking a nibble out of the risk of mass murder" (p. 141) is undoubtedly a worthy cause for our nation. In order to be effective, statutes and policies, as well as training techniques and security devices (see Chapter 7), must be empirically informed. Laws, policies, and procedures based on raw emotion and inaccurate stereotypes about mass shooting events and perpetrators, especially those driven by political agenda from any source, will fail our country. The only way to increase safety, even minutely, is to continue researching mass shootings and use the findings to inform the design of new measures to reduce the likelihood of their occurrence and decrease lethality in the case of an attack.

5

The "Usual Suspects" as Causal Factors

Myth: "I don't let games like *Call of Duty* in my house. You cannot tell me that a kid sitting in a basement for hours playing *Call of Duty* and killing people over and over and over again does not desensitize that child to the real-life effects of violence."
　　　—Chris Christie, governor of New Jersey (in Lichtblau, 2013)

Mass shootings often leave people with one lingering question: why? While some shooters leave behind clues that can help to answer this (see Chapter 8, for example), the reality is that such a question rarely, if ever, is answered. To merely say, however, that the shooting happened because "bad people do bad things" has been rejected due to its simplicity. Instead, in an effort to "do something" about the problem, a number of potential causal factors for mass shootings have been identified. Among these, there are three that stand out as the most prevalent of explanations—guns, mental health, and violent media. Termed the "usual suspects" (see Schildkraut, Elsass, & Muschert, in press; Schildkraut & Muschert, 2013), these three areas of concern often are where most attention is paid.

When it comes to these usual suspects, shootings like Columbine, Virginia Tech, Aurora, and Sandy Hook can be what Kristin Goss (2015) calls a "shocking 'focusing event'" (p. 203). While the national discourse about these topics may exist prior to a mass shooting, they usually do so in the background, yet are jolted into the spotlight once such an event occurs as the public demands attention be given to these factors (Goss, 2015). Such scrutiny may manifest itself in the form of criminalizing firearms and law-abiding owners, stigmatizing individuals with mental health concerns, or condemning violent video games (Schildkraut et al., in press; Schildkraut & Muschert, 2013). Other responses may take shape in the form of legislative responses aimed at regulating some or all of these perceived issues (Schildkraut & Hernandez, 2014; Soraghan, 2000).

In this chapter, we explore each of these and other causal factors in more depth. We consider how each is framed by and through the media, particularly after high-profile shootings. We also explore how media coverage of these causal factors translates into public opinion, as well as other reactions, such as moral panic. We further examine how such reactions may manifest through political responses in the form of legislative change.

GUNS

In the wake of mass shooting events, there is no topic more controversial than the weapons themselves. In fact, of the "usual suspects," guns consistently are the most referenced of the three (Schildkraut, 2014; Schildkraut & Elsass, in press; Schildkraut et al., in press; Schildkraut & Muschert, 2013). Those individuals who support gun control measures typically suggest that with stricter laws and regulations, the shootings may not have occurred (Kleck, 2009; Schildkraut et al., in press; Schildkraut & Muschert, 2013; Wallace, 2015). Conversely, advocates for gun rights argue that the presence of armed citizens may have stopped the shooter and saved lives.

A driving force behind the gun control debate is public opinion, and this has been shown to be influenced by the occurrence of mass shootings. The Pew Research Center for the People & the Press (2000), for example, found that in the year following the Columbine High School shooting, support for gun control was at an all-time high (see also Carlson & Simmons, 2001; Connelly, 1999; Saad, 1999; Smith, 2002). Specifically, 66 percent of respondents expressed support for stricter regulations; conversely, only 29 percent favored the protection of owners' rights (Pew Research Center for the People & the Press, 2000). Similar trends also were apparent in polls conducted by Gallup (Carlson & Simmons, 2001; Saad, 1999) and the *New York Times* (Connelly, 1999). Greater support for gun control versus owners' rights was found after the 2007 Virginia Tech shooting, with 60 percent of individuals polled preferring tighter regulations (Pew Research Center for the People & the Press, 2014). Around 58 percent of respondents also expressed such support following Sandy Hook (Saad, 2012a; Swift, 2014).

In later polls beyond the immediate aftermath of Columbine, however, support for gun control was found to decrease (Blumenthal, 2012; "DC mass shooting," 2013; Goss, 2015; Pew Research Center for the People & the Press, 2014). Instead, more individuals favored the right to carry for gun owners ("DC mass shooting," 2013; Doherty, 2015; Pew Research Center for the People & the Press, 2014; Saad, 2012a). Following the 2012 shooting at a high school in Chardon, Ohio, 54 percent of people opposed gun control, compared to just 38 percent of those who expressed their support ("DC mass shooting," 2013). In fact, support for gun rights also eclipsed approval for stricter regulations following shootings in Tucson (Madison, 2011; Pew Research Center for the People & the Press, 2011), Aurora (Blumenthal, 2012; "DC mass shooting," 2013; Pew Research Center for the People & the Press, 2012a), and Washington, DC, Navy Yard ("DC mass shooting," 2013). Still, these shootings failed to have the same significant impact on the gun control movement, regardless of which side of the debate one fell, that Columbine had.

In response to these public reactions, elected representatives often feel pressure to "do something" to address the perceived problem. There are two possible ways in which this can be accomplished—either enforce those laws that are already in place or pass new ones (typically under the belief that the existing ones do not work or the shooting would not have occurred had stricter legislation existed). While the public appears to be torn on which of these options is the better choice (Pew Research Center for the People & the Press, 2000; Saad, 2012a; Wozniak, 2015), politicians most commonly opt to introduce new pieces of legislation. Within one year of the Columbine shooting, for example, over 800 pieces of legislation had been introduced at the state and federal levels combined (Schildkraut & Hernandez, 2014; Soraghan, 2000). Despite the flurry of activity, only approximately 10 percent of these bills successfully were enacted into law (Schildkraut & Hernandez, 2014; Soraghan, 2000). In the first 75 days after the Sandy Hook shooting, a total of 23 bills were introduced at the federal level solely focusing on new gun control measures (Schildkraut, 2014). At the state level, New York passed one of the most comprehensive gun control packages (Hernandez, Schildkraut, & Elsass, 2015; "NYSAFE Act," n.d.), and other states, including Connecticut, followed suit.

There are several key areas that typically are the main focus of this type of gun control legislation. The first is what is called "the gun show loophole" (Kleck, 2009; Schildkraut & Hernandez, 2014). This refers to the ability to buy, sell, or transfer firearms between private individuals who are unlicensed through transactions taking place at gun shows (Wintemute, 2013). This issue first became a point of concern following Columbine when it was discovered that three of the four firearms used in the attack had been purchased at a gun show by a friend of the shooters (Kleck, 2009; Schildkraut &

Hernandez, 2014). Further compounding the situation was that the sale took place in the form of a straw purchase (having someone buy a gun on your behalf), as neither of the shooters were old enough to be in possession of any of the weapons at that time (Kleck, 2009; Schildkraut & Hernandez, 2014). One of the shooters, Eric Harris, had identified the gap in a school paper on the Brady Law that allowed these transactions to occur: "the biggest gaping hole is that background checks are only required for licensed dealers ... not private dealers ... private dealers can sell shotguns and rifles to anyone who is 18 or older" (Jefferson County Sheriff's Office, 1999b, p. 26,538), and the two gunmen specifically sought out dealers who did not conduct background checks (Schildkraut & Hernandez, 2014; Soraghan, 2000). Several politicians actually had introduced legislation aimed at addressing this gap before the shooting had taken place, though it did not pass.

Despite that the public routinely supports background checks at gun shows (Saad, 2012a; see also Barry, McGinty, Vernick, & Webster, 2013; Carlson & Simmons, 2001; Doherty, 2015; McGinty, Webster, Vernick, & Barry, 2013; Wozniak, 2015), these pieces of legislation are never enacted. In fact, multiple attempts at closing the loophole after the shooting failed at each introduction (Schildkraut & Hernandez, 2014), though the state of Colorado was successful in passing a ban on straw purchases (Soraghan, 2000). Following Sandy Hook, a bill to extend the background check system's use to transfers between private individuals more broadly was introduced, but failed before it even made it to a hearing (Goss, 2015). One reason such legislative efforts may be unsuccessful, as Goss (2015) points out, is that "people react more strongly to the threat of real, present-day losses (e.g., gun liberties) than to the prospect of theoretical gains in the future (e.g., a reduction of gun violence)" (p. 204).

A second area of gun control reform that often receives attention in the wake of a mass shooting is the types of weapons that are available to the general public. Since the 1960s, public opinion polls consistently have indicated opposition for banning handgun ownership for anyone except law enforcement (Pew Research Center for the People & the Press, 2012c; Saad, 2012a). Handguns, however, receive far less attention in the discourse than assault weapons, even though they are used far more frequently in these shootings (Fox & DeLateur, 2014; Mayors Against Illegal Guns, 2013), as discussed in the prior chapter. Assault weapons typically are compared to military-grade guns and utilize a semiautomatic firing mechanism (Kleck, 2009). The semiautomatic feature, however, is not solely limited to assault rifles; many handgun models also employ this technology. This mechanism allows for new cartridges to load into the chamber after the weapon is discharged, meaning that the only additional action needed by the shooter between rounds is pulling the trigger; consequently, they are able to fire more rapidly.

Interestingly, assault weapons have been banned in the past. In 1994, Congress passed the Violent Crime Control and Law Enforcement Act, or Federal Assault Weapons Ban (AWB) as it is more commonly known (Schildkraut & Hernandez, 2014). The law declared that it was "unlawful for a person to manufacture, transfer, or possess a semiautomatic assault weapon" (18 U.S.C. §§ 921–922) and further identified a list of 19 different firearms that were banned under the provision. The criteria to determine whether or not a particular gun met the criteria of an assault weapon, and therefore prohibited under the Act, was included (18 U.S.C. §§ 921–922; see also Singh, 1999). In the crafting of the AWB, Congress included what is called a sunset provision, which meant that the law would be effective only for a certain amount of time—in this case, 10 years (Singh, 1999). At the end of the term, the law either would have to be renewed or, as in the case of the AWB, would expire. Since the AWB lapsed, members of Congress, including gun control advocate Carolyn McCarthy, have introduced legislation trying to reinstate the original ban or implement a revised version, but all attempts have been unsuccessful.

One potential explanation for the failure to pass regulations on assault weapons, particularly at the federal level, could be these laws' perceived effectiveness. One of the guns used by Columbine shooter Dylan Klebold—the IntraTEC Tec DC-9—expressly was prohibited under the original AWB, which was in effect at the time of the attack. Similarly, an assault weapons ban was in place in the state of Connecticut at the time of the Sandy Hook shooting. The Bushmaster rifle used as the primary weapon may not have been prohibited at the time of the crime, though it was outlawed following the attack.

With all of the concerns raised over assault weapons, particularly after high-profile events such as Columbine and Sandy Hook, a consistent proportion of individuals still favor restricting these types of guns (see, generally, Blumenthal, 2012; Madison, 2011; Omero et al., 2013; "Post-ABC poll," 2013). At the same time, much like control measures overall, support for a federal assault weapons ban, even since its introduction in 1994, continues to decline. In fact, in some polls, as much as a 25 percent drop has been witnessed (Doherty, 2015). Further, depending on the poll, opposition for a ban has been found to exceed the support for such a measure (Pew Research Center for the People & the Press, 2012b; Saad, 2012a). One potential fact for this shift in support is that the AWB has had almost no effect on the number of mass shootings taking place (Fox & DeLateur, 2014).

Another area targeted in legislative efforts, particularly related to assault weapons, is the size of the magazines they can hold—that is, how many bullets the gun can fire between reloads (Kleck, 2009). Individuals who support the ban of larger magazines argue that prohibition could help reduce the lethality of mass shootings because people would have more time to escape or engage the shooter as they reloaded, which would have to be done more frequently (Best, 2013; Kleck, 2009). Such a measure was included in the original AWB—magazine capacities were limited to 10 rounds (Kleck, 2009; Schildkraut & Hernandez, 2014). Anything larger than this was considered to not be suitable for civilian use and was prohibited, at least until the time the ban expired (Kleck, 2009; Schildkraut & Hernandez, 2014). Still, given that many shooters use multiple guns and come prepared with numerous magazines and rounds of ammunition, attempts to regulate the size of these clips ultimately may be irrelevant (Schildkraut & Elsass, in press). Despite this, public support for such limitations persists (Barry et al., 2013; Doherty, 2015; McGinty et al., 2013; Pew Research Center for the People & the Press, 2012c; Saad, 2012a). Still, this support has failed to translate into enacted legislation, even after the Aurora, Colorado, movie theater shooter used a 100-round drum in his attack (Dao, 2012).

Kleck (2009) has argued that mass shootings (in schools) are the worst possible case for gun control because those measures that are proposed actually better address more ordinarily occurring crimes (e.g., aggravated assaults, armed robberies) as opposed to random acts of violence. Furthermore, a greater problem exists with how shooters obtain their weapons, which the majority of proposed remedies do not directly address. For instance, the shooters at Virginia Tech, Tucson, and Aurora each should have been disqualified from being able to purchase or personally own firearms under the Gun Control Act of 1968 because of mental health issues (Schildkraut & Hernandez, 2014), as we discuss in the next section. Instead, each of these perpetrators legally passed all of the necessary background checks to obtain their weapons; thus, it is important to consider that the gaps in the reporting systems are more to blame than the laws themselves. Other perpetrators, particularly those who are juveniles, often use guns that belong to a family member, as was the case with the Heath High School (1997) and Thurston High School (1998) shootings. The Sandy Hook shooter also had access to a number of firearms that his mother legally had acquired. A third way in which the shooters procure weapons is by theft, as was done by the shooters at Westside Middle School (1998) in Jonesboro, Arkansas (though the theft actually was from a family member who had secured their weapons in their home) (Kleck, 2009; Schildkraut & Hernandez, 2014). Consequently, in any of these scenarios, the legislation proposed in their wake could not adequately have prevented the shootings. Thus, the reality is that many of the measures discussed here, which are proposed to prevent statistically rare events (mass shootings), actually instead are regulating a much broader group, many of whom are responsible, law-abiding gun owners.

MENTAL HEALTH

Mental health also has been at the forefront of concern in the wake of mass shootings. In fact, concerns over mental health as a causal factor have been evident in the public discourse as early as the 1966 University of Texas shooting (Heilbrun, Dvoskin, & Heilbrun, 2009). Commentary following the rampage speculated that a malignant tumor found at the base of the gunman's brain had caused, at least in part, the shooting (Eagleman, 2011; Heilbrun et al., 2009). Yet this was debunked in the final report issued on the shooting, which found no evidence of neurological abnormalities ("Governor's committee," 1966). Among the recommendations made by the committee following the shooting was the development of a mental health program on campus accessible to both students and faculty as well as additional resources for the university's counseling services.

Following the 1999 Columbine High School shooting, it appeared that the public, in their search for answers as to why the shooting happened, began grasping at straws, and mental health was such a straw. In their 2001 report, the Columbine Review Commission (CRC) indicated that one of the gunmen, Eric Harris, had been taking the drug Luvox at the time of the shooting. In fact, his autopsy revealed that he had levels consistent with a therapeutic dosage in his system at the time of his death (CRC, 2001). Luvox typically is used to treat obsessive-compulsive disorders, but also has been prescribed as an antidepressant (CRC, 2001; "Fluvoxamine," n.d.), a revelation that likely sparked concerns over the shooter's mental health. One survivor of the shooting sued the pharmaceutical company that made Luvox, claiming that the drug either contributed to or caused the rampage (*Taylor v. Solvay Pharmaceuticals, Inc.*, 2004). The case later was settled out of court (Pankratz, 2003; *Taylor v. Solvay Pharmaceuticals, Inc.*, 2004).

Despite the amount of attention the Columbine shootings garnered, it was not until the 2007 Virginia Tech shooting that the issue of mental health as a causal factor took center stage (see Schildkraut, 2014). In August 2007, the Virginia Tech Review Panel (VTRP) released their findings after concluding their investigation of the shooting. One of the main areas of focus in the report was shooter Seung-Hui Cho's mental health. The report indicated that at an early age, following his family's immigration to the United States from South Korea, the shooter was diagnosed with selective mutism, which is a social anxiety disorder, as well as major depression (VTRP, 2007). As a result, he was dissuaded from attending Virginia Tech due to its size and distance from his home, but enrolled anyway in the fall of 2003.

While attending Virginia Tech, the shooter exhibited a number of, what later would be considered to be, warning signs. His writings became increasingly violent, so much so that a number of his professors began documenting their encounters with him (VTRP, 2007; see also Roy, 2009). His behavior also grew more hostile and threatening to those around him (VTRP, 2007). Some students stopped attending classes when they became fearful of him; one professor had Cho removed from his class and he was mentored one-on-one by the head of the English Department.

The shooter's erratic behavior extended outside of the classroom as well. In November 2005, he appeared at the dorm room of a female student wearing a hat and sunglasses, introducing himself as his imaginary twin brother "Question Mark" (VTRP, 2007, p. 45). The student alerted the Virginia Tech Police Department (VTPD), who visited the shooter but let him off with a warning to leave her alone. The shooter subsequently made an appointment with the Cook Counseling Center to seek help, but failed to show up as scheduled. The following month, another female student found writings on her dorm room door that mirrored messages he had sent to her through Facebook. He was let off with a second warning from the VTPD after the student declined to press charges.

The following day, however, the VTPD was back at the shooter's dorm room following a call about a suicide threat (VTRP, 2007). He was taken back to the department, where a member of the local community service board (CSB) pre-screened him for mental illness. A temporary detention order was issued based on the CSB screener's finding that he was mentally ill, refused to seek voluntary treatment, and posed an imminent danger to himself and others (Bonnie, Reinhard, Hamilton, & McGarvey, 2009; VTRP, 2007). He then was transported to a local behavioral health center, where he underwent observation and evaluation. Despite findings consistent with the CSB screener's report, the judge ordered outpatient treatment at the shooter's commitment hearing, which he never followed up on.

Similar to the Virginia Tech shooter, Jared Loughner, the man who shot Congresswoman Gabrielle Giffords and 18 others, killing 6 of them, in 2011, had a long documented history of mental health concerns. In the months and years leading up to the shooting, his behavior had grown increasingly irregular. He was paranoid that the government was trying to control him and sometimes spoke in random strings of words that did not make sense (Cloud, 2011; Pickert & Cloud, 2011). At Pima Community College, his classmates grew increasingly fearful of his behavior, with some noting that they expected him to commit a shooting right at the school (Pickert & Cloud, 2011). He had five contacts with the college's police department before his expulsion in 2010 (Corella, 2013; Pickert & Cloud, 2011). His parents had noticed increasingly strange and erratic behavior but did not seek a mental health evaluation, ultimately writing the oddities off as a side effect from drugs they assumed him to be taking, though a drug test they required him to submit to came back clean (Corella, 2013). They did, however, eliminate his access to weapons within the home after Pima Community College recommended so in its report coinciding with his expulsion. The shooter, successfully passing a background check, was able to secure a handgun from a local sporting goods store; yet when he went to a Wal-Mart to purchase additional ammunition on the morning of the shooting, his behavior was so alarming that the clerk lied to him and said they were out of stock.

Following the shooting and after entering an initial plea of not guilty in May 2011, the gunman underwent examination by two medical experts who diagnosed him as suffering from schizophrenia and associated delusions (Harris & Kiefer, 2011; Lacey, 2011a). He was disruptive in court and, after one outburst, had to physically be restrained and removed by marshals (Lacey, 2011a). Accordingly, the judge ruled him unfit to stand trial and remanded him to a federal psychiatric facility for treatment (Harris & Kiefer, 2011; Lacey, 2011a). The following month, a federal judge ruled that the shooter could be forcibly medicated, though his attorneys argued it violated his constitutional rights (Graham, 2011). In September 2011, the shooter was ordered to undergo further treatment in an attempt to enable him to stand trial (Lacey, 2011b). Finally, a year and a half after the shooting, he was found competent to stand trial and pled guilty in exchange for the removal of a possible death sentence (Kiefer, 2012). On November 8, 2012, he formally was sentenced to life in prison without the possibility of parole (Duke, 2012).

The case of Aurora, Colorado, movie theater shooting suspect James Holmes also has raised questions regarding mental health. Prior to the shooting, he had sought counseling from several psychologists affiliated with the University of Colorado, where he was a PhD student (Coffman, 2012). This included Dr. Lynne Fenton, the school's medical director for student mental health services who also specializes in schizophrenia ("James Holmes," 2012). During sessions with Dr. Fenton, the shooter revealed that he had homicidal thoughts multiple times per day but never had specifically spoken of specific threats or targets, which limited her abilities to have him placed on a psychiatric hold (Frosch, 2015). Similar statements had been made to others outside of the realm of doctor-patient confidentiality. Four months prior to the shooting, he told a classmate he wanted to kill people (Riccardi & Elliott, 2012).

Though the judge entered a plea of not guilty on his behalf when his lawyers indicated they were not yet ready to proceed, they did indicate that they intended to pursue an insanity defense (CNN Staff, 2013; Healy, 2013). Such a defense seemed likely as the shooter had appeared dazed and out of touch with reality at his first court appearance, which was televised for the world to see (Pearson, 2012). In early June 2013, the court accepted the shooter's insanity plea (Sandell, McKinley, & Ng, 2013) and ordered him to undergo a mental health evaluation (Elliott, 2013). When that evaluation later was deemed to be flawed, the court then ordered a second examination (Jojola, 2014). The prosecution declared in their opening statements that the evaluations found the shooter was sane (Villapaz, 2015). During his trial, the shooter's defense team presented evidence to support their claim of mental illness, including testimony from the neuropsychologist who evaluated him (Snowdon, 2015) as well as testimony from an expert in schizophrenia (Johansson, 2015). On July 16, 2015, the jury found the shooter guilty (and not legally insane) of all 165 counts, including 12 charges of first-degree murder (Johnson & Rascon, 2015). The sentencing phase began on July 22, 2015, with the shooter eligible for the death penalty (Johnson & Rascon, 2015). On August 7, 2015, however, he was sentenced to life in prison without the possibility of parole (Almasy, O'Neill, Weisfeldt, & Cabrera, 2015).

Five months after Aurora, mental health concerns again were highlighted following the Sandy Hook shooting. This was due in large part to the revelation that the shooter had been diagnosed with Asperger's syndrome (Sedensky, 2013). Asperger's is a highly functioning form of autism (Rochman, 2012), yet as Lori Shery, the president of an advocacy group for the disorder, points out:

> The media's continued mention of a possible diagnosis of Asperger syndrome implies a connection between that and the heinous crime committed by the shooter. They may have just as well said, "Adam Lanza, age 20, was reported to have had brown hair." (in Harmon, 2012)

As Shery points out with this quote, what escapes the discourse about Asperger's and the autism spectrum more broadly is how this disorder is linked with violence. According to one doctor, "aggression in autism spectrum disorders is almost never directed to people outside the family or immediate caregivers, is almost never planned, and almost never involves weapons" (Dr. Catherine Lord, in Harmon, 2012; see also Rochman, 2012). Additionally, research on Asperger's patients has found no weapon usage among study samples, and only about 2 percent have been found to be aggressive toward someone outside their family (Harmon, 2012; see also Park, 2014). In most cases, any violent acts committed by a person with Asperger's are targeted at themselves (Park, 2014).

To people searching for answers after the shooting, none of this mattered. Asperger's syndrome and autism became a place to lay blame, despite how far the United States had advanced in overcoming the stigmatization of mental health issues. Mental health advocates rallied to combat misperceptions about these disorders in the midst of intense public scrutiny (Rochman, 2012). Autism Speaks reported a 130 percent increase in calls and emails in just five days after the shooting from concerned parents wondering how to help their children avoid a similar fate or how they could protect them from backlash for being essentially "guilty by association" (Park, 2014; Rochman, 2012). Liza Long (2012) penned a blog called "I am Adam Lanza's mother," chronicling the struggles she faced each day with her son, Michael, whom she believed to be autistic based on a diagnosis from a medical professional (later determined to be one of several misdiagnoses of his condition) and the fear she had that he could resort to similar violence (see also Gupta, 2014; Park, 2014). Posted the day after the shooting, the blog quickly went viral, and two years later, after a leading expert read her story, Michael was diagnosed with bipolar disorder and treated with the necessary medications; he has not experienced another violent episode since (Gupta, 2014).

In a rare move unseen with family members of most other mass shooters (Susan Klebold, mother of one of the Columbine perpetrators, is the other exception—see Klebold, 2009), the Sandy Hook gunman's father, Peter Lanza, sat down with Andrew Solomon of the *New Yorker* for a one-on-one interview. In it, he opened up about the struggles that he and ex-wife, Nancy, faced raising the shooter, particularly after his diagnosis of Asperger's syndrome (Solomon, 2014). Peter went on to note that "Asperger's makes people unusual, but it doesn't make people like this (a killer)," even suggesting that schizophrenia was a more likely culprit for the massacre (para. 23). Even the massacre itself, particularly as it related to the shooter's planning—demolition of his computer, leaving behind photos of him with a gun held to his head, and exhibiting increasing instability leading up to the attack—was at odds with what is known about autism and related disorders (Park, 2014). Researchers have found that people with autism spectrum disorders also often suffer from other mental illnesses—depression and anxiety are among the most common—but that the overlapping of symptoms makes diagnosis difficult, if not impossible (Park, 2014; Solomon, 2014). Still, despite all of the research available on these mental health topics, there is no concrete explanation as to why Sandy Hook or any other mass shooting has occurred. As such, we continue to struggle with how to resolve a problem that is unable to specifically be attributable to a given source (or causal factor).

How to address the issue of mental health in the wake of mass shootings has been a point of contention. The Virginia Tech shooting, for one, identified a number of key issues, both in the state and in the nation as a whole. The series of events related to the commitment of the shooter a year and a half before the rampage never was reported to the state's Central Criminal Records Exchange (CCRE) as required by Virginia code (VA Code § 37.2-819; see also Schildkraut & Hernandez, 2014). As a result of failed reporting by the court clerk, the shooter was not flagged when he went to purchase the firearms used in the shooting and was able to acquire them legally. Then-governor Timothy Kaine quickly signed an executive order aimed at closing the loophole that had allowed the shooter to pass the necessary background checks and required reporting to all relevant databases (Schildkraut & Hernandez, 2014). At least 12 other states enacted similar legislation to improve reporting (Brady Campaign Press Release, 2011).

The biggest legislative change came in the form of the NICS Improvement Amendments Act, signed into law by President Bush in early 2008 and aimed at improving the national instant criminal background check system (NICS, 2007). In order to improve reporting at a national level, the Act designated $875 million in federal funding to be disbursed over five years to state courts in order to establish or overhaul existing reporting systems for firearm eligibility. An additional $500 million was added for states to use to update criminal history reporting in order to disqualify those gun owners who had prior records. The overarching goals of the Act were to improve the frequency of updating records and the speed of reporting new cases as well as promoting coordination between state and federal agencies.

In the nearly six years between the Virginia Tech and Sandy Hook shootings, little change actually occurred. In the first five years alone, only $50 million of the $1.3 billion allocation by the NICS Improvement Amendments Act had been claimed (Brady Campaign Press Release, 2011; Witkin, 2012). While almost a million new records were added to the NICS, the Brady Campaign (2011) noted that more than double the number of records disqualifying people from purchasing firearms should have been in the system, and as many as 24 states had submitted less than 100 mental health records (see also Witkin, 2012). During the same time period, mental health budgets at both state and federal levels were reduced drastically due to the recession (National Alliance on Mental Illness [NAMI], 2013).

Yet following the Sandy Hook shooting, there appeared to be a renewed interest in the topic of mental health, particularly as it relates to mass shootings. In a campaign headed by Vice President Joe Biden, the federal government pledged $100 million toward mental health care (Fox, 2013). While the legislation at the federal level was quieter than after past shootings,

37 states added new or changed existing budgets for mental health spending (Mukherjee, 2013; Simon, 2013; "States restore," 2013). A number of these measures addressed things like early detection and intervention for mental health issues, violence prevention (particularly as it related to firearms), and treatment and civil commitment (Hernandez et al., 2015; NAMI, 2013). Understanding the impact that the Sandy Hook shooting may have had on this legislation proves difficult, if not impossible (see Hernandez et al., 2015), as these changes also coincided with the passing of the Affordable Care Act (42 U.S.C. § 18001, 2010) and the Mental Health Parity and Addiction Equity Act of 2008 (Beronio, Po, Skopec, & Glied, 2013). Still, this does not stop speculation that both budgetary and legislative changes were sparked by the Sandy Hook shooting (NAMI, 2013). Despite the advances in the discussion and action related to mental health care in this country, it continues to be a usual suspect in the wake of mass shootings.

VIOLENT MEDIA

While typically receiving the least attention of the "usual suspects" (see Schildkraut, 2014), the potential role of violent media as a causal factor for mass shootings often still is present in both the public and the political discourse following such an event (see also Lawrence & Birkland, 2004; Rocque, 2012). As with the quote at the onset of this chapter, people argue that entertainment media has a desensitizing effect on those who consume it, either causing them to be violent or reinforcing such tendencies that already may have been present. As De Venanzi (2012) astutely notes, "violent movies and video games ... have been converted into objects of fear" (p. 262). In return, campaigns are launched to regulate the television, film, music, and video game industries in an attempt to prevent these violent products from falling into the hands of the next mass shooter. Yet the broad reach of the media industry often is not considered in such a crusade.

The trend of criminalizing violent media in the wake of mass shootings was evident early on with Columbine. When it was revealed that the gunmen had a considerable interest in "Goth rock" bands, such as Rammstein and KMFDM, these and similar artists immediately were vilified for the shooting (Powers, 1999; Schildkraut & Muschert, 2013). In particular, it was Marilyn Manson who was the most criticized and often blamed for the shootings, despite that it later was revealed that the shooters actually did not listen to his music (Bell, C., 2012; Cullen, 2009; D'Angelo, 2001; Willis, 2015). Two years after the shooting, protests erupted in Denver when Manson was scheduled to perform in the upcoming Ozzfest concert series (Walsh & Mazza, 2001). The backlash was so intense and widespread that the rocker ultimately pulled out of the show (D'Angelo, 2001).

Beyond the music, another form of media was criticized heavily after the shooting. As Cullen (2009) notes, "the pop culture artifact most associated with the Columbine massacre" was a movie—*Natural Born Killers* (p. 197). Oliver Stone's film chronicles a pair of serial killers as they embark on a murder spree across the country while simultaneously avoiding capture by law enforcement (Frymer, 2009). Diary excerpts from the Columbine shooters revealed the boys' fascination with the movie, so much so that they used "NBK" as the codename for their attack (Cullen, 2009; Frymer, 2009; Larkin, 2007). Though *Natural Born Killers* has been framed as having the strongest impact on the Columbine rampage (Larkin, 2007), other movies, including *The Matrix* and *The Basketball Diaries*, also were suggested to be influential on shooters both from Columbine and from other similar events (Birkland & Lawrence, 2009; Springhall, 1999; see also *Sanders v. Acclaim Entertainment, Inc.*, 2002). Similarly, the popular Korean film *Old Boy* was said to have inspired the Virginia Tech massacre (Corliss, 2007; Kellner, 2008a; Schildkraut, 2012b; Serazio, 2010), and "commercial movies depicting mass shootings" were among the items seized as evidence from the Sandy Hook shooter's home (Sedensky, 2013, p. 26).

Discourse on violent media following earlier shootings, such as those at Columbine (*Sanders v. Acclaim Entertainment, Inc.*, 2002) and Heath High School in West Paducah, Kentucky, a year and a half earlier (*James v. Meow Media, Inc.*, 2002), emphasized the role of violent computer games, such as *Doom* and *Quake*. *Doom*, in particular, has been characterized as one of the earliest first-person shooter games where players also can engage with others over the Internet (Nizza, 2007). In addition to allowing players to compete across predesigned levels, it enables them to create their own scenarios (Simpson & Blevins, 1999). One of the Columbine gunmen even was said to have created a level that mirrored the school so that he could test and improve his plans for the shooting.

Though Columbine was not the first incident in which the shooters had been avid video game players, it became the platform on which special interest groups could campaign against this particular form of media (Ferguson, 2011; Gaudiosi, 2011). In addition to the political crusade against violent media, others took a stand in the fight by suing the manufacturers of the games and movies. In 2002, the family of Dave Sanders, the only teacher to be killed at Columbine, filed a wrongful death suit against a number of media companies, including New Line Cinema, Nintendo, Sega, Atari, Sony Computer Entertainment, and Time Warner (*Sanders v. Acclaim Entertainment, Inc.*, 2002). The suit alleged that "but for the actions of the Video Game

Defendants and the Movie Defendants, in conjunction with the acts of the other defendants herein, the multiple killings at Columbine High School would not have occurred" (p. 1268). The case was dismissed before oral arguments even were made. That same year, parents of the victims of the 1997 Heath High School shooting in West Paducah, Kentucky, filed suit against media companies, including several of those in litigation with Dave Sanders's family. Similarly, they argued that regularly playing video games, watching movies, and visiting Internet sites had " 'desensitized' Carneal [the shooter] to violence and 'caused' him to kill the students of Heath High School" (*James v. Meow Media, Inc.*, 2002, p. 687). Their case also was dismissed.

Despite the failure of these lawsuits to confirm the liability of the violent media industry in mass shootings, others continued to try to label these products as causes. More recently, however, the discourse on violent media following such attacks has shifted toward the role of video games. Specifically, first-person shooting games, such as *Call of Duty* and multiple editions of its sequels, *Black Ops* and *Modern Warfare*, have been at the center of a firestorm of controversy, particularly as some reported that the Sandy Hook shooter spent hours each day playing the game (Henderson, 2012; Jaccarino, 2013; see also Ferguson, C. J., 2014; Fox & DeLateur, 2014). Other shooters, including those from the 2011 Tucson and 2012 Aurora attacks, also have been reported to be avid gamers (Jaccarino, 2013). In the case of the 2011 Oslo, Norway, shooting, the gunman reportedly used the game as a training simulation (Guadiosi, 2011; Jaccarino, 2013; see also Ferguson, 2008; Fox & DeLateur, 2014; Markey, French, & Markey, 2015).

Early research into the effects of gaming violence (e.g., Anderson, 2004; Funk, Balducci, Pasold, & Baumgardner, 2004; Gentile, Lynch, Linder, & Walsh, 2004; Uhlmann & Swanson, 2004) purports a causal link between playing violent video games and aggressive behavior. Anderson (2004), for example, suggests that playing violent video games increased the likelihood of violent behavior in real life. Gentile and colleagues (2004) share similar findings, noting that greater exposure to violent video games is linked to increased hostility, more frequent arguments with authoritative figures (teachers), poor performance in school, and greater likelihood of participating in physical altercations. Funk et al. (2004) found that exposure to violent video games among children was correlated with decreased empathy toward others as well as attitudes supportive of violence. Pro-violence attitudes also were supported by exposure to violent movies. Using an implicit associations test, Uhlmann and Swanson (2004) found that study participants who played the violent video game (as opposed to a more passive offering) exhibited more aggressive traits.

Strasburger and Donnerstein (2014) have suggested that video games in particular may have a greater impact on individuals than other forms of media (e.g., television shows or movies) due to "the process of identification with the aggressor, active participation, repetitive actions, a hostile virtual reality, and reinforcement for aggressive actions [which] are all strong mechanisms for the learning and retention of aggressive behaviors and attitudes" (p. 721). Yet in spite of this, they caution that no such causal link actually has been found, particularly as it relates to mass shooters. Similarly, more recent studies do not support a relationship between video game violence and mass shooters or even people more generally (e.g., Ferguson, C. J., 2014; Ferguson & Olson, 2014; Fox & DeLateur, 2014; Markey, Markey, & French, 2014). Ferguson and Olson (2014), for instance, found that among children with clinically elevated mental health symptoms, no evidence of increased bullying or delinquent or criminal behaviors existed when they played violent video games. Such a finding is particularly important as Strasburger and Donnerstein (2014) point out that most research on gaming effects concentrates on "normal" participants rather than those with some form of mental health issue. Ferguson (2011) also offers caution in drawing causal links between violent video games and mass shooters, particularly as events more commonly are perpetrated by older individuals. Effects of the media, however, typically are attributed to younger gunmen. In a separate study examining the relationship between violent crimes (homicides and aggravated assaults) and video games (using sales, release dates, and Internet searches for guides for such games), Markey, Markey, and French (2014) found that there actually is a *negative* relationship, meaning that increased exposure to violent video games leads to a *decrease* in real-world violence.

The public also has weighed in on various forms of media as a causal factor for violence. In a survey conducted by Gallup less than a month after the Columbine shootings, 62 percent of the over 1,000 adults questioned indicated that violence in the media was to blame for similar brutality in schools (Newport, 1999). Additionally, 83 percent expressed support for restricting the sale of violent entertainment media (Carlson, 2002). More than half of these same respondents believed it was the government's responsibility to regulate the level of violence in video games (58 percent), on television (56 percent), and on the Internet (65 percent). In a poll conducted just five days after the Sandy Hook shooting, 78 percent of the 1,009 respondents indicated that decreasing the depiction of gun violence in the media would be effective at preventing mass shootings in schools (Newport, 2012).

Attempts have been made by politicians to regulate various forms of media, such as video games. In 2005, California governor Arnold Schwarzenegger signed into legislation a bill that required violent video games to be labeled accordingly (CA Assem. Bill 1179, 2005). Sales and rentals of such games to minors were prohibited, and anyone found in violation of the law could be fined up to $1,000 per incident. A key problem with the legislation, as Thorsen (2005) points out, is that the term "violent" was broadly defined and would eliminate most games. Similar legislation had been passed in both Illinois (Broache, 2006) and Michigan (Associated Press, 2006c); each later was found to violate the First Amendment and deemed unconstitutional (Associated Press, 2006c; Broache, 2006). The Entertainment Merchants Association (EMA), which had been instrumental in the Illinois and Michigan cases, joined by the Entertainment Software Association (ESA), challenged the California law, noting that the overly strict regulations ultimately could harm the video game industry. After an injunction and then a victory for the EMA and ESA, Governor Schwarzenegger appealed the District Court's decision, and the case eventually found itself before the U.S. Supreme Court (*Brown v. Entertainment Merchants Association*, 2011). In a 7-2 opinion, the Supreme Court upheld the lower court's decision, noting that video games were protected under the First Amendment and did not meet the threshold for content-based exceptions.

What often escapes the discourse about violence in the media is just how many people consume it. For instance, Marilyn Manson has sold over 50 million albums worldwide to date ("Marilyn Manson," n.d.). In just its opening weekend alone, *Natural Born Killers* grossed over $11 million (BoxOffice.com, n.d.). In its first week of release, *Call of Duty: Black Ops 2* sold more than 11 million copies (Kain, 2012). Thus, despite all of the millions of people that consume these various forms of entertainment media and do not commit a mass shooting, these still remain as one of the "usual suspects."

Mass shootings themselves have, in various forms, taken a starring role in popular media. Well-known teen shows throughout the years, including *Buffy the Vampire Slayer* (1997: Season 2, Episode 3), *7th Heaven* (1998: Season 3, Episode 7; 2001: Season 6, Episode 2), *One Tree Hill* (2006: Season 3, Episode 16), and *Glee* (2013: Season 4, Episode 18), all have featured episodes with a school shooting in the storyline. Prime time crime dramas, including *Law and Order* (2001: Season 11, Episode 22), *CSI* (2001: Season 2, Episode 4), *Law and Order: SVU* (2003: Season 5, Episode 2), *NCIS* (2006: Season 3, Episode 18), and *Criminal Minds* (2011: Season 7, Episode 4), each have highlighted similar content. A number of popular movies, including the aforementioned *The Basketball Diaries*, also have portrayed school shootings. Several movies—including Ben Cuccio's *Zero Day* (2003) and Gus Van Sant's *Elephant* (2003)—specifically depict the Columbine shooting.

In addition to the large and small screens, mass shootings also have found a place in the lyrics of a number of popular songs. The 1972 song "Sniper" by Harry Chapin is about the 1966 University of Texas shooting. A number of songs, including "I'm Back" (2000) and "Rap God" (2013) by Eminem, "The Anatomy of a School Shooting" (2004) by Ill Bill, and "Cassie" (2005) by Flyleaf, specifically reference the Columbine massacre, the shooters, or the victims by name. Other songs, such as Pearl Jam's "Jeremy" (1991), Alice Cooper's "Wicked Young Man" (2000), and P. O. D.'s "Youth of a Nation" (2001), reference school shootings more generally. It is, however, the 2011 song "Pumped Up Kicks" by the band Foster the People that has drawn considerable criticism. Despite being labeled as a "perky pop ditty with just enough low-fi murkiness to make it hip" (Johnson, 2011, para. 3), the song features lyrics chronicling the struggles of a shooter preparing for his attack. It is, however, the song's chorus of "All the other kids with the pumped up kicks/you better run, better run, outrun my gun/all the other kids with the pumped up kicks/you better run, better run, faster than my bullet" that has raised the most red flags. Despite the song's success on the industry charts, a number of stations quickly pulled it from their rotation after Sandy Hook (" 'Pumped Up Kicks,' " 2012; Quan, 2012). Ke$ha's song "Die Young" (2012) also was pulled from the airwaves following the shooting (" 'Pumped Up Kicks,' " 2012).

WHO ELSE IS TO BLAME?

While much of the discourse on causal factors after mass shootings is centered upon these "usual suspects," there are additional outlets that may be criminalized through the search for the ever-elusive answer to the question "why?" From a lack of religion (Brooks, 2007; Seelye, 1999) to high school subcultures (see, generally, Larkin, 2007; Lewin, 1999) and the isolating environments of colleges and universities, a number of purported causes extend beyond the shooters themselves, who rarely are criminalized (Schildkraut & Muschert, 2013). Instead, the causes of the shootings often are perceived as being more complex. Some have gone so far as to suggest that the environmental design of suburban communities, such as Littleton, breeds mass shooters (Hamilton, 1999).

Still, arguably one of the easiest "suspects" to be critical of is people as it is much easier to lay blame when "someone should have done something." Following Columbine, for example, the school resource officer, Neil Gardner, was suggested to have facilitated the lethality of the shooting because he engaged with the gunmen (CRC, 2001). Such a statement fails, however, to account for the fact that he likely had no training on active shooter situations, originally had been responding to a diversionary explosion the shooters set up in nearby Clement Park, and was outside, leaving the shooters with free-range of the school until SWAT teams entered the building. The Jefferson County Sheriff's Office (JCSO), the agency charged with leading the response to the shooting and subsequent investigation, also was blamed for their handling of the incident, though not necessarily believed to be directly liable for the attack. The daughter of Dave Sanders, the only teacher to be killed in the shooting, sued JCSO and other county-level agencies for violating her father's due process rights and failing to act in a timely manner that may have saved his life (*Sanders v. The Board of County Commissioners of the County of Jefferson, Colorado*, 2001). The court sided with Sanders, and she was awarded a $1.5 million settlement; JCSO maintained that it engaged in no wrongdoing associated with Dave Sanders's death (Associated Press, 2002b).

Other lawsuits filed by Columbine victims and their families (or the latter in the case of those who had been killed) were less successful ("Judge dismisses," 2001). In fact, all other cases (*Castaldo v. Stone*, 2001; *Ireland v. Jefferson County Sheriff's Department*, 2002; *Rohrbough v. Stone*, 2001, 2002; *Ruegsegger v. Jefferson County Board of County Commissioners*, 2001; *Ruegsegger v. Jefferson County School District R-1*, 2001; *Schnurr v. Board of County Commissioners of Jefferson County*, 2001) claiming that the school and JCSO had failed to prevent the shooting were dismissed (see also "Judge dismisses," 2001). Despite a federal judge finding there was no evidence of negligence on the part of JCSO in the rescue of Patrick Ireland, one of the survivors in the library, they later settled for $117,500 ("Injured Columbine student," 2004). Parents of two of the slain children at Sandy Hook—Noah Pozner and Jesse Lewis—similarly filed suit against Newtown and its school board, alleging that each were negligent as it related to security on the day of the shooting (*Lewis v. Town of Newtown*, 2015; see also Altimari, 2015). The lawsuit still is pending at the time of this writing.

In the aftermath of both Columbine and Sandy Hook, lawsuits were filed against gun manufacturers and distributors as well. Ireland sued the owner of the gun show at which the shooters had acquired three of their four guns, alleging that he had failed to have safety precautions in place to prevent minors from acquiring firearms (*Ireland v. Jefferson County Sheriff's Department*, 2002). The problem, however, is that as discussed earlier, they did not purchase the guns themselves as they were not old enough at the time; instead, their friend did so on their behalf. Ireland also sued the specific dealer who had sold the shotgun used to wound him (*Ireland v. Jefferson County Sheriff's Department*, 2002); the case later was settled out of court, as was a similar claim by other families of slain victims (Associated Press, 2003a).

In 2015, nine families of victims of Sandy Hook joined together and filed suit against Bushmaster International, the manufacturer of the gun used in the shooting (*Soto et al v. Bushmaster Firearms International, LLC et al*, 2015). The plaintiffs argued that the company was negligent in its manufacturing of the gun and making it available to the public (*Soto et al v. Bushmaster Firearms International, LLC et al*, 2015; see also Milford & Dolmetsch, 2014; Ziv, 2014). The case, originating in state court, was moved to federal district court after Bushmaster filed to have the suit transferred, as it would have a better chance of being dismissed (Richinick, 2015a). Under a federal shield law enacted in 2005, gun manufacturers are protected against lawsuits related to people being killed with their products (Goss, 2015; Richinick, 2015a). The families of the victims quickly responded, trying to get the case pushed back to state court (Stewart, 2015). Though the case remains open at the time of this writing, on October 1, 2015, a district court judge ruled that the case was to be returned to state court ("First victory," 2015).

On one occasion, the owner of the location of the shooting was the target of blame and litigation. In 2013, victims and family members of those killed in the Aurora, Colorado, theater shooting the year prior filed suit against the company who owned the venue (*Traynom v. Cinemark USA, Inc.*, 2013). They alleged, among other things, that the theater's failure to provide added security in anticipation of increased patrons for the movie, the absence of security devices on the theater door (leading out to the gunman's car parked directly behind the auditorium, which he accessed at least once just prior to the shooting), and failure to provide emergency response protocols and training to their employees potentially could have prevented the attack. The theater's motion to dismiss the case ultimately was denied, though the judge refused to enter a summary judgment. The case, however, was reintroduced the following year after both sides had additional time for discovery (*Axelrod v. Cinemark Holdings, Inc.*, 2014). For a second time, the court held that the case would not be dismissed at the theater's motion (*Axelrod v. Cinemark Holdings, Inc.*, 2014; see also Patten, 2014). In 2014, the Brady Center to Prevent Gun Violence filed a separate suit on behalf of the parents of Jessica Ghawi, who was killed in the attack (Brady Campaign Press Release, 2014). The suit named online sellers of the ammunition and other equipment (e.g., gun magazines and body armor) used in the shooting, noting that their negligence enabled the perpetrator to amass an arsenal of over 6,000 bullets, a 100-round drum, and ballistics gear.

A growing trend in the blame game is to point the finger of guilt at the shooters' parents. After Columbine, anywhere from 20 to 51 percent of people polled blamed the Harrises and Klebolds (AllPolitics, 1999; Gillespie, 1999; Pew Research Center for the People & the Press, 2000; Saad, 1999).

Several articles (Belkin, 2009; Brooks, 2004) purported this number to be as high as 85 percent, though the polling data never were recovered. One Gallup poll reported that nearly 50 percent of respondents believed that parents should be held legally responsible if their child committed a crime using their gun (Saad, 1999).

The public was not the only group pointing fingers at the shooters' parents. In fact, while others, as discussed above, were suing Jefferson County, the sheriff's office, the school district, and gun manufacturers, one family— the parents of Isaiah Shoels, who was killed in the shooting—sued the parents of the perpetrators (CNN, 1999). Just over a month after the shooting, the Shoels family filed a wrongful death suit for $250 million, alleging that the shooting occurred as a result of the parents' failure to supervise their children. In 2003, they were ordered by a judge to accept a settlement of $366,000 on their claim (*Shoels v. Stone*, 2003; see also CNN Library, 2015b; *Shoels v. Klebold*, 2004). Five other families also sued the shooters' parents, though the details of their settlements never were released (CNN Library, 2015b). In the interim, the remaining 30 families reached settlements with the Harrises and Klebolds, totaling approximately $1.6 million (CNN, 2001). Additional settlements were reached with those individuals who had helped the shooters secure their firearms. Similar lawsuits also had been associated with pre-Columbine shootings at Heath High School in West Paducah, Kentucky, and Westside Middle School in Jonesboro, Arkansas (Belkin, 1999).

While most believed that the Columbine shooters' parents' guilt was indirect, in that they were not aware of what their sons had been planning but should have been, many following the Sandy Hook attack treated Nancy Lanza, who was killed by her son prior to his rampage, as an accessory to murder. Family members of the victims in particular pointed to a breakdown in parenting and an ease in accessibility to the firearms and ammunition that were kept in the home (Kuruvilla & Chinese, 2013; Quijano, 2013). It was those guns that took her life and the life of 26 others at the elementary school (Kuruvilla & Chinese, 2013). Nancy, a gun enthusiast, had shared her hobby with the perpetrator as a way for them to stay connected; they had taken gun safety courses together as well (Sedensky, 2013). She even had planned to purchase him a pistol of his own for Christmas. Despite her attempts at teaching responsible gun ownership to her son, the estate of Nancy Lanza was sued by multiple families for damages stemming from the shooting (Sgueglia & Sanchez, 2015; Tepfer, 2015). On August 3, 2015, the case was settled for $1.5 million to be divided equally among the 16 families (De Avila & King, 2015). Additionally, she was vilified in the media. In one op-ed, for example, Emily Miller (2013) remarked, "We can't blame lax gun-control laws, access to mental health treatment, prescription drugs or video games for Lanza's terrible killing spree. We can point to a mother who should have been more aware of how sick her son had become and forced treatment" (para. 30, 31). Other media outlets shared similar sentiments.

Arguably one of the most proffered causal factors for mass shootings, particularly in events involving adolescent perpetrators, is bullying, a term that has become a buzzword in the media discourse after such attacks (Schildkraut, 2012b). This trend, like others discussed in this chapter, began after Columbine as society struggled to understand why the shootings had occurred. Larkin (2007) points out that bullying had occurred at Columbine, typically instigated by the jocks against the social outcasts, and has been rationalized as an unfortunate side effect of the social ladder that is high school (both in Littleton and across the nation). Reports vary as to whether Harris and Klebold actually were bullied (e.g., Brown & Merritt, 2002; Cullen, 2009; Larkin, 2007). Research has shown, however, that the perpetrators themselves had bullied others (Larkin, 2007). As Tonso (2009) points out, bullying occurs in schools across the nation every day, yet few adolescents choose to engage in mass shootings as a form of revenge. Still, this does not stop the media from speculating that the tormenting of the shooters by their peers was the cause for this and other attacks. Even when shooters, such as Chardon High School gunman T. J. Lane, were well liked and had a strong social network of friends (Caniglia, 2012; Thomas, 2012), the media still attempts to insinuate that they were bullied (CBS News, 2012a).

WHY ARE THE SHOOTERS NOT MORE RESPONSIBLE?

The usual suspects and other potential causal factors discussed in this chapter highlight one very important trend: in the wake of a mass shooting, the discourse focuses on blaming everyone and everything but the person who pulled the trigger. As noted earlier in the chapter, it is too simplistic of a response to say that bad people do bad things, nor in a number of cases can the shooters be held responsible because they commit suicide. Even when they can be, their actions often are reasoned away by emphasizing issues such as mental health, which take the lead in the blame game (see also Schildkraut & Muschert, 2013). While we may never fully understand "why" these events take place, we are able to gain a better understanding by continuing a comprehensive discussion about the individual, community-level, and sociocultural causes of this type of violence (Henry, 2000, 2009; Muschert, 2007a; Muschert, Henry, Bracy, & Peguero, 2014; Schildkraut & Muschert, 2013). Such a discussion should include the media, but also must incorporate individuals from academia, politics, and the public alike (Harris & Harris, 2012; Schildkraut & Muschert, 2013).

6

Mass Shootings around the Globe

Myth: "This type of mass violence does not happen in other advanced countries."

—President Barack Obama (in Richinick, 2015b)

In the barrage of media coverage that follows mass shootings in this nation, remarks often are made by politicians, writers, and reporters about how such events are almost exclusively a U.S. phenomenon. The quote above, made as part of President Obama's response to the July 17, 2015, shooting at the Emanuel A. M. E. Church in Charleston, South Carolina, is indicative of similar statements that have followed other shootings. In fact, in one article published following the September 16, 2013, shooting at the Navy Yard in Washington, DC, by the satirical news source *The Onion*, writers noted that the American public is

> [t]otally into and [has] indeed fully embraced deadly public shootings as part of the rich tapestry of American life, akin to baseball or apple pie. . . . They are undeniably an American tradition at this point. ("Desperate nation tries getting on board," 2013, para. 2, 5)

Though *The Onion* is not given the same level of credibility as other news sources due to its humorous slant on serious topics, this statement is highly indicative of public sentiment—that mass shootings are an American issue.

While the president followed the above comment by noting that "it doesn't happen in other places with this kind of frequency," this often was lost in the media coverage of the Charleston shooting ("Obama on Charleston," 2015, para. 7). Instead, writers and reporters focused on the initial statement as a way to generate fear and hysteria and reinforce the belief that mass shootings are a U.S. problem. The quote at the beginning of this chapter was emphasized so heavily that thousands of news articles utilized it as the headline within hours of the statement being made. Additionally, news stations superimposed the quote along the bottom ticker for their shows.

The reality is, however, that the United States is not the only country that experiences mass shootings. Other countries have had extremely lethal and high-profile shootings, yet few of these receive the same level of media attention in this nation. For example, a cursory examination of the *New York Times* for 30 days following several of these shootings (see, generally, Chyi & McCombs, 2004; Muschert & Carr, 2006; Schildkraut, 2012a, 2014; Schildkraut & Muschert, 2014) reveals that two shootings in Germany, occurring in 2002 and 2009, each received mention in only six articles. Shootings in schools in Finland in 2007 and 2008 were covered in just four stories and one article, respectively. In fact, only one shooting—a 2011 multisite attack in Norway—received comparable coverage (71 articles) in the *Times* to higher saliency cases in the United States, including Columbine (1999), Tucson (2011), and Sandy Hook (2012).

In this chapter, we challenge the perception (or myth) that mass shootings are a U.S. phenomenon. Specifically, we explore mass shootings that have occurred in other nations around the globe using a case study approach. From there, we consider the broader picture in terms of how many events have transpired internationally and how these numbers compare with those from the United States. We further consider why, if any, disparity in the statistics exists and how that may contribute to beliefs about these events.

NORTH AMERICA

When individuals think of North America and mass shootings, they most immediately associate the two with the United States. After all, as noted at the onset of this chapter, claims makers, including politicians and the media, typically frame mass shootings as a problem inherent to this country. Yet what often is not discussed is that such incidents also have taken place in Canada. These events have occurred at a lesser frequency than in the United States, but have been costly in terms of the number of lives claimed.

On August 28, 1972, William Lepine, also known as William McConnell, went on a murder spree in the Kettle Valley area of British Columbia (Canadian Press, 1972a, 1972b; United Press International, 1972b). The 27-year-old gunman was a mental patient who, several weeks earlier, had escaped from an institution near Vancouver (United Press International, 1972b). In the 100-mile-long spree, he killed six people and wounded three others using two firearms (Canadian Press, 1972a, 1972b; United Press International, 1972a, 1972b). After an intensive manhunt, police arrested the suspect (United Press International, 1972a). Following his charging, the shooter underwent a psychiatric evaluation (Canadian Press, 1972c); he later was found not guilty by reason of insanity on all six counts (Canadian Press, 1974).

The Parliament Building in Québec City, the capital of Québec, also was the site of a mass shooting. On May 8, 1984, Denis Lortie, a 25-year-old corporal in the Canadian Army, entered the building armed with two submachine guns and a pistol (CBC, 2014a; Martin, 1984). He then made his way throughout the building to the Assembly Chamber, where the Parliament had been meeting but let out minutes earlier (CBC, 2014a; Martin, 1984). The building's sergeant-at-arms ultimately intercepted the shooter and was able to convince him to surrender to military police. He had killed 3 and wounded 13 others in the attack (CBC, 2014a). Prior to the rampage, he dropped an audiotape off at a local radio station that detailed his plans and provided motivation—he was unsatisfied with a number of the province's policies and the federal government (Martin, 1984). While he was convicted in his first trial in 1985, the verdict was overturned due to legal errors (CBC, 2014a). He pled guilty to lesser charges (second-degree murder) two years later, and was paroled in 1996 (CBC, 2014a).

In a more recent episode, 23-year-old Christopher Husbands opened fire in the food court at the Eaton Centre shopping mall in Toronto on June 2, 2012 (CBC, 2014b). By the end of his rampage, one person had been killed and seven others were injured, one of whom died nearly two weeks later (Edmiston & O'Toole, 2012). The shooter fled the scene, but surrendered to police two days later (National Post Staff, 2012). Though the two deceased victims and the shooter all had gang ties, law enforcement ruled out such activity as the cause for the attack (Edmiston & O'Toole, 2012). It also later was revealed that at the time of the shooting, the gunman was on house arrest stemming from a sexual assault charge (Edmiston & O'Toole, 2012; National Post Staff, 2012). The shooter ultimately was found guilty of two counts of second-degree murder and additional other charges stemming from the attack (CBC, 2014b). In 2015, he was sentenced to 30 years in prison without the possibility of parole (Hasham, 2015). In a tragic twist of fate, 24-year-old aspiring sportscaster Jessica Ghawi had been at the mall but left the food court moments before shots rang out (Boesveld & Cross, 2012). She was killed just over a month later in the Aurora, Colorado, movie theater shooting.

Similar to the United States, Canada has also experienced incidents of mass murder in schools. On May 28, 1975, 16-year-old Michael Peter Slobodian opened fire at the Brampton Centennial Secondary School outside of Toronto, killing an art teacher and another student during the attack (Associated Press, 1975a). An additional 13 people were wounded by gunfire before the shooter committed suicide. Nearly five months later, on October 27, 1975, in the Ontario city of Ottawa, 18-year-old Robert Poulin opened fire at the St. Pius X Catholic High School (Sherring, 2012). Using a pump action shotgun, he killed one and wounded five others before committing suicide. Prior to his rampage, the perpetrator had raped and stabbed to death an acquaintance at his home before heading to the school.

While these two Ontario shootings consistently are referenced as Canada's earliest school shootings (e.g., Associated Press, 1975a; Sherring, 2012), two other events are better known and more lethal. On December 6, 1989, 25-year-old Marc Lépine entered the Université de Montréal École Polytechnique in Montreal, Quebec (Associated Press, 1989b; Bindel, 2012). Armed with a rifle and hunting knife, he entered an engineering classroom and ordered most of the men to leave. He then opened fire on the remaining women, killing six instantly; the remaining three were wounded. He continued shooting throughout the school. By the time he committed suicide, the shooter had killed 14 women and 14 others (10 women and 4 men) were wounded. A suicide note found with the body indicated that the shooter specifically targeted women as he believed them to be feminists who had ruined his life ("The Montreal massacre," 2007). The École Polytechnique massacre has been described as the worst mass shooting in Canadian history (Associated Press, 2006e).

Nearly 20 years later, gunfire erupted at Dawson College, also located in the city of Montreal. On September 13, 2006, 25-year-old Kimveer Gill entered the campus armed with multiple weapons and made his way to the school's cafeteria. Once inside, the gunman opened fire, killing 1 and wounding 19 (Associated Press, 2006e; Struck, 2006). Responding officers engaged the shooter, who was hit in the arm by police fire in the attack (Alfano, 2006; Struck, 2006). While early reports suggested that law enforcement had taken down the shooter (Alfano, 2006; Struck, 2006), it later was revealed that he committed suicide (Alfano, 2006; Associated Press, 2006e). Further investigation into the shooter's history revealed that he had been fascinated by the 1999 Columbine shooting, suggesting that his selection of the cafeteria and wearing of a trench coat during the attack both were done to mimic the earlier event (Associated Press, 2006e).

Unlike Canada, the number of mass shootings in Mexico is few and far between. One event that received international attention was the July 31, 2015, shooting in San Jerónimo de Juárez. Oscar Flores, a 24-year-old former soldier, shot and killed 11 people and wounded several others during his rampage (McKinley, 2005). The shooter was wounded during the subsequent chase and later died of his injuries. Prior to his rampage, he also had stabbed his nephew to death and assaulted two police officers.

CENTRAL AND SOUTH AMERICA

By classifying events internationally with the definition established in Chapter 2, we see that, of all of the continents (excluding Antarctica), Central and South America are home to the fewest number of mass shootings. In fact, only one Central American country actually has experienced a single shooting; several events have taken place in South American countries. Further, in either area, there have been no documented cases of what have previously been labeled as workplace shootings. Even school shootings, which often gain particularly high levels of attention, even in other parts of the world, are especially rare occurrences.

On September 28, 2004, a 15-year-old student opened fire on his school in Carmen de Patagones, Argentina, just over 600 miles from Buenos Aires (BBC News, 2004). He killed three students and wounded five others before he was arrested by law enforcement. A separate attack took place in 2011 at Tasso da Silveira Municipal School, located in Realengo, Brazil, on the outskirts of Rio de Janeiro (Fick & Lyons, 2011). On April 7, 23-year-old Wellington Oliveira, armed with two revolvers, shot and killed 12 children and wounded 12 other people. The gunman was wounded by police fire and committed suicide shortly thereafter.

Brazil has been the site of another mass shooting, one occurring outside of a school, less than 15 years earlier. Genildo Ferreira de França, a 27-year-old who had served with the 7th Battalion of Combat Engineers, went on a shooting rampage in Santo Antonio dos Barreiros on May 21, 1997 ("Former soldier," 1997). Fifteen people lost their lives in the attack and several others were wounded. The gunman was killed in a shootout with responding law enforcement.

Other countries in South America also have experienced deadly mass shootings. On June 2, 2000, policeman Luis Navarette killed seven and wounded two others when he opened fire on a military patrol near El Tabon, El Salvador, located less than 150 miles from the capital city of San Salvador ("Authorities say," 2000). The gunman, who appeared to be intoxicated at the time of the shooting, was taken into custody by the military and police. Just over three weeks later, on June 24, a different gunman opened fire at a dance club in Bogotá, Colombia (BBC News, 2000). Eleven people were killed and seven others wounded in the shooting ("Las víctimas de la taberna," 2000).

EUROPE

If any continent is most commonly compared to the United States in terms of mass shootings, it is Europe. While the quantity of incidents still is lower by comparison, there have been a number of high-profile shootings through various countries receiving national and even international media attention. This particularly is true for school shootings, as several countries, including Germany and Finland, have experienced deadly, high-profile events. Additionally, it is Europe that is home to the most lethal mass shooting to date.

On July 22, 2011, Norway was riveted by what remains, to date (and using the definition proposed in Chapter 2), the largest fatality mass shooting event worldwide. That day, 32-year-old Anders Breivik opened fire on a camp run by Norway's largest youth political organization, Worker's Youth League, or AUF as it is known, on the island of Utøya (BBC News, 2011). Disguised as a police officer, he shot and killed 67 people (BBC News, 2011; Rayner, 2011; Sollid et al., 2012). Two others died (one fell and the other drowned) as they tried to escape; over 100 people were wounded in the attack (Andersen et al., 2012). Prior to the Utøya rampage, the shooter also had set off a car bomb outside of government offices in Oslo, killing 8 and wounding over 200 others (Rayner, 2011; Sollid et al., 2012). Police later revealed that during the Utøya rampage, the gunman had called their emergency line twice to negotiate his surrender but hung up each time and continued shooting (Price & Sandelson, 2011). He eventually surrendered to police without incident when they arrived on the island (Rayner, 2011). His 2012 trial concluded with him being given the maximum sentence of 21 years, though through the Norwegian process of containment, his sentence could be extended in 5-year increments (Lewis & Lyall, 2012).

Following the Utøya shooting, it appeared that attention shifted, at least in part, to such events on the European continent. Still, few events took place. One such incident was the February 24, 2015, shooting in Uherský Brod, located in the Czech Republic. At 12:30 p.m., 63-year-old Zdeněk Kovář entered the busy Družba restaurant and began shooting patrons at close range (Stoklasa & Vodstrcilova, 2015). After a two-hour standoff, during which time police tried to negotiate with him, the shooter committed suicide as the tactical unit entered the restaurant (Janicek, 2015). A total of eight people were dead and one other was wounded seriously (Janicek, 2015; Stoklasa & Vodstrcilova, 2015).

Yet the tragedy in Norway, while both the country's and the world's deadliest mass shooting, was not the first such incident in Europe. In fact, just several months earlier, on April 9, 2011, another attack had taken place in the Netherlands (Associated Press, 2011; Sekularac, 2011). Armed with several firearms, one of which served as the primary weapon in the attack, 24-year-old Tristan van der Vlis entered the Ridderhof mall in Alphen aan den Rijn, located approximately 20 miles from Amsterdam. Six people were killed before the shooter committed suicide (Associated Press, 2011; Quinn, 2011). An additional 16 people were wounded in the shooting (Sekularac, 2011).

Mass shootings in Europe, however, have been occurring for more than 100 years. One of the earliest documented events occurred on September 14, 1900, in Pastena, Italy. The gunman, Gaetano Longo, killed nine people and wounded two others before retreating to a nearby cemetery and committing suicide ("Flashes from the wire," 1900; "Italian runs amok," 1900). On August 30, 1912, 25-year-old Hermann Schwarz opened fire in the town of Romanshorn in Switzerland ("Madman shoots," 1912). He killed seven and wounded six others before taking off on foot; he later was captured after having been shot during the chase.

On September 4, 1913, 38-year-old German Ernst August Wagner drove to Mühlhausen an der Enz, set fire to several parts of the village, and began shooting ("Mad teacher kills," 1913). During the attack, 15 people were killed and another 16 injured by gunfire ("Man who slew 15," 1914). Prior to his rampage, the gunman also had killed his family at their home in Degerloch ("Mad teacher kills," 1913; "Man who slew 15," 1914). The shooting ended when, as he paused to reload, the perpetrator was disarmed by three bystanders, who beat him to near death ("Mad teacher kills," 1913). Law enforcement found him early the next morning lying in the street; he later was declared not guilty by reason of insanity and sent to an asylum ("Man who slew 15," 1914), where he lived until his death in 1938 (Maher & Spitzer, 1993). A year after the German rampage, on July 13, 1914, Italian Simone Pianetti opened fire on the village of Camerata Cornello, where he lived (Lorenzi, 2012; "Simone Pianetti," n.d.). He killed seven people before retreating into the mountains; he was never arrested nor his body recovered ("Simone Pianetti," n.d.).

In later years, as Europe experienced the rise and fall of the Nazi regime and World War II and its aftermath, other mass shootings took place. In the Spanish village of Tarragona, 26-year-old Jose Marimon opened fire at a farm on May 21, 1928 ("Maniac amok," 1928). He killed 10 and wounded 2 others before fleeing the scene ("Cable news," 1928; "Maniac amok," 1928). Several days later, after an intense manhunt from police and villagers, the gunman was found; he was shot and killed when he refused to surrender ("Cable news," 1928). On April 26, 1930, an unknown assailant opened fire on children performing the national dance outside the village hall in Zidilje, Yugoslavia ("5 killed," 1930). Five people were killed and six seriously wounded. On February 11, 1937, Polish peasant Wasyl Tymkow shot and killed seven people in the village of Domitrowka before committing suicide ("Peasant kills," 1937).

For several decades, few mass shootings took place in Europe; this changed as the continent approached and entered the 1980s. On November 18, 1979, for instance, 25-year-old Odon Renard opened fire on a crowd of spectators at a soccer match in Hannut, located just outside of Brussels, Belgium (United Press International, 1979). He killed 2 and wounded 12 others before being taken into custody. Six people were killed and four others wounded when 27-year-old Cevdet Yilmaz opened fire on a Delft, Netherlands café on April 5, 1983 (van den Heuvel & Houses, 2009). The shooter was apprehended and later sentenced to life in prison.

On August 19, 1987, England was shattered by what became known as the Hungerford massacre ("Massacre toll rises," 1987). In a rampage of shootings lasting just over six hours, 27-year-old Michael Ryan killed 16 people, including his mother and a responding police officer. An additional 16 people were shot but survived the attack. At the end of his rampage, the gunman barricaded himself in a room at the nearby Community Technical College, where he exchanged shots with police before ultimately committing suicide. The massacre is the most lethal in Great Britain's history and one of the most deadly in all of the United Kingdom.

Less than two years later, on April 30, 1989, England once again was riveted by news of a mass shooting as 22-year-old Robert Sartin opened fire in Monkseaton (BBC News, 2009b). He killed 1 person and wounded 14 others before being taken into custody by an unarmed police officer; he later was institutionalized after being found to suffer from schizophrenia. That same year, news of a mass shooting also broke in France. On July 12, 1989, 31-year-old farmer Christian Dornier went on a shooting rampage in the village of Luxiol (United Press International, 1989). A total of 14 people were killed in the attack; 8 others were wounded by gunshots. Among the victims were the shooter's mother and sister, who both died, and his father, who was injured but survived. He was apprehended by law enforcement after a chase and subsequent shootout, and later was institutionalized after being found not responsible due to mental illness (Michel, 2009).

Incidents took place across Europe during the 1990s. On March 4, 1992, 37-year-old Erminio Criscione opened fire in the Lugano district of Switzerland, killing six and wounding six others (Associated Press, 1992). He later hung himself in his jail cell. On June 11, 1994, seven people were killed and three others injured when 24-year-old Mattias Flink opened fire in a Falun, Switzerland, park ("Killer released," 2014; "Swedish mass murderer," 2014). He was sentenced to life in prison, which later was commuted to a set term; the shooter was released in 2014 on the 20th anniversary of the shootings ("Killer released," 2014). The same year as the Swiss attack, on December 4, 25-year-old Tommy Zethraeus opened fire at a Stockholm, Sweden, nightclub, killing 4 and wounding up to 20 others, though reports are inconsistent as to the latter ("2 convicted," 1995). He later was convicted and sentenced to life in prison; a person found to have helped him plan the attack was given 10 years imprisonment for their actions ("Killer at nightclub," 1995). The village of Podvinje, Croatia, was the site of a shooting on April 14, 1998, when 50-year-old Antun Mataić opened fire on patrons at a local café, killing seven and wounding one ("Najteži zločini," 2006). He fled the scene and committed suicide a short distance away.

A number of high-profile mass shootings took place across Europe following the turn of the century. On September 27, 2001, 57-year-old Friedrich Leibacher, dressed as a police officer, opened fire on the Zug Parliament in Switzerland, less than 20 miles from Zurich (BBC News, 2001). A total of 14 people were killed and 18 others wounded in the attack (Ochsenbein, 2011). Just before committing suicide, the gunman detonated a homemade bomb (BBC News, 2001). Six months later, on March 27, 2002, 33-year-old Richard Durn opened fire on a town council meeting in Nanterre, a suburb of Paris, France (BBC News, 2002). He killed 8 of the council members and wounded 19 others before being overpowered by bystanders. After being taken into police custody, he confessed to the crime, later committing suicide by throwing himself from a window after interrogation (Esterbrook, 2002). That same year, on August 25, 2002, 40-year-old off-duty police captain Sergey Semidovskiy killed 5 and wounded 10 others after opening fire outside a bar in Yaroslavsky, Russia ("Primorye rampage," 2002). He died two days later from cardiac arrest after an unsuccessful suicide attempt.

In 2005, Italy was the site of another public mass shooting, following nearly 50 years without such an incident. On June 28, 54-year-old Angelo Sacco killed three and wounded nine others in a rampage shooting in Bogogno (BBC News, 2005). After a nine-hour standoff, the shooter was taken into custody; he later was sentenced to life in prison. In 2010, a pair of shootings in two different countries also garnered attention. On June 2, 2010, 52-year-old taxi driver Derrick Bird opened fire in the county of Cumbria, England, near the Scottish border (BBC News, 2010; "Taxi gunman," 2010). Over a two-hour span, he killed 12 and wounded 11 others, though some reports indicated that the total number of people injured was as high as 25 (Armed Police Working Group, 2011; BBC News, 2010; "Taxi gunman," 2010). He committed suicide in a nearby wooded area (Armed Police Working Group, 2011; "Taxi gunman," 2010). Three months later, in the town of Lörrach, Germany, 41-year-old Sabine Radmacher opened fire at the local hospital, killing 3 (one of whom was both stabbed and shot) before being shot dead by responding officers (Graham & Schimroszik, 2010). Eighteen additional people were wounded in the attack on September 19, 2010 ("Autopsy reveals," 2010).

As noted, European countries also have experienced their share of mass shootings in schools. A number of these events received considerable media attention, in part for their high death toll. For those occurring after Columbine, their linkage or comparison to the shooting also helped to drive coverage and interest. Many shooters were reported to have modeled their attacks after the Columbine perpetrators or to have idolized or worshipped the gunmen.

The 2002 shooting at the Gutenberg-Gymnasium in Erfurt, for example, has been called "Germany's Columbine" (Lemonick, 2002, p. 36). On April 26, 2002, 19-year-old Robert Steinhäuser, a student who had been expelled for forging a medical note, entered the school armed with a pump-action shotgun and semiautomatic pistol (Erlanger, 2002). After changing his clothes in one of the campus's bathrooms, he went classroom to classroom, shooting primarily at teachers (Erlanger, 2002; Hooper, 2002). A total of 16 people were killed, including one responding police officer who was shot in the head; an additional person was wounded in the gunfire (Erlanger, 2002; Hooper, 2002; Lemonick, 2002). One of the school's teachers, Rainer Heise, was able to lure the shooter into a storeroom, where he locked him inside until authorities could take him into custody (Hooper, 2002; Lemonick, 2002). While in the room, the shooter committed suicide.

Nearly seven years later, another high-fatality mass shooting occurred in a German school, this time in the town of Winnenden. On March 12, 2009, 17-year-old Tim Kretschmer entered the Albertville-Realschule school just after 9:30 a.m. (BBC News, 2009a). He opened fire on three separate classrooms, hitting most of his victims in the head. As law enforcement arrived on scene, the shooter fled, first killing a gardener in a nearby park, then carjacking a passing motorist about 30 minutes after the attack began (BBC News, 2009a; Reuters, 2009). He ordered the driver toward Wendlingen, a town about 25 miles away. Once there, the shooter jumped out of the vehicle and entered a Volkswagen dealership, where he killed several more people (BBC News, 2009a). As police arrived at the showroom, the gunman engaged in a shootout, ultimately fleeing the building as he continued to fire indiscriminately at anyone he passed. The rampage ended when the shooter committed suicide. A total of 15 people had been killed (12 at the school) and 9 others wounded (Reuters, 2009).

Finland also had a pair of high-profile mass shootings in schools. On November 7, 2007, 18-year-old Pekka-Eric Auvinen entered Jokela High School in the country's Tuusula district (Ministry of Justice, 2009). Armed with a semiautomatic pistol, he arrived through the school's main entrance and opened fire. Among those shot were the school's principal as she tried to convince him to surrender and the school nurse as she tended to wounded students. He also unsuccessfully tried to burn the school down, but was unable to get the engine fuel to ignite. Approximately 44 minutes after the shooting began, the perpetrator went into one of the restrooms and shot himself in the head. He was found by police an hour and a half later, still alive; he died hours later at the hospital from his wounds (Ministry of Justice, 2009; "Nine dead," 2007). A total of eight people, including the principal and nurse, had been killed and one other injured.

Less than a year later, the town of Kauhajoki, located in western Finland, experienced a similar tragedy. On September 23, 2008, 22-year-old Matti Saari entered the Seinäjoki University of Applied Sciences, also armed with a semiautomatic pistol (Cser, 2008). In a pair of classrooms, the gunman shot and killed nine students and a teacher and wounded one other; others were injured in the shooting (Pohjanpalo, 2008). The perpetrator also had ignited a number of fires around the school and detonated a petrol bomb in the business class where most of the victims had been killed (Cser, 2008). Like the Jokela shooter, the gunman attempted to commit suicide but was found alive by law enforcement (Pohjanpalo, 2008). Similarly, he died several hours later at a nearby hospital (Cser, 2008). The Kauhajoki shooting had been the deadliest attack on a college campus after Virginia Tech and also Finland's most lethal shooting (Pohjanpalo, 2008).

Despite that these incidents received prominent attention given their timing after Columbine, several other attacks in schools also occurred before the shooting. On June 20, 1913, 29-year-old Heinz Schmidt opened fire at St. Mary's Catholic School in Bremen, Germany ("Kills 3," 1913). He killed two in the shooting (a third died from falling down stairs as she tried to escape) and wounded 21 others ("Kills 3," 1913; Schlott, 2013). Two additional girls died several weeks later of complications stemming from their gunshot wounds (Schlott, 2013). The shooter was apprehended by police and taken to a mental institution, where he was held until he died in 1932, having never been tried for the shooting ("Kills 3," 1913; Schlott, 2013). Seventy years later, on June 3, 1983, 34-year-old Karel Chavra went on a shooting rampage at a comprehensive school in Eppstein-Vockenhausen in West Germany (Associated Press, 1983; United Press International, 1983a). During his 30-minute rampage, a teacher, police officer, and 3 students were killed; 14 others were wounded. The shooter then committed suicide as additional law enforcement arrived on scene.

One of the most well-known pre-Columbine incidents was the shooting at the Dunblane Primary School in Scotland. On the morning of March 13, 1996, 43-year-old Thomas Hamilton drove to the school and entered near the gymnasium (Clouston & Boseley, 2013; The Stationery Office, 1996).

Armed with four handguns (two pistols and two revolvers) and nearly 750 rounds of ammunition, he opened fire on a PE class (The Stationery Office, 1996). Over the next three to four minutes, during which time he exited and reentered the gym several times, the shooter killed 17 people and wounded 15 others (The Stationery Office, 1996; see also Clouston & Boseley, 2013). Then, using one of the revolvers, he committed suicide (The Stationery Office, 1996). The Dunblane massacre remains the deadliest shooting incident in the United Kingdom's history.

Workplace shootings, those that are perpetrated by current or former employees of a company, appear to be less common in Europe than in the United States, but still have occurred. On July 3, 1956, 30-year-old baking assistant Giuseppe Molinari went on a two-hour rampage in Busto Arsizio, Italy ("Italian killer," 1956). During that time, in which he engaged in a shootout with responding law enforcement, the gunman killed four people and wounded five others before turning the weapon on himself. Nearly 40 years later, on July 1, 1992, 25-year-old Frank Zoritch entered a machine tool factory in Besancon, France, where he previously had been employed (Agence France-Presse, 1992). He opened fire, killing six and wounding five others before committing suicide.

Twenty years later, on November 7, 2012, 30-year-old Russian lawyer Dmitry Vinogradov shot and killed six people and wounded two others in a pharmaceutical office in Moscow where he once had worked (Stewart, 2012; see also BBC News, 2012; CBS News, 2012b). After the 18-second rampage, at which time he ran out of ammunition, the shooter was subdued by security guards and taken into police custody (BBC News, 2012; CBS News, 2012b; Stewart, 2012). Prior to his rampage, the shooter had posted a hate manifesto online (*Russia Today*, 2012; Stewart, 2012). He was sentenced to life in prison the following year and ordered to pay restitution to his victims and a fine for publishing his manifesto (*Russia Today*, 2013). While the Besancon factory shooting received virtually no coverage, the latter Russian attack was heavily covered throughout international media outlets, particularly as it followed the high-fatality shootings in Norway and Aurora, Colorado. In fact, *Russia Today* (2012, 2013) consistently called the shooter their country's equivalent of the Norway gunman.

ASIA AND THE MIDDLE EAST

There have been a number of incidents of mass violence in Asia and the Middle East. For instance, on the same day as the December 14, 2012, shooting at Sandy Hook, 22 children and 1 adult were injured when a man wielding a knife went on a rampage in an elementary school in central China

(Newcomb, 2012). Targeted incidents of violence using firearms are less common in schools in Asia and the Middle East. China, in particular, has no recorded episode of a mass shooting in a school.

Other countries, albeit a handful, however, have experienced such violence. On March 30, 1997, 48-year-old Mohammed al-Nazari killed 6 people and wounded 12 others in a pair of schools in San'a, Yemen ("Around the world," 1997). Within days, he had been tried, convicted, and executed for the crime ("Around the world," 1997; "Yemen executes," 1997). On June 6, 2003, 17-year-old Anatcha Boonkwan opened fire at the Pak Phanang school in Nakhon Si Thammarat in Thailand, killing two students and wounding four others before police arrested him (Associated Press, 2003b; "Schoolyard killings," n.d.). Years later, on March 6, 2008, 26-year-old Alaa Abu Dhein opened fire at a Jerusalem, Israel, seminary school (Glickman, 2009). In less than 20 minutes, he had shot 19 people, 8 of whom died (Glickman, 2009; Zino, 2008). An armed student who witnessed the attack shot the gunman dead (Zino, 2008). The following year, on April 30, 2009, 29-year-old Farda Gadirov killed 12 people and wounded 13 others before committing suicide in a rampage on the Azerbaijan State Oil Academy in the capital city of Baku (BBC News, 2009c; Mehtiyeva, 2009).

While mass shootings in schools have not been particularly common in Asia and the Middle East, such episodes in workplaces have seemed to occur slightly more frequently by comparison. On January 26, 1962, 41-year-old Tsui Yin killed seven and wounded four in a rampage at the school at which he worked in Taipei, Taiwan ("Berserk man," 1962). He later was executed for the killings ("Teacher who slew," 1962). More than 30 years later, on October 21, 1995, 16-year-old orderly Edgardo Fernandez killed eight and wounded three in a shooting at a hospital near Manila in the Philippines before being taken into police custody ("Philippine hospital orderly," 1995). Police sergeant Chaiyaworn Hiranwadee, age 50, killed five and wounded five others at a station in Chumphon, Thailand, on June 11, 1997, before committing suicide ("Massacre at police station," 1997).

Eight people were killed and five others injured on July 31, 2002, when 48-year-old Ahmed Mansour opened fire at a Beirut, Lebanon, ministry office where he was employed (Associated Press, 2002a). He was arrested at the scene (Associated Press, 2002a) and executed 18 months later (Karam, 2004). Samarendra Deka, a 22-year-old constable, killed seven and wounded two others before he was shot dead by police in Baramulla, India, on November 27, 2004 (Ahmad, 2004; "Shocked & sleepless," 2004). Just two months later, 31-year-old Jonathan Moreño killed 8 and wounded 30 others in a rampage near a police station in Kalibo in the Philippines (Burgos, 2005). The shooter also was killed in the attack.

As noted at the outset of this section, China has never witnessed a mass shooting in schools. The country, however, is not immune to such violence in other locations. Four people were killed and six injured when Ting Yung opened fire near Shanghai on June 22, 1934 ("Man runs amok," 1934). The shooter later was apprehended by law enforcement. On September 20, 1994, military officer Tian Minjian killed more than 15 people and wounded over 30 during his rampage shooting across Beijing (Fu, 1994; Tofani, 1994). The gunman was killed by a responding police officer (Fu, 1994). More recently, 62-year-old Jieming Fan killed six and injured four others before being arrested for his June 22, 2013, attack at a Shanghai chemical company (Associated Press, 2013a).

Mass shootings also have occurred in other countries across Asia. On July 23, 1983, 28-year-old Ramesh Sharma, a police constable, killed 14 people in a rampage at the Pashupatinath Temple in Mandsaur, India (United Press International, 1983b). An additional nine people were wounded before the gunman was shot and killed by a responding police officer. The Kali Devi temple in Chihandanda, Nepal, was the site of a similar attack on December 14, 2005, when 26-year-old Basudev Thapa killed 11 people and wounded 19 others before he was shot dead (Associated Press, 2005).

Yemen also has been the scene for mass shootings outside of schools. On April 27, 1997, Abdullah Ahmed Barkani killed eight and wounded one other at a polling station in Mukayras before being apprehended by police ("Yemen soldier kills 8," 1997). Nine people were killed and one injured on July 30, 2003, when Mohsen Yehya Munser opened fire on individuals studying the Qur'an at a local mosque; the shooter was subsequently arrested ("Death toll in Yemen," 2003). On May 30, 2008, 26-year-old Abdullah Saleh al-Kohali opened fire at a mosque in Bait al-Aqari (CBS News, 2008). Eight people were killed and nearly two dozen wounded before the gunman was taken into custody; he was executed by firing squad the following year (Al-Mahdi, 2009; see also CBS News, 2008). Ali Rasheed killed six people and wounded four others in a similar attack after a prayer at a Hamalan mosque on June 10, 2011; he subsequently was arrested by police (Yemen Post Staff, 2011).

Along with growing border tensions, countries such as Israel and Iran also had to contend with several episodes of mass shootings. On August 1, 2009, a LGBT association center in Tel Aviv, Israel, was the site of such an event when an unknown perpetrator killed two people at a youth function (Amichai, 2009; Seynor, 2013). At least 10 others were wounded in the attack. Just over three weeks later, on August 25, a 65-year-old man known only as Mohammad killed 6 and wounded 11 others during a rampage in Shahriar near Tehran, Iran (Joshi, 2009). After his arrest, the gunman indicated that he had intended to kill several others.

AFRICA

In one of the earliest recorded mass shootings on the continent, farmer Stefanus Swart killed eight people in Charlestown, South Africa, on May 6, 1927 (Lorenzi, 2012; Webster, 2005). Three others were wounded before he committed suicide. In later years, the country would experience other similar tragic incidents. On January 20, 1992, 30-year-old Carel "Kallie" Delport killed 9 and wounded 19 others in a rampage through Ladysmith, engaging in a shootout with police before being taken into custody (Renfrew, 1992). Later that same year, on August 25, police constable L. S. Hasenberg opened fire at the prison complex in Goedemoed where he was employed, killing eight before turning the gun on himself ("PC kills eight," 1992). Bulelani Vukwana killed 11 people and wounded 6 others before committing suicide in a rampage shooting in Mdantsane on February 9, 2002 ("Jilted man," 2002). Five months later, on July 1, 2002, 31-year-old former police officer Christo Brian Fortune killed four and wounded nine others in a shooting in Postmasburg ("Postmasburg killings," 2002). Eight people were killed and two others wounded when 42-year-old Chippa Mateane went on a shooting rampage in Gauteng on April 3, 2006 (Eliseev & Cherney, 2006). He was shot and killed by police during the attack.

Other countries across Africa experienced similar tragedies to those shootings in South Africa. On December 4, 1977, 38-year-old policeman Banda Khumalo killed 13 and injured 16 others before being shot and killed by responding officers in Bulawayo, Rhodesia (United Press International, 1977). Suleiman Khater, a 24-year-old soldier in Ras Burqa, Egypt, killed eight and wounded four others before being apprehended by police on October 5, 1985 ("Egyptian who shot," 1986). He was tried, convicted, and sentenced to life in prison, but committed suicide by hanging just 10 days after his hearing. Egypt also was the site of a mass shooting on August 21, 2013, as Omar Abdul Razeq Abdullah Rifai killed 15 people and then committed suicide in the village of Mayt al-Atar (Agence France-Presse, 2013).

On May 10, 1998, Rwandan soldier Viateur Nkurunziza killed six people and wounded three others before he was shot dead in Gikongoro (Reuters, 1998). The following year, on October 8, 1999, six people were killed and three others injured by 21-year-old Jean-Claude Ndayisaba during his rampage in Ruyaga, Burundi (IRIN, 1999). He was apprehended and later sentenced to death. On November 11, 2001, soldier Bawa Michael opened fire in Kaduna, Nigeria (Kwaru, 2002). He killed seven before being taken into custody, and later was sentenced to death for his crimes. In the town of Siakogo, located approximately 75 miles from the Kenyan capital of Nairobi, Peter Karanja killed 10 people in a November 6, 2010, rampage before being arrested

("Kenyan police officer," 2010). On May 12, 2013, Ethiopian federal police officer Fekadu Nasha killed 12 and wounded 2 others in a shooting in Bahir Dar before committing suicide ("Police named officer," 2013).

Uganda also experienced several highly lethal attacks in the 1990s and 2000s. On June 26, 1994, Richard Komakech killed 26 people and wounded 13 others during a rampage killing on Naguru in the capital city of Kampala (Bwire, 2015). Six months later, on December 26, 1994, 28-year-old Alfred Ogwang killed 13 and wounded an additional 14 people when he opened fire at a dance at the Kamwenge Trading Centre (Bwire, 2015); he was arrested after fleeing the scene ("Policeman massacres 12," 1994). In a more recent event, Nicholas Mucunguzi opened fire at a bar in Kampala on May 2, 2009 (Karugaba & Bekunda, 2009). A total of seven people were killed and six injured; the gunman committed suicide at the scene.

AUSTRALIA AND NEW ZEALAND

Since 1923, when the first mass shooting on the continent was recorded, Australia and New Zealand have had a relatively small number of events. In fact, just 10 shootings over nearly 100 years appear to meet the definition outlined in Chapter 2. Further, only one shooting has occurred in the new millennium. Despite relatively low numbers of mass shootings, however, a number of these events have been highly lethal.

The Waikino schoolhouse massacre was the earliest known mass shooting in these countries. Occurring on October 19, 1923, just outside of the town of Waihi, New Zealand, farmer Christopher John Higgins entered the schoolhouse intending to kill all of the students (Smith, P. J., 2013). Confronted by the school's headmaster, Robert Reid, the gunman opened fire. Reid was shot twice in the face as he tried to calm down the angry shooter, though he ultimately survived (Anderson, 2012; Smith, P. J., 2013). Two young boys were killed while eight others were wounded (Smith, P. J., 2013). For several hours after the initial attack, the gunman exchanged fire with responding police officers, ultimately giving himself up and being taken into custody (Anderson, 2012; Smith, P. J., 2013). He was convicted on two counts of murder and sentenced to execution, though the Parliament later commuted his sentence to life in prison, where he remained until his death in 1937. Over 90 years later, the Waikino schoolhouse shooting remains New Zealand's only recorded school shooting.

Several other shootings have occurred in schools across Australia. In the first recorded school shooting in Australia, a 13-year-old boy opened fire at Orara High School in Coff's Harbor, located in New South Wales, on June 19, 1991 (Associated Press, 1991a). He shot three people, including two teachers, before being subdued by other students and taken into police custody; all survived. The investigation revealed that, on the day of the attack, the student had been sent home for behavioral issues.

On August 3, 1999, 38-year-old Jonathon Brett Harrocks opened fire at a bar on the campus of La Trobe University in Melbourne, Australia ("Leon Capraro," n.d.). He shot two, killing one instantly; the second victim survived her injuries (Forbes-Mewett, McCulloch, & Nyland, 2015). Staff members in the restaurant restrained the shooter until police arrived and he was taken into custody ("Leon Capraro," n.d.). He later was sentenced to life in prison with the possibility of parole after 23 years of time served.

Several years after the La Trobe shooting, on October 21, 2002, 36-year-old student Huan Yun Xiang, more commonly known as "Allen," opened fire on an econometrics class at Monash University, also located in Melbourne (Forbes-Mewett et al., 2015; Murphy, Ketchell, & Heasley, 2002). Two students were killed and five others were injured in the attack (Murphy et al., 2002). After being disarmed and restrained by several people in the room, he was taken into police custody without further incident. In 2004, the shooter was found not guilty by reason of mental impairment and remanded to a local psychiatric hospital (Australian Associated Press, 2004).

The majority of mass shootings in Australia and New Zealand have taken place outside of school settings—and were considerably more lethal. On August 9, 1987, 19-year-old Julian Knight, a discharged army cadet, opened fire on passing cars in the Clifton Hill community of Melbourne (Cowan, 2007). In what has become known as the Hoddle Street massacre, 7 people were killed and 19 others were injured before the shooter was captured following a 30-minute police chase (Cowan, 2007; "Hoddle Street Massacre," n.d.). He was convicted and given a life sentence ("Hoddle Street Massacre," n.d.). Later that year, another mass shooting occurred in Melbourne, just over three miles from the site of the Hoddle Street massacre (Australian Associated Press, 2007). On December 8, 1987, 22-year-old Frank Vitkovic opened fire at the office of the Australia Post located on Queen Street in Melbourne (Australian Associated Press, 2007; Willox & Darby, 1987). He killed eight and wounded five others (Australian Associated Press, 2007). Some of the office workers were able to wrestle the rifle away from the shooter, who then fled to a ledge of the building, ultimately falling to his death as he tried to evade capture (Australian Associated Press, 2007; Willox & Darby, 1987).

Several years later, New Zealand experienced what remains (to date) the deadliest mass shooting on its soil. On November 13, 1990, 33-year-old David Malcolm Gray opened fire in his community (Hunt, 2014; Jones, 2005). After killing his neighbor, the gunman set the house on fire, ultimately killing the neighbor's daughter and a friend (Hunt, 2014; Jones, 2005;

Roughan, 2012). He then continued shooting others nearby, including responding police officers. After a house-by-house search that continued into the following day, law enforcement found the shooter, who engaged in a gunfight with them (Hunt, 2014). He was struck five times by police gunfire and died 20 minutes later while en route to the hospital (Hunt, 2014; Roughan, 2012). By the time the massacre ended, 13 people, excluding the perpetrator, had been killed (11 by gunfire and 2 by arson) and 3 others were wounded (Hunt, 2014; Jones, 2005; Roughan, 2012).

The following year, 33-year-old Wade Frankum went on a murder rampage in a coffee shop located in a mall in Strathfield, a suburb of Sydney, Australia (Walker, 2015). On August 17, 1991, after sitting in the café for approximately two-and-a-half hours, he grabbed a knife out of his bag and stabbed a girl sitting behind him to death. Abandoning the knife, he pulled out a semiautomatic rifle and began shooting other patrons in the café. Police quickly arrived on scene and engaged the shooter as he tried to carjack a woman. Realizing he could not escape, the gunman committed suicide. A total of seven people were killed (including the girl who had been stabbed to death) and six others wounded in the rampage.

For the next several years, no mass shootings occurred in either New Zealand or Australia. On April 28, 1996, this changed as Australia experienced its worst mass shooting and what has become one of the most lethal events of this type worldwide (Associated Press, 1996b; CNN, 1996). After arriving at the historic Port Arthur prison site located in Tasmania, 29-year-old Martin Bryant ate lunch at the park's café ("Port Arthur massacre," n.d.; "The Port Arthur massacre," n.d.). Once he finished his meal and returned his tray, he opened fire on the crowded restaurant, killing or wounding nearly every patron (Associated Press, 1996a). He continued shooting as he made his way through the gift shop and parking lot areas, returning to his vehicle, and firing as he drove around the park. After carjacking another vehicle and taking a man hostage, he drove to a nearby bed and breakfast, where, earlier, he had killed its owners (Associated Press, 1996a; CNN, 1996; "Port Arthur massacre," n.d.). Following a standoff with police that lasted into the next day, the shooter set the guest house on fire and fled, ultimately being taken into custody (Associated Press, 1996a, 1996b; CNN, 1996). In total, 35 people had been killed and an additional 19 wounded in the shootings ("Gunman's life sentence," 1996). Though he initially pled not guilty, the shooter later changed to a guilty plea and was sentenced to 35 life sentences with no possibility of parole ("Gunman's life sentence," 1996; "Laughing," 1996; "Port Arthur massacre," n.d.).

Less than a year after the tragedy at Port Arthur, neighboring New Zealand was shocked with its fifth mass shooting of the decade (Brockett, 1997). On

February 8, 1997, 24-year-old Stephen Anderson opened fire at the Raurimu Lodge, killing four people and wounding four others (Brockett, 1997; CNN, 1997). He then moved to a neighboring property, where he shot and killed a fifth individual (CNN, 1997). Using planes and helicopters, police quickly were able to track and apprehend the shooter. Investigation into the shootings revealed that prior to the rampage, the gunman also had killed his wife. The shooter, who had a history of mental illness including schizophrenia, was found not guilty by reason of insanity and remanded to a psychiatric hospital in December 1997 (Louisson, 1997; "Raurimu killer," 2000). By 2000, he was temporarily allowed special leave ("Raurimu killer," 2000), and finally was released back into the community in 2009 (Francis, 2011; Reid, 2009). Less than two years after his release, however, the shooter was recalled to the psychiatric hospital for undisclosed reasons (Francis, 2011).

COMPARING THE NUMBERS: THE UNITED STATES AND ABROAD

As the prior discussion on mass shootings internationally indicates, these events, unlike President Obama's quote at the beginning of this chapter following the Charleston church shooting, are occurring in countries other than the United States. In fact, mass shootings have been found both in advanced nations and in those that are perceived as less developed. Therefore, the president's claim that "this type of mass violence doesn't happen in other advanced countries" is not substantiated (see also Herring & Jacobson, 2015). It is important to note, however, that our comparison looks solely at mass shootings across independent nations. It does not, as President Obama's statement entails, consider mass murder as a form of "mass violence" more broadly, which would include bombings, knifings, and attacks classified as terrorism.

But what about President Obama's claim that such violence (again in terms of mass shootings) does not happen in other places with this type of frequency? In order to answer that question, we first must define "frequency." Simply stated, most dictionaries will note that the term refers to "the number of times that something happens in a particular period" ("Frequency," n.d.). In an analysis we conducted for *Politifact* in response to the president's statement after Charleston, we compared mass shootings across 11 separate nations between 2000 and 2014 (in Herring & Jacobson, 2015). Just considering the frequency of events in terms of a dictionary definition, the president's statement would have been true—the United States had 133 identified events during that period, while Germany had 6, China had 4, Canada had 3, and Finland, Australia, and Mexico each had 2. One event was found in each England, France, Norway, and Switzerland during the same time frame.

This interpretation is problematic, however, for several reasons. First, these countries do not all have the same population. Using 2014 data from the Central Intelligence Agency (n.d.), we find that the U.S. population was nearly 319 million. Only China had a larger population, with over 1.35 billion; Mexico was the third largest with just over 120 million. The remaining countries each had populations of less than 100 million citizens with two countries—Finland and Norway—having just over 5 million each. Essentially, these data show that the number of events in their raw form, or the dictionary definition of "frequency," are not comparable because the countries were not all equal to begin with.

A second issue now arises in trying to compare numbers to determine the legitimacy of President Obama's claim—the fact that all mass shooting events themselves are not equal. It is true that the United States has more shootings in terms of raw numbers. Yet there remains considerable variation between events. For instance, even just considering what Schildkraut (2014) terms "highly salient events," or those that received the most media attention, events are not equal in terms of the number of victims. Looking at just fatalities, for example, the 2011 Tucson shooting had 6 fatalities, Aurora had 12, Fort Hood had 13, Sandy Hook had 27, and Virginia Tech had 32 (Schildkraut, 2014). Similar differences are found in the number of injuries and total victims, as well as across those events that received less (or even no) media coverage. As discussed throughout this chapter, variation in events also occurs in shootings that have happened in other countries.

Thus, since not all events are equal, trying to draw a meaningful comparison by looking at a raw number of shootings is futile. One way to address such a problem is to examine these mass shootings per capita, or in rates per 100,000 people in the population. This is a format that academic researchers and national statistical agencies (such as the Bureau of Labor Statistics, the Bureau of Justice Statistics, and even the Federal Bureau of Investigation [FBI] in their annual Uniform Crime Report) use to compare types of crimes across localities (cities, states, and even nations) that are not the same size. A classic example is comparing homicide rates in U.S. cities to determine which city has the "worst" problem. In 2013, there were 414 murders in Chicago and 156 in New Orleans (FBI, 2014). At first glance, it appears that homicide is a more "frequent" occurrence in Chicago. In order to compare these two cities, however, we have to be mindful of the populations—there were 2,720,554 citizens in Chicago but only 377,022 in New Orleans in 2013. When these numbers are recalculated into rates, what we find is that Chicago experienced 15.2 homicides for every 100,000 people in its population. By comparison, the rate in New Orleans was 41.4 murders per 100,000 people, meaning that there is a greater statistical occurrence of homicide in this city.

Using per capita rates to compare mass shootings across multiple countries is beneficial because 100,000 people is equitable no matter what country is being analyzed. In our *Politifact* analysis (see Herring & Jacobson, 2015), we compared rates by both fatalities and the total number of victims (a combination of deaths and injuries). What we found is that despite the United States having the most number of mass shooting *incidents*, the *rate* of those killed (0.15 per 100,000) is lower than in Norway (1.30), Finland (0.34), and Switzerland (0.17). The same pattern emerges when looking at the total number of victims.

Still, there are a few notes when interpreting such statistics. First, the data used to compute these rates are aggregated for the first 14 years of the new millennium. As a result, looking at the rates of mass shootings annually would yield a different outcome, as not all countries had mass shooting events each year. Additionally, some events can be considered outliers, or those events that are deviations from what is considered "normal" or typical. In her analysis, Schildkraut (2014) found that, on average, there were 4.2 fatalities and 8.8 total victims per U.S. mass shooting between 2000 and 2012. Consequently, the highly salient cases discussed earlier are exceptions, not the rule. Similar extremely lethal events and those with large total victim counts were found in other countries, thereby potentially skewing the numbers, particularly when the country has a smaller population. It is not to say that these numbers are wrong, misleading, or manufactured—they simply must be interpreted with caution.

A final concern for comparing events cross-nationally is the very definitional challenge we tackled in Chapter 2. What is considered a mass shooting in the United States is not necessarily considered the same thing in other countries. Depending on which continent an event is located, other labels may come into play when trying to define a particular event. For example, episodes of mass violence (shootings or otherwise) in Central and South America often are associated with drug crimes and cartel violence. Similarly, throughout Europe and the Middle East, these attacks quickly are labeled as terrorist activities, such as the September 2004 siege on a Beslan, Russia, school, where 334 people were killed (more than 20 by gunfire and the remaining when bombs exploded) and more than 800 injured when over 30 Chechen militants took the school hostage for three days before Russian forces intervened ("Beslan bell tolls," 2012; "3 days," 2014). In Africa, terrorism, ethnic violence, or religious warfare can be used as an identifier for these shooting rampages.

Take, for instance, the January 7, 2015, mass shooting at the offices of the *Charlie Hebdo* satirical newspaper in Paris (Withnall & Lichfield, 2015). At approximately 11:30 a.m. local time, brothers Chériff and Saïd Kouachi stormed the publication's offices and opened fire (BBC News, 2015). They killed 11 people inside and wounded 11 others (Withnall & Lichfield, 2015). A responding law enforcement officer was the 12th person killed in the attack (BBC News, 2015; Withnall & Lichfield, 2015). The pair escaped the scene and, after a hostage siege two days later at a printing firm in nearby Dammartin-en-Goële, the gunmen were killed in a shootout with law enforcement (BBC News, 2015).

Despite that the *Charlie Hebdo* attack bears a similar resemblance to other mass shootings discussed through this chapter, the finding that the gunmen had terrorist acquaintances and that the attacks received praise from organizations such as al Qaeda meant that it quickly was labeled an act of terrorism (e.g., Aboudi, 2015). As such, based on the definition posed in Chapter 2, this and similarly labeled incidents are excluded from most mass shootings databases, ours included. If such events were included, it is probable that the statistics would show even less disparity in terms of the "frequency" of mass shootings in other countries. As we noted earlier in Chapter 2, however, there is no all-encompassing definition that will include every single event.

Such considerations are just another factor that must be taken into account when determining the extensiveness of the mass shootings phenomenon. Countries around the globe have experienced similar events, some even more deadly than those occurring on U.S. soil. We also see that in order to draw a meaningful comparison between these nations, we must, as the old saying goes, "compare apples to apples." Due to the definitional issues that plague all countries, it is nearly impossible to capture all events of mass shootings around the globe. What we can say for certain, however, is that mass shootings are not solely an American problem.

Preventing Mass
Shootings

Myth: "If it [a bullet] hits you anywhere on the body, it'll hurt you. But it's not going to kill you. As the students put them on and line up in the hallway, they develop a shield like the Romans and Greeks used to lock together, so it gives them added protection."
— Stan Schone, managing partner of Dyneema, manufacturer of the Bodyguard Blanket (in Nelson, 2014)

Though they are statistically rare, mass shootings generate a substantial amount of concern in the general public and among policy makers tasked with protection. This heightened concern, coupled with the level of media attention that they garner, make them appear to be more commonplace than they really are (Elsass, Schildkraut, & Stafford, 2014; Schildkraut, 2012b; Schildkraut, Elsass, & Stafford, 2015; Schildkraut & Muschert, 2014). As news of a mass shooting hits the airways, discussions focusing on how to prevent future events begin almost simultaneously, with politicians, pundits, and the general public all weighing in. These conversations often are even more passionate when a shooting takes place in a school, leading to the majority of products and preparation tips being centered on those locales. The discourse in these instances typically centers on a call for improved and/or additional security measures (Schildkraut, Elsass, & Muschert, in press), encompassing topics such as a search for the motivation behind the shooting, early identification of potential threats and warning signs, police presence, gun control and gun rights, mental health, preparation and training, and new inventions to keep us safe.

Mass shootings, regardless of the location in which they take place, most often result in an outcry by the media, politicians, and public for increased and improved security measures. Addington (2009) points out that a normal reaction to a violent event, such as a mass shooting, is for "people who are fearful of crime [to] respond by trying to reduce their risk of experiencing victimization" (p. 1428). In fact, Crepeau-Hobson, Filaccio, and Gottfried (2005) found that, when a mass shooting occurs in a school, the first tactic employed to address parental fear of a school shooting is to install security that is tighter and more visible. Furthermore, in the wake of a mass shooting, especially when they occur at a school, media reports—similarly at the local (e.g., Gjovaag, 2014; "Mass. Officials," 2014; Ryan, 2014), state (e.g., Barnes, 2014; Graff, 2014; Schrank, 2014; Suder, 2014), and national (e.g., Eckersley, 2014) levels—are full of stories focusing on the need to increase security measures. But with regard to the prevention and mitigation of lethality in mass shooting events, what does better security really mean, and does it necessarily entail the adoption of *more* security measures and devices?

After a mass shooting occurs, people rush to find answers and ways to prevent future events, or at the very least, reduce the lethality of potential attacks. Subsequently, a wide range of tips and security devices are offered in order to achieve greater safety, preparedness, and protection. This chapter explores the call to action that tends to erupt after a mass shooting event, especially in the wake of a school shooting. We discuss a number of safety devices and prevention strategies that have been introduced, and contextualize these products and tips in their effectiveness against this potentially lethal violence. The chapter also includes recommendations for prevention and fatality reduction, as well as how to properly assess proffered proposals in these areas.

THE IMPORTANCE OF CONSIDERING THEORY

While it is impossible to completely eliminate the risk of mass shootings, there are ways in which the occurrence of these events, and the subsequent lethality when a shooting does take place, can be minimized. In order to be effective, however, proposed solutions must be grounded in academic theory and scholarly research rather than be built upon a foundation of emotion and politics. The use of academic theory, in particular, can help inform future efforts to reduce risk as well as provide testable propositions to determine if a specific proposed solution is effective.

One particularly useful theory for this purpose is Lawrence Cohen and Marcus Felson's (1979) routine activity theory, which comes out of the discipline of criminology. Routine activity theory provides a core on which to base proposed measures aimed at reducing the occurrence of mass shootings and minimizing the number of fatalities when they do take place. The theory suggests that criminal opportunity is increased when a motivated offender and a suitable target converge in the absence of a capable guardian (Cohen & Felson, 1979). Therefore, according to routine activity theory, three necessary components must exist for crime—including mass shootings—to occur: a suitable target, a motivated offender, and the lack of a capable guardian (Cohen & Felson, 1979). It follows, then, that crime is not likely to occur in the presence of a capable guardian or when a target's suitability is reduced.

Once the initial shock of a mass shooting subsides, the public wants answers as to why a shooter chose to commit such a heinous act. Yet, the search for motivation rarely is fruitful and often even less comforting. Instead, it generally is assumed that the shooter was mentally ill, evil, or some combination of the two, and therefore an anomaly. This goes hand in hand with routine activity theory, which does not consider the actual motivation of the offender, instead assuming that all offenders are equally driven (Cohen & Felson, 1979). As a result, policies that attempt to reduce the motivation of a potential offender are ill suited to address possible preventative strategies for mass shootings. In the absence of a consideration of motivation, the focus often quickly turns to future prevention, or at least the reduction of lethality. This generally ends in calls for improved safety, generally including the adoption of additional security measures.

INCREASING GUARDIANSHIP

Capable guardians include individuals, objects, and devices designed to prevent crime from taking place—for example, guards (armed or unarmed), alarm systems, dogs, and security cameras, as well as other interventions. Two important functions are performed by a capable guardian in order to disrupt criminal opportunity: (1) the guardians provide protection and oversight for the target; and (2) they act as a control or deterrent for the offender. In the case of potential mass shootings, increasing capable guardianship improves these two functions, thereby reducing the likelihood of an attack occurring. While this seems straightforward, people have been at odds with one another as to how to increase guardianship in the real world.

The cornerstone of guardianship is capability, according to routine activity theory (Cohen & Felson, 1979); yet this point often is overlooked and ignored. It is not enough to increase guardianship generally because only an increase in *capable* guardianship will reduce the likelihood of crime. The issue is complicated further as people try to define what *capable* guardianship actually entails in the real world. Every prevention strategy and device introduced for the purpose of thwarting mass shootings is not capable (despite being marketed as such), and therefore, likely to be either ineffective or counterproductive. *Capable* guardianship is that which is grounded in empirical research. Therefore, it is vital that prevention strategies and security inventions introduced with the purpose of reducing mass shootings through increasing capable guardianship be developed and designed upon a foundation of research findings produced by rigorous methodology. Failure to do so will result in, at the very least, a static, unimproved level of security, and possibly an actual decrease in safety.

One of the first areas we see a concentration on in the wake of a mass shooting centers on preparation and training. Arguably the strongest recommendation to come out of the Columbine Review Commission's [CRC] (2001) report is the need to be prepared for these types of emergencies. In the report, the CRC (2001) makes a number of recommendations communicating a need for comprehensive crisis response plans, advanced planning for critical emergencies, training of school resource officers, and plans for the early detection of potential perpetrators. School security experts in particular stress the importance of preparation (Graham, Shirm, Liggin, Aitken, & Dick, 2006; Schneider, 2007, 2010a, 2010b; Tuoti, 2014). This has spurred schools, as well as other venues including workplaces, malls, and movie theaters, and first responders, to push for better preparation through enhanced training and crisis response planning (e.g., Bruzda, 2015; Gentile, 2015; Marcelo, 2014; Plotts, 2014; Safe and Sound, n.d.a, n.d.b; Stevenson, 2014).

Every mass shooting provides things to be learned, and those lessons, if accepted and analyzed thoroughly, help to guide our path toward better preparation in the future. For example, the attack in Columbine showed us the need for drafting and implementing crisis response plans (Mitchell, 2014) and better training of first responders, including school resource officers, on how to deal with these types of events. Today, most schools have developed and adopted a crisis plan that includes procedures for how to deal with mass shooting events (Elliott, 2015; Graham et al., 2006). In a post–Virginia Tech world, universities have designed more thorough emergency notification systems and recognize the need for their continued evaluation in order to help keep students, faculty, and staff safer by having a way to get instructions and information out to them (Schildkraut, McKenna, & Elsass, 2015). This need was highlighted by the emergency notification system failures at Virginia Tech on the day of Seung-Hui Cho's rampage (Schildkraut, McKenna, & Elsass, 2015; Schneider, 2010a, 2010b; Virginia Tech Review Panel [VTRP], 2007). Recently, the tragedy at Sandy Hook underscored the need for the constant evaluation of enacted crisis plans so that they can be modified to adapt to the changing needs of a particular school (Safe and Sound, n.d.b). Moreover, this provides an opportunity to adopt new procedures as cutting edge research findings dictate (Safe and Sound, n.d.b).

In the wake of these tragedies, we have seen a push to be better prepared, especially in schools. Crisis response teams and task forces have been established (e.g., Bruzda, 2015; Kittle, 2014) for the purpose of assessing safety and designing plans and procedures to increase their preparedness. These groups typically also are tasked with establishing procedures and schedules for enacting drills for possible crisis events, including mass shootings. Doing so is in line with the recommendation made by the Sandy Hook Advisory Commission (SHAC, 2015) that "the law should require schools to undergo periodic training and drilling of school safety and security plans" (p. 72).

It is the recognition of a need for training that has spurred organizations across the nation into actively practicing their crisis response plans. Nowhere has this been the case more than in schools. More and more, schools are putting their faculty and staff through active shooter training (Payne, 2014), with many adopting the ALICE safety plan (e.g., Buell, 2014; Johnson, M., 2014). ALICE, which stands for alert, lockdown, inform, counter, and evacuate, was developed after Columbine and aims to teach schools and businesses how to survive a mass shooting event (ALICE, n.d.b). There even have been reports of school nurses receiving specialized medical training focusing on mass shootings (e.g., Lea, 2015). Recently, this training has translated to active shooter situations in locations other than schools. In the July 23, 2015 rampage at a movie theater in Lafayette, Louisiana, two teachers who had received active shooter training at their schools were credited with saving lives when they instinctively put that knowledge into action (Balingit, 2015).

Another commonly enacted protocol is for schools to practice their active shooter plan. In fact, Sandy Hook Elementary School had practiced their evacuation plan just days prior to the rampage (McCormack, 2012). Schools across the nation have followed suit, drilling students, faculty, and staff on the procedures for dealing with an active shooter situation (e.g., Daly, 2014; DaSilva, 2015; Forman, 2014; Hayes, 2014; Smith, 2014; Wind, 2014). These drills, however, have not always been met with praise. As one news report illustrates, parents have complained that active shooter drills are too scary, citing worries over increased anxiety and trauma for their children (Ferguson, C., 2014). Despite this criticism, a consensus exists with regard to the need for preparation and training for responding to mass shootings, which undoubtedly allows for increased guardianship while simultaneously reducing the suitability of targets.

Following mass shooting events, such as Columbine, Aurora, and Sandy Hook, gun control proponents often call for stricter regulations on firearms including banning assault weapons and large capacity magazines and further restricting locations that guns legally can be carried (see Chapter 5). The argument is that lax regulations increase the likelihood of a mass shooting occurring or maximize an event's lethality (Haider-Markel & Joslyn, 2001). These propositions are based on the idea that if potential mass shooters were unable to secure weapons, had a more difficult time getting firearms, or at the very least were restricted by having to reload their weapons more often, lives would be saved. Gun rights advocates, on the other hand, assert that fewer restrictions should be imposed on firearm acquisition and ownership so that people are better able to protect themselves and others. Often, gun rights supporters lobby for reduced regulations concerning carrying a weapon, including relaxing the restrictions on where firearms legally can be carried. The rationale is that by allowing law-abiding citizens to carry firearms in a wider variety of environments, the likelihood of an armed individual being present to engage the shooter and use deadly force to protect potential victims is increased (Haider-Markel & Joslyn, 2001).

In line with gun rights activists' argument, a number of states have considered allowing firearms on their campuses, both on secondary and college campuses. While some have pushed to allow concealed carry permit holders to bring their weapons on school grounds (e.g., Clark, 2014; Grossfeld, 2015), others have considered providing specialized training to teachers and arming them (e.g., Creason, Walmer, & Vaughn, 2014; "Texas training," 2014) or volunteers (e.g., Kinsey, 2014), having safety designees (e.g., "Evers files," 2014; Kennedy, 2014), or even outfitting schools with guns (e.g., Pinckard, 2014). To date, there are eight states that have passed laws that allow for concealed-weapons permit holders to carry their firearms on college campuses: Colorado, Idaho, Kansas, Mississippi, Oregon, Texas, Utah, and Wisconsin (Fernandez & Montgomery, 2015). Gun control proponents, on the other hand, strongly oppose the allowance of firearms on educational campuses, arguing instead that gun restrictions should become even tighter. In order to help ensure that gun free zones, including schools, remain as such, gun-sniffing dogs recently have been introduced in some districts (Associated Press, 2014a). There is support, however, in the gun control camp for increasing the number of armed law enforcement officers in these environments, as well as in other public places.

In an effort to find a compromise between the two sides of the firearms debate, it often has been proposed that the number of armed peace officers in public places should be increased (e.g., Bergquist, 2014; Clark, 2015; Coburn-Griffis, 2014; D'Amico, 2015; McKinney, 2014; Solochek, 2014; Stankiewicz, 2014). This includes the introduction of or increase in the number of officers patrolling schools, again arguing that having an armed police officer on hand could deter a potential shooter, or reduce the lethality of a shooting by creating the ability to resolve it more quickly. Yet, there was an armed school resource officer present on the day of the Columbine shooting, who quickly was joined by a nearby off-campus officer who heard the call and responded. In fact, according to the CRC (2001),

> The greatest death toll occurred in the library after School Resource Officer Neil Gardner exchanged gunfire with Eric Harris, forcing the murderous pair into the school and the library where ten students were shot to death during an uninterrupted 46-minute assault on defenseless students. (p. 6)

Accordingly, some have asserted that placing armed law enforcement at every school would do nothing to prevent such attacks. As Senator Dianne Feinstein (D-Calif.) points out, "there were two armed law enforcement officers at that campus [Columbine], and you see what happened—15 dead" (in Terkel, 2012, para. 9).

Clearly, the presence of an armed police officer on the Columbine High School campus on April 20, 1999, was not enough to deter the shooters, nor is it clear if the officer was able to reduce the lethality of the rampage, as the CRC (2001) insinuated that he actually inadvertently may have increased the death toll by driving the shooters into the library. This may be due in large part, however, to the officer having received little specialized training on how to respond to a mass shooting situation (CRC, 2001), which did not prepare him for the rampage that would take place at Columbine High School. Compounding the issue was the fact that the SWAT team that responded to Columbine followed protocols that prevented them from entering the school immediately, allowing for the rampage to last for 47 minutes rather than to be neutralized quickly (CRC, 2001). In another attack, James Holmes opened fire in an Aurora, Colorado, movie theater in 2012; the first police officer was on scene within 83 seconds and in 21 minutes, 51 police cars had arrived (Noe, 2013).

It is clear that the faster first responders can get on the scene of a mass shooting, the better the outcome for all involved. Not only is this true for law enforcement, but the more rapidly the emergency medical personnel respond, the quicker injured people receive medical attention and are transported to the hospital. This is very likely to help reduce the lethality of these types of events, as was the case in the Aurora rampage. The first ambulance arrived on the scene within 3 minutes, resulting in all victims being relocated to the hospital in 55 minutes (Noe, 2013). Every victim who left the scene of the theater shooting alive ultimately survived (Noe, 2013), likely due to the rapid response of the first responders.

With regard to the presence of armed law enforcement officers specifically, there still have been situations in which their presence resulted in the speedier resolution of a mass shooting. In 2006, 19-year-old Alvaro Castillo fired upon his school and was apprehended at gunpoint by the school's resource officer, Corporal London Ivey ("Deputy hailed," 2006). Castillo had murdered his father before arriving at the school and opening fire. While the effectiveness of armed police at deterring potential mass shooters has not been fully clarified, it is clear that unless armed officers receive specialized training on the proper procedures to take in the case of an active shooting event, they can potentially do more harm than good. In 2012 outside of the Empire State Building, 58-year-old Jeffrey Johnson shot and killed a former coworker (Ariosto, 2012). Two nearby NYPD officers opened fire on the gunman, killing him. In the process of firing 16 rounds on a busy New York City street, however, 9 bystanders were injured (Ariosto, 2012). This event brings to the forefront the need for better training for law enforcement (and the general public) in the event of a mass shooting.

A number of high profile mass shooting events, including the shootings at the University of Texas and Columbine High School, have resulted in the creation of active shooter training initiatives, including the Advanced Law Enforcement Rapid Response Training (ALERRT) Active Shooter Response Program (ALERRT, n.d.). In fact, ALERRT's (n.d.) curriculum, which offers nine grant-funded courses for first responders that utilize scenario-based training exercises, "has become the national standard in active shooter response training" (para. 2). This program now has been adopted by numerous states and law enforcement agencies. What ALERRT is striving to do is create law enforcement officers who are *capable* guardians and are therefore prepared to effectively respond to an active shooter during a rampage with the purpose of ending the attack quickly, thereby reducing the loss of life.

An attack can only be ended quickly, however, if officers are alerted and able to respond rapidly. This is a large hurdle as commonly the response time for law enforcement to reach the scene is longer than the total time the shooting takes. The attack at Columbine lasted 47 minutes; however, this is an anomaly for school shootings, mainly as a function of the lack of protocols for responding SWAT teams on how to handle this type of event (CRC, 2001). Most events are over in five minutes or less (Blair, Nichols, Burns, & Curnett, 2013). Thus, unless an armed police officer not only already is on scene but also is anticipating the attack, the length of time a rampage lasts is a function of normal police response times.

Often, shooters commit suicide upon the arrival of the police (Kalish & Kimmel, 2010); thus, it is likely that the sooner the police can reach the scene, the more quickly the incident will be resolved, even if they are unable to directly neutralize the shooter. Winning the 2014 New Product of the Year award in the category of crisis management from *Security Products* magazine, BluePoint Alert aims to, among other goals, reduce police response time to schools ("Bluepoint Alert's school safety solution," 2014). The product, which builds upon traditional panic buttons and security systems, is painted blue and resembles a typical fire alarm (BluePoint Alert Solutions, n.d.). It works by acting as a security system that automatically contacts police and provides them with an initial location of the shooter when it is engaged (BluePoint Alert Solutions, n.d.). Simultaneously, it communicates the threat throughout the building, including to those in charge, in turn letting the shooter know that the police are en route (BluePoint Alert Solutions, n.d.).

While it is unclear at this time whether or not BluePoint Alert's product will be able to achieve its goal of getting law enforcement officers on the scene more quickly in the case of a mass shooting, it likely is a step in the right direction over traditional panic buttons. Traditional panic buttons can be found in a wide variety of public spaces including businesses and schools, the latter of which was facilitated largely by the mass shooting at Virginia Tech (Rasmussen & Johnson, 2008). In fact, they are the most commonly used form of duress alarms in elementary and secondary schools (Garcia, 2003). These devices work by alerting police to the location of an emergency situation (Schneider, 2001). While often touted as providing instant police response (Levkulich, 2014), Petrosino, Fellow, and Brensilber (1997) point out that these devices largely are ineffective due to the rapid nature of crime, including mass shootings. Recently, they also have been introduced in a wearable, wireless form (Fiel, 2015).

Moreover, panic buttons are expensive (Graham et al., 2006) and require routine testing to ensure they remain in working order. They typically are used so infrequently that if the need for routine tests is ignored, broken equipment can go unnoticed. This was undoubtedly the case during Paul Ciancia's rampage that took place at Los Angeles International Airport on November 1, 2013, which killed one person and injured three others. On the day of the shooting, there were 12 panic buttons located throughout the terminal where the attack took place, two of which were found to be broken ("Phone system," 2014). Furthermore, one Transportation Security Administration (TSA) agent claimed to have pressed a working button, yet there remained a substantial lag in law enforcement's response time ("Phone system," 2014). Whatever the case, it is clear that while well trained law enforcement officers absolutely are capable guardians, they are much more successful when they are alerted quickly and at the start of a rampage. Anything, including poorly designed or malfunctioning technology, which increases their response time, simultaneously decreases their ability to be *capable* guardians.

As of late, we have seen an increase in militaristic technology for improving capable guardianship in order to prevent or reduce the lethality of mass shootings (Bidgood, 2014). One novel product with this goal that recently has been suggested is the ShotSpotter gunfire detection system (De Benedetti, 2015). ShotSpotter, acknowledging the gap between the length of active-shooter incidents and police response times, has developed what essentially is a gunfire-locater system (Johnson, K., 2014; SST, n.d.). While this has been in place on the outside of the College of Art and Design in Savannah, Georgia, for the last two years, the first fully functioning interior gunfire-detection system was scheduled to be up and running on the campus during the 2014–2015 school year (Johnson, K., 2014).

The ShotSpotter system, which can distinguish between a gunshot and other loud sounds such as a firecracker or a door slam and does not record conversations because they are not loud enough triggers, works through the installation of microphones and other equipment (De Benedetti, 2014). Upon detection of a gunshot, the system automatically notifies the police, pinpointing a shooter's exact location at each subsequent shot (De Benedetti, 2015). Though it is unknown whether this technology is going to prove to be beneficial, it is interesting in that it is the first of its type; however, cost remains an issue. The vice president of SST, the company that makes Shot-Spotter, did not release installation fees, choosing instead only to say that the school will be required to pay a sum less than the cost of their fire alarm system, amounting to "a few thousand dollars per year" (De Benedetti, 2015, para. 11). Still, it remains to be seen if the trend toward militaristic technology will result in capable guardianship, and cost for such technology is certainly an issue.

As previously stated, not all guardianship is necessarily *capable*, and it is *capable* guardianship that is required to disrupt the convergence of a motivated offender and a suitable target, according to routine activity theory (Cohen & Felson, 1979). One attempt at increasing security in the wake of these tragedies that has been less effective in reducing the occurrence of mass shootings is the installation of security cameras throughout U.S. society (Schneider, 2010b). Closed-circuit security systems, allowing for the monitoring of public and private spaces alike, are commonplace today. The vast majority of businesses, including movie theaters, shopping malls, a wide variety of workplaces, and even an increasing number of both public and private schools, have been outfitted with cameras in the hope of deterring crime, including mass shootings. Yet, it remains unclear to what extent these devices have reduced the occurrence of mass shooting events or the lethality of such incidents.

In fact, a number of attacks have taken place in full view of security cameras that the shooters knew were in existence. In the 2013 Washington,

DC, Navy Yard shooting, 34-year-old contractor Aaron Alexis opened fire at a facility where he previously had been employed, killing 12 people and wounding 3 others (U.S. Department of Defense, 2013). This attack was carried out in full view of a closed-circuit security system that the shooter likely knew was operating. In other events, shooters have not just ignored the presence of security systems, but appreciated that their attacks would be captured on camera. The two perpetrators of the 1999 Columbine shooting were fully aware that their school was equipped with an extensive security system, yet they killed 13 people and wounded 24 others in full view of the cameras before committing suicide. Additionally, a number of shooters have used video equipment to record messages to the general public before an attack. For example, the perpetrators of the shootings at Columbine High School, Virginia Tech, in 2007, and in Santa Barbara in 2014 all utilized video equipment to communicate with the media and the general public, which suggests that they would not find the use of closed-circuit security systems in their target locations to be an adequate deterrent (see Chapter 8 for an in-depth discussion of this topic).

Another commonly employed attempt at increasing guardianship is to install metal detectors (Rasmussen & Johnson, 2008; see also Nevel, 2014; Rahman, 2015). Studies have shown that some schools use them only randomly, even as little as once a month, and those with just handheld wands bring out the devices at large sporting events or if they suspect a student to be armed (Schneider, 2007). With regard to their effectiveness, Schneider (2001) found the results to be mixed as there typically are too many entry points on school campuses for all to be covered by a metal detector. In fact, during the 2005 massacre at Red Lake High School in Red Lake, Minnesota, 16-year-old Jeffrey Weise, upon entering the school, immediately killed an unarmed security guard manning a metal detector. Furthermore, these devices pose practicality issues as they require students' school arrivals to be staggered in order to allow sufficient time for processing and they necessitate personnel to be hired to operate the machines (Frost, 2014; Haeck, 2014; Schneider, 2001). Outside of schools, metal detectors still do little to deter potential mass shooters. In the 2013 shooting at the Los Angeles International Airport, the perpetrator breached the metal detectors with a firearm in order to gain access into the terminal ("Phone system," 2014). This is unsurprising as reports have indicated that the TSA allows hundreds of prohibited items, including weapons, to get past them and into secure areas every day (Greenblatt, 2012; Halsey, 2015).

It is vital to remember that we want to adopt security measures that studies have shown to be effective in making us safer. When considering ways to increase guardianship, in order for tactics to be effective and therefore *capable*, it is important that they rest upon continued scientific research focusing on the realistic impact of each proposed intervention. We must resist the urge to draft statutes and procedures on the basis of fear, emotionality, and political agendas; instead, we must create both public and private policy with new research findings as its cornerstone.

REDUCING THE SUITABILITY OF TARGETS

Another way to work toward the prevention of mass shootings or the reduction of fatalities, as entailed in routine activity theory, is to decrease the suitability of potential targets, as doing so disrupts the convergence of the three necessary components—a suitable target, a motivated offender, and the lack of capable guardianship (Cohen & Felson, 1979). This helps make individuals (as targets) appear less attractive to the offender, and this often is achieved by restricting a shooter's access to them. Merely restricting access is not sufficient—doing so is not always practical as well—and it is imperative that all techniques aimed at reducing lethality in a mass shooting event be realistic and workable in the real world.

In striving to decrease the suitability or attractiveness of potential targets, we often focus on restricting a shooter's access to possible victims, usually by outfitting doors with locks that can quickly be engaged in the event of a threat (Schneider, 2010b). Research has shown that in mass shooting events, there never has been an individual killed behind a locked door (Blair et al., 2013). Commonly, shooters are seeking easy targets; therefore, barriers put in place, such as locked doors, act as a deterrent as perpetrators tend to continue seeking out more accessible potential victims rather than spending time working to breach a particular entry point (Blair et al., 2013). This was the case at both Columbine and Sandy Hook, as the shooters in each of these attacks passed up potential victims sheltering in place behind locked doors in favor of more accessible targets—either in rooms that could not be secured, such as the library at Columbine (CRC, 2001) or in classrooms at Sandy Hook where teachers were unable to go into the hallway to lock their door from the outside because of the risk of facing the perpetrator (SHAC, 2015).

Almost all schools—over 92 percent—report having a plan in place for a lockdown of the school in the case of an emergency (Graham et al., 2006). When considering door locks for the purpose of access control in the case of an active shooter, however, consideration must be given to the types of locks being used. Spring latches, found on the average doorknob, are relatively useless, and deadbolts, while more effective, cannot be used in many areas, such as on designated exit doors in public places (Schneider, 2007, 2010b). Lock-and-key systems are another option, but it is imperative that they can be engaged from the inside of the room to be secured or you risk coming face to face with the shooter, as was the dilemma at Sandy Hook (SHAC, 2015).

Recognizing this danger, an elementary school teacher from Iowa designed a device she named the Sleeve, which allows rooms to be secured in seconds from the inside without needing to be installed beforehand or requiring the use of a key. The Sleeve, made of carbon steel and able to withstand over 550 pounds of force, is a slide-on cover that fits over the joints on the control arm of a door (Reinwald, 2014). The issues with securing individual doors also have been identified by other inventors, who then designed special door-stops to bypass the shortcomings of more traditional lock systems (Rawdon, 2014). One such invention, the Barracuda Intruder Defense System, which was designed by a firefighter in Ohio, is a freestanding device that acts as a doorjamb, securing the door in place (Slinger, 2014) and can be attached to either outward or inward swinging doors (Bilco, n.d.). This is a unique advantage as mass shooting experts (see generally, Hayes & Hayes, 2014; Martin, 2008; Martin & Snyder, 2011) advocate installing doors so that they open inward and can be barricaded; however, doing so often is against fire code, especially in schools. Further, as is pointed out by the Ohio building standards board, which is against using these types of devices, they require special training (Welsh-Huggins, 2015).

In another attempt to bypass the fire code issue, many places have considered electronic access control systems, which utilize door hardware that automatically secures at the push of a button (Schneider, 2010b; see also Forman, 2014; Peterson, B., 2014). This creates the ability for instantaneous lockdowns. While this appears to be a good option on the surface, Schneider (2010b) highlights a number of serious drawbacks for these types of systems, including high cost, inherent and unforeseen technical difficulties, the need for power, issues surrounding location, and considerations concerning biometrics. When these are used for access control through a main entrance to a building, which often is controlled by a buzzer system, as has been adopted by many schools (e.g., Harte, 2014), there is an additional problem of piggybacking or tailgating. These problems reduce the ability for these systems to be practical in many locations. Even when installed, there remain serious concerns not solely limited to fire hazards. In fact, Sandy Hook had a system in which visitors had to be buzzed into the school at the front entrance; however, this failed to stop the attacker as he shot his way through the glass entrance door and proceeded to enter the building (SHAC, 2015).

Recently, environmental and architectural designs have been considered for tactics to reduce the likelihood of a mass shooting. Using environmental design to reduce crime has a long tradition in criminology, having a specialty within the discipline devoted to the endeavor. After Sandy Hook, this has become a more popular idea with respect to mass shooting prevention. In fact, Sandy Hook's new school has heavily invested in this technique, striving for invisible security (Barrineau, 2014; Peterson, S., 2014). The layout of the new campus, which broke ground in October 2014, is set back deep into the forest and has only roadway entrance, routed through two wetland areas that act as natural barriers, ending in a security gate (Peterson, S., 2014). Another natural barrier incorporated in the design is a rain garden that sets off the pathways to the school's front entrances (Peterson, S., 2014).

Additionally, the entire building curves around the parking lot allowing for a clear view of any and all approaching visitors (Peterson, S., 2014). The classrooms are organized into three separate wings perpendicular to the body of the school permitting each to easily be quarantined from the rest of the campus (Peterson, S., 2014). Furthermore, each classroom has the ability to be locked from the inside, which addresses the issue faced by teachers during the shooting that occurred on the original campus. Glass panels on the class-room doors are situated far enough away from doorknobs that intruders would be unable to break the impact-resistant glass and unlock the door (Peterson, S., 2014). Unquestionably, the designers of Sandy Hook's new school have taken environmental criminology into account in their plans for the future campus (Barrineau, 2014), and in doing so, have taken clear steps toward reducing the suitability of potential targets inside.

Not all attempts to increase security (and therefore reduce target suitability) are equal, and a number of less effective, practical, and even counterproductive prevention strategies and devices have been proposed and adopted. As Borum, Cornell, Modzeleski, and Jimerson (2010) point out, "many of the school safety and security measures deployed in response to school shootings have little research support" (p. 27). For example, some schools have suggested taking the concept of door locks a step further by considering the installation of lockdown mechanisms, whereby all interior and exterior doors immediately are secured with the push of a single button (Schneider, 2001, 2007). There is no doubt that this would reduce the time it takes to secure a building; however, these systems often require an override code that generally only is known to a select few individuals at any given location (Schneider, 2007). This increases the danger, particularly with fire safety, as technological malfunctions could prove to be deadly if there was no one available to enter the override code.

Other examples of poorly designed security inventions that were introduced after Sandy Hook focus on making common items bulletproof, including blankets, backpacks, clothing, and whiteboards, or bulletproofing physical aspects of schools and businesses, such as windows (Associated Press, 2014c).

Bulletproof whiteboards recently have made a splash on the security market (Cloud, 2014; Frankel, 2014). Pitched as an educational tool that doubles as lightweight armor with the ability to withstand a shotgun blast from a foot away, the bulletproof whiteboard craze has been sweeping the country of late, with sales recorded in every state (Cloud, 2014). The University of Maryland Eastern Shore reportedly spent $60,000 on them last year alone (Connor, 2013), and after they were featured on the *Today* show, "orders began pouring in from all over the country" (Cloud, 2014, para. 3). This is just the beginning of the bulletproofing trend.

The Bodyguard Blanket (n.d.) is a bright orange bulletproof shield made from a material similar to Kevlar that was designed to protect students from bullets and falling debris (in the event of a natural disaster like a tornado or earthquake). In an active shooter incident, students put the blanket on like a backpack and then duck and cover (Associated Press, 2014c), basically freezing in place, which is in direct opposition to academic research that points to higher rates of survival when potential targets try to flee from a shooter (Blair et al., 2013). In fact, the FBI (n.d.) recommends that if you find yourself in an active shooter situation, you should first try to escape. Only when fleeing is not a safe option do they advise hiding. If you find yourself face to face with a shooter, the FBI advocates engaging the attacker and fighting back. This technique also is supported by the ALICE training institute, which has been adopted in a wide variety of schools and businesses across the country (ALICE, n.d.b).

Bulletproof backpacks are a similar product to the bulletproof blanket. Product designers describe them as flexible, pistol-rated armor disguised as a standard backpack (Bidgood, 2014; Dewey, 2012; McClanahan, 2015). BulletBlocker (n.d.), one of the first companies to design and market these backpacks, now also makes bulletproof clothing, including underwear (Cloud, 2014), iPad cases, and notebooks, as well as "school bag survival kits" (Stein & Cherkis, 2014, para. 7), which contain a first aid kit and shelter supplies, including toilet paper, water, and a space blanket. It is unclear why many of the items contained in these survival kits would be necessary or helpful in the case of a mass shooting. Additionally, where are children supposed to put their books and other school supplies if their bulletproof backpack is overflowing with survival gear?

In fact, this is just the tip of the iceberg when it comes to concerns about bulletproof products marketed to schools and businesses under the guise of increased safety through reducing the suitability of potential targets. In keeping with the bulletproofing trend, a number of businesses and schools have hired companies to modify their existing structures in order to make aspects of them bulletproof. In recent years, especially since the shooting at Sandy

Hook, the installation of protective safety glass for windows and doors has become much more commonplace (e.g., Barrineau, 2014; Colli, 2014; Harte, 2014; Levulis, 2015; Martin, 2014; Peterson, S., 2014; Reynolds, 2014).

Beyond bulletproofing, there have been some inventions and suggestions for reducing the suitability of potential targets in mass shooting events that are absurd. One such recommendation includes throwing canned food at an active shooter:

> The procedure will be the same as we have done in the past with the addition of arming our students with a canned food item. We realize at first this may seem odd; however, it is a practice that would catch an intruder off-guard. The canned food item could stun the intruder or even knock him out until the police arrive. The canned food item will give students a sense of empowerment to protect themselves and will make them feel secure in case an intruder enters their classroom. (Kalin, 2015, para 4)

The ridiculousness of this plan is evidence that we, as a society, are allowing fear to propel us into a state of hysteria in which solutions are adopted regardless of their realistic ability to keep us safe. Real, workable, grounded, legitimate plans for increasing safety and security for the purpose of preventing a mass shooting or reducing the lethality of an event never will be arrived at through raw emotion and fear. We must design products and plans from a level-headed, empirical perspective in order to truly be safer. This undoubtedly entails the continuation of academic research on mass shootings and the consideration of those studies' findings when products and plans are being developed.

There are other serious concerns raised when judging products marketed to keep people safe in the case of a mass shooting. The first concern has to do with risk. As outlined in Chapter 4, mass shooting events are exceedingly rare. In fact, when considering school shootings in particular, which commonly are mistaken as being on the rise in the United States, they actually have occurred "throughout the history of formal education" (Rocque, 2012, p. 304). Today, the risk of a child being a victim of a school shooting is less than .00005 percent (Schildkraut & Elsass, in press). In other words, a student has a greater likelihood of being struck by lightning than being killed at school (Donohue, Schiraldi, & Ziedenberg, 1998; see also Bernard, 1999). Borum and colleagues (2010) note that even the "highly publicized series of school shootings in the late 1990s that culminated in the 1999 Columbine shooting occurred at a time when student victimization was declining" (p. 29).

The question then becomes whether or not we should be spending an exorbitant amount of money on items that are designed—typically with little to no empirical influence—to increase safety in the event of a crime that is extraordinarily rare. Bulletproof blankets, for example, cost approximately $1,000 apiece (Associated Press, 2014c). With the extremely tight budgets faced by many schools today, this undertaking seems to become even more inappropriate, as money inevitably must be pulled from other educational endeavors in order to fund these projects. An additional criticism is that these companies are capitalizing on public fear. As many products have not actually been found to increase security, with some even being counterproductive, we seriously must question the use of educational funds to purchase products capitalizing on fear, which many have pointed out, pose psychological risks especially to children (e.g., Schreck & Miller, 2003). Most often, these are little more than knee-jerk reactions that accomplish nothing but making us feel safer, even if increased security actually is not occurring.

PROACTIVITY, COOPERATION, AND EVALUATION

One lesson that emerges each time a mass shooting takes place is the need for people to be proactive in order to increase the likelihood that these types of events are prevented or at least their lethality is reduced when they do occur, as enhanced safety necessarily requires early intervention (ALERRT, n.d.; Do, 2014; Sherman, 2014). Being prepared necessarily encompasses being proactive; however, proactivity takes a variety of forms, including creating tactics for identifying potential shooters before they attack, setting up systems to disseminate information to potential targets in the case of a mass shooting, and training people on what to do should a shooter target their location. All of these things work together to foster a "culture of preparedness" (McKay, 2014), which likely not only reduces the number of fatalities when a mass shooting occurs but also increases the probability of an attack being thwarted before it is carried out.

Rarely are school shootings impulsive, as most shooters plan their assaults and provide clues or warning signs that an attack is being considered (Wike & Fraser, 2009). Leakage is a significant issue, with the Centers for Disease Control (2006) reporting that nearly 50 percent of shooters gave some kind of public warning (see also Chapter 8). Schildkraut and colleagues (in press) highlight the existence of warning signs prior to a mass shooting. It has been asserted that when considering safety in schools in particular, "student silence is our worst enemy" (Halbig, 2000, p. 34). Yet, what realistically can be done to identify and act upon these red flags? Beyond that, how do we follow up on tips while still preserving the constitutional rights of the potential suspect?

Wike and Fraser (2009) outline six prevention strategies for the early identification of potential attackers: strengthening school attachment, reducing social aggression, breaking down codes of silence, establishing resources for troubled and rejected students, bolstering security, and increasing communications within the school as well as between it and outside agencies. By implementing these strategies, potential shooters may be identified more readily, as people are likely to feel comfortable expressing their concerns. This is especially important as research has found that most averted shootings are the result of someone reporting rumors or threats (Madfis, 2014). In order to translate this into the real world, schools, communities, and law enforcement agencies have introduced a wide range of avenues for the purpose of early identification, including hotlines, the monitoring of social media, and public outreach campaigns urging people to report suspicious behavior.

Many schools have started confidential hotlines where people can report campus crime and threats to school safety, including references made to perpetrating a mass shooting. Recognizing the success that hotlines for anonymous crime reporting has enjoyed, having long been employed by police departments and private businesses alike, states as well as individual school districts have implemented similar tactics to improve school safety (e.g., Associated Press, 2014d; D.A.R.E., 2014; "Free safety tip line," 2014; McCoy, 2015). According to the U.S. Department of Justice (2002), school crime hotlines are effective and relatively inexpensive, costing approximately $20 per month to operate. For example, a hotline established in a single high school in San Francisco says that the number of criminal incidents on campus decreased within the first month it was in operation (U.S. Department of Justice, 2002). Still, while effective, the use of crime tip hotlines in schools is not as straightforward as one might think. As Hanson (2002) points out, we must be careful to balance school safety with the constitutional rights of the subject, as acting on anonymous tips may affect students' search and seizure rights guaranteed under the Fourth Amendment.

By fostering a culture in which people are proactive about identifying potential threats and feel comfortable reporting their concerns, however, police hope to be able to stop more attacks before they are committed. This proved to be the case when a woman in Waseca, Minnesota, noticed some strange occurrences at a storage facility and chose to report the bizarre behavior to police (Brumfield, 2014). In doing so, she prompted an investigation by law enforcement who uncovered an elaborate plot by the 17-year-old occupant of the storage locker to commit both familicide and a school shooting (Brumfield, 2014).

Another technique used for the early identification of potential mass shooters is the monitoring of social media. The use of social media by perpetrators and potential attackers to relay their frustrations and plans as well as leave behind their final words has been a more recent development in the realm of mass shootings (see Chapter 8 for a complete discussion of this phenomenon). While this trend undoubtedly is disturbing, it does provide an opportunity for the early identification of individuals contemplating committing an attack (Walker, 2014). In fact, early identification through social media monitoring recently has proven to be fruitful. In South Pasadena, California, for example, two teenagers who planned to commit a school shooting were apprehended by police after investigators discovered their postings on social media (CNN Newsroom, 2014). In 2014, a threat against the school district in Flushing Township, Michigan, was discovered on a social networking application called After School (Emery, 2014). While no incident at Flushing Township High School ultimately occurred, it is possible that the swift response of police and school officials to alert the school community and general public deterred the potential shooter. Interestingly, a letter sent to parents notifying them of the threat also was published on Flushing Community Schools' Facebook page (Emery, 2014). This underscores the use of social media not only by shooters and potential attackers but also by those working to prevent attacks. Furthermore, it has become common for politicians to advocate for the monitoring of social media to thwart a wide variety of crimes, including mass shootings, as well as to solve cases (e.g., McCarter, 2014).

There is a question, however, as to how law enforcement can differentiate between real threats and sarcastic or joking comments. The FBI and the U.S. Secret Service, as well as the U.S. Department of Education, advocate using a threat assessment approach to achieve this goal (Borum et al., 2010). The idea is that while any person can make a threat, few have the planning, preparation, and persistent violent drive necessary to actually perpetrate an attack (Borum et al., 2010). Research suggests that a threat assessment approach has the potential "to provide . . . effective, practical, and less punitive alternatives to zero tolerance" (Borum et al., 2010, p. 34).

This approach may have proved fruitful in a case from New Braunfels, Texas, in which a 19-year-old man was arrested after posting on Facebook that he wanted to shoot up a kindergarten (MacCormack, 2013). He was charged with making a terroristic threat; he contends that his purpose was not to scare anyone, but rather that he was "trying to be witty and sarcastic" (MacCormack, 2013, para. 3). With regard to constitutional rights, the line is blurred as to what constitutes a legitimate threat versus an expression protected under the First Amendment.

The success of hotlines and social media monitoring has been due in large part to public campaigns, especially in schools, urging people to report those who make threats or comments alluding to violence. The National Association of Students Against Violence Everywhere (n.d.), for example, is a founding partner of the National Youth Violence Prevention Campaign, which works to raise awareness and educate school communities and the general public on "effective ways to prevent or reduce youth violence" (para. 1), urging people to take all threats seriously and report them to officials. Campaigns of this nature have played a central role in increasing awareness about the need for being proactive, including the reporting of threats and red flags in order to assist in the early identification of potential shooters.

An additional aspect of proactivity with regard to mass shootings has to do with plans to get information out to potential victims as well as the general public in case of an attack. Clear plans for the distribution of time-sensitive information to potential targets are crucial in a mass shooting situation, and challenges regarding the dissemination of information differ depending on the type of location being targeted (Fox & Savage, 2009; Gow, McGee, Townsend, Anderson, & Varnhagen, 2009; Gulum & Murray, 2009; Hamblen, 2008; Kepner, 2010; Latimer, 2008; Mastrodicasa, 2008; Schildkraut, McKenna, & Elsass, 2015; Schneider, 2010a, 2010b; Stephens, Ford, Barrett, & Mahometa, 2014; Young, 2008). For example, emergency notification plans created for a school are likely not to be helpful for a workplace or a mall. Even within general types of locations, there are differences, as an elementary or secondary school's emergency notification system is likely to be ineffective for a sprawling university campus, though they are both considered schools. Therefore, it is imperative that emergency notification systems are designed to reflect the unique challenges presented by location types as well as specific considerations unique to a single place.

College campuses are a good example of a type of location that has made emergency notification a priority. The shooting at Virginia Tech in 2007 that left 32 people dead and 23 wounded really brought the need for better emergency notification systems to the forefront. Though there was a system in place, a number of failures occurred on the day of the attack, as outlined in the report by the VTRP (2007). Recognition of these weaknesses at Virginia Tech has resulted in researchers committing themselves to investigating how to improve emergency notification systems so that their effectiveness is increased in similar situations.

One of the most supported findings centers on the need for a multimodal notification system in order to increase the delivery of messages to the intended recipients (see Gow et al., 2009; Gulum & Murray, 2009; Halligan, 2009; Hamblen, 2008; Kepner, 2010; Latimer, 2008; Mark, 2008; Mastrodicasa, 2008; Schneider, 2010a; Stephens, Barrett, & Mahometa, 2013; Stephens et al., 2014; Young, 2008). A multimodal system encompasses a range of communication formats—for example, text messaging, email, campus computer systems, classroom tickers, and social media, among others—which simultaneously are used to deliver a message in the event of an emergency on campus (Kepner, 2010). These alert systems should be redundant across a variety of different modes (Schildkraut, McKenna, & Elsass, 2015; Schneider, 2010a). This overlap is likely to foster a sense of urgency among recipients, while such a response is improbable when a single mode is utilized (Stephens et al., 2014). By designing and employing a multimodal emergency notification system that is tailored to the specific needs of an individual location, schools and businesses are, without a doubt, taking a proactive approach to being prepared in case of a mass shooting. Yet, it is not enough to merely set these systems and plans in place, as constant training and evaluation are a necessity to help prevent an incident or reduce its lethality.

Undeniably, ongoing education and training regarding responses to prevention of, preparation for, and response to mass shooting events are vital, having been recognized as such by both the grassroots movement and the academic community. In order to be proactive, it is imperative that individuals be educated about not only the realistic potential risk for mass shooting events (see Chapter 4) but also ways in which to respond if they are faced with a mass shooting situation. In order to achieve a high level of preparedness, education and training must be a collaborative effort between members of the community, both on a small scale (as in the case of schools or workplaces) and on more far-reaching platforms (such as the city, county, and state), as well as between locations and law enforcement and other first responders (Graham et al., 2006).

After Columbine, the need for collaboration between schools and first responders, including police officers, regarding prevention of and response to mass shootings was widely agreed upon as necessary in order to better handle this phenomenon. This point was clearly outlined by the CRC (2001) in their recommendations. Recognizing this, community leaders across the nation have made cooperation for the purposes of prevention of and response to mass shootings a priority. Schools, in particular, have paved the way for increased cooperation between administrators, faculty, staff, students, parents, and first responders (e.g., Davis, 2014; Feijo, 2014; Loughman, 2014).

Community collaboration also is critical. Parents should be involved in and educated on the development of crisis response plans. According to the U.S. Department of Education (2007), nearly 60 percent of principals report having made an effort to obtain parental input in school security efforts since Columbine (see, generally, Nott, 2014; Pigee, 2014). By making collaboration a priority, these individuals can approach crisis preparation efforts from a proactive and multidisciplinary angle, which allows for an increase in efficiency and planning. More efficient and better planned protocols for what to do should a mass shooting event take place will result in reduced lethality.

Thus, potential threats must be identified and emergency response plans should be designed to meet the individual needs of a specific locale. Schools, for example, present different environmental and architectural security challenges than other places, such as malls, movie theaters, and workplaces, and have different types of potential targets, both of which impact the design of mass shooting response plans and procedures.

Once plans and procedures are developed, it is essential that individuals be educated about the protocols, which can be achieved through information sharing, training, and practice sessions. Drills for a number of emergency types, including mass shootings, should be conducted routinely. This will ensure that all people, especially the key players charged with overseeing the development and implementation of emergency planning, are up to date on the most current protocols and clearly understand their roles in a variety of crisis scenarios, including mass shootings. Once plans are in place, it is crucial that there be ongoing assessment of the strategies and protocols, as doing so will illuminate weaknesses in response implementation as well as highlight areas for improvement.

As the SHAC (2015) points out, "a plan that sits on a shelf simply collects dust" (p. 72), and it therefore is ineffective at keeping people safe (Fast & Fanelli, 2003). In their Straight-A School Safety model, Safe and Sound (n.d.a) stresses that "school safety is a *process*, not a *product*" (para. 3), implying that security is a dynamic process with no end. In fact, Safe and Sound (n.d.a) contends that when safety protocols becomes routine, the security of our schools is undermined. In order to combat this, its model is designed as an iterative process that continually builds upon itself as schools assess their needs, act to design and implement plans to meet those requirements, and audit those protocols for the purpose of refining the procedures in place, before starting the process over again (Safe and Sound, n.d.b). Safe and Sound's (n.d.a) model, and much of their tool kits encompassed within, easily are adaptable to a number of different locations that have the potential to become mass shooting sites. Many schools have heard this message loud and clear (e.g., Enos, 2014; Nevel, 2014; Thibeault, 2014). The biggest takeaway point, regardless of location type, is that consistent evaluation and adaptation based on the findings of those assessments is vital for remaining prepared for the possibility of a mass shooting.

WHERE DO WE GO FROM HERE?

While it is impossible to ever fully reduce the risk of mass shootings to 0 percent, there are ways to minimize the opportunities for these events to occur and diminish their subsequent lethality when they do take place. In order for these strategies to be effective, however, they must not be based upon emotion or politics, but rather be grounded in academic research. Thus, potential security measures and enhancements, prevention strategies, and legislation aimed at reducing the frequency and/or lethality of mass shootings must be adequately assessed through continued scientific research focusing on the impact of different interventions. As Rocque (2012) contends, "more research is needed before firm policy conclusions can be made" (p. 304). Furthermore, much as response plans need to be adequately assessed and refined, the research itself must continue and evolve (Harris & Harris, 2012). Accordingly, public and private policy should be drafted in response to new academic research findings rather than statutes and procedures being created out of fear and increased emotionality. The stage has been set for a national dialogue on mass shooting prevention, but the success of this conversation hinges on our ability to put our emotions, assumptions, and political agendas aside and instead focus our attention on the findings of rigorous research to inform proposed public policy initiatives, prevention and mitigation strategies, and safety inventions.

8

Mass Shootings in a Mediatized Society

Myth: "To prevent a horror like this, we have to anticipate it. To anticipate it, we have to understand it or at least recognize warning signs. So far, we've got nothing—no understanding, no warning signs, no explanation. Just a bewildering mystery."

—*The News Tribune*, 2014

Over the years, the attention paid to mass shootings has continued to increase, due in part to high profile events (e.g., Columbine, Virginia Tech, Aurora, and Sandy Hook), which are covered extensively by the media. At the same time, this increased interest also can be attributed to advances in technology. No longer are people required to gather around the clunky old black-and-white television sets of the 1940s and 1950s. Instead, they are able to stream news more quickly, thanks to technological advents like the Internet and smartphones. To keep up with the demands of more tech-savvy news consumers, media organizations have had to shift their practices in order to remain competitive for ratings.

Media organizations, however, are not the only entities using technology to their advantage. Since the 1999 Columbine High School shooting, a number of perpetrators have transmitted messages to the public (both successfully and unsuccessfully) via the media (Oksanen, Hawdon, & Räsänen, 2014). While some shooters have relied on traditional video formats to leave behind their final words, others, particularly in more recent years, have employed social media platforms, including YouTube (see Sumiala & Tikka, 2011a), which is a file sharing network. In this section, we review four cases where mass shooters have produced multimedia manifestos that provide insight into their motivations and their attacks. We also explore how mediatized communication by the shooters is received and reciprocated by online fan communities through various social networking sites. Finally, we consider the role of leakage—that is, others knowing about a shooting before it is set to happen—and how often this occurs beyond the critical clues these gunmen directly offer in their own media packages.

COLUMBINE AND THE BASEMENT TAPES

While the Columbine shooting set the mold for how mass shootings would be covered by the media in the years to come, it also changed the way in which the perpetrators of such events communicated their motivations, or in some instances, their plans prior to the attack. With earlier shootings, such as those at the University of Texas or All-Tech Investments and Momentum Securities, the gunmen left behind what equate to suicide notes. In some instances, these documents provide insight into the motivation behind such rampages; in others, the perpetrators may leave behind few clues as to why the shootings have occurred. What all of these earlier messages have in common, however, is how they were written—traditional pencil-and-paper notes.

Columbine is a prime example of how shooters have become more technologically savvy. In what has become one of the most controversial and highly sought-after pieces of evidence in the case, Eric Harris and Dylan Klebold compiled a series of five videos, later dubbed the "Basement Tapes," prior to their rampage (see Gibbs & Roche, 1999; Larkin, 2009). The videos have been considered to be the only definitive answers to why the shooters chose to engage in their attack (Larkin, 2009). Extremely graphic in nature, the tapes were sealed by the Jefferson County Sheriff's Office (JCSO) after they had been viewed by just a handful of individuals, including reporters from *Time* magazine (Gibbs & Roche, 1999).

The Basement Tapes chronicle the weeks leading up to the shooting at Columbine. Filmed at a series of locations, including in the shooters' homes and vehicles, the videos provide an in-depth look into the meticulous planning they had conducted to prepare for the attack (JCSO, 1999a). In one video, the perpetrators engaged with one another and further interact with their guns and a number of the improvised explosive devices that lay openly around them in their home (JCSO, 1999a; Schildkraut, 2012b). They ridiculed school projects, the upcoming prom, and the gun show dealers who had sold several weapons to a friend on their behalf. In other segments, the shooters contemplated which Hollywood producer would direct a movie about their attack and discussed how many people they wanted to kill (Gibbs & Roche, 1999). In one clip, one of the shooters remarked how "it is a weird feeling knowing you are going to be dead in 2½ weeks" (JCSO, 1999a, p. 10375). The final segment of the videos showed the gunmen, on the morning of their attack, saying goodbye as they contemplated what their impending actions would do to their parents (Gibbs & Roche, 1999).

Over two years after the shooting, many different media outlets had tried—albeit unsuccessfully—to gain access to the Basement Tapes. In December 2001, *The Denver Post* sent a letter requesting that the tapes and other evidence recovered from the shooters' homes be released to the public (see *Fleming v. Stone*, 2006). Sheriffs John Stone, who was in office on the day of the attack, and his successor, Ted Mink, continually denied each request. In a later statement, Mink (2006) justified his decision to withhold the tapes by noting that they essentially were a call to arms for any other potential shooters, including an instruction manual of sorts for how to plan and implement a similar attack. Prior to his statement, both the FBI's Behavioral Analysis Unit and the National Center for the Analysis of Violent Crime had reviewed the tapes and provided similar recommendations (*Fleming v. Stone*, 2006).

The Denver Post did not give up their fight to get the documents unsealed. In fact, they took their case all the way up to the Colorado State Supreme Court after the district courts refused to overturn JCSO's decision not to release the material to the public (Schildkraut, 2012b). While the State Supreme Court did overturn the lower court's decision, they still created a provision that allowed Sheriff Mink to use a balancing test when determining what materials to distribute. Though he elected not to release the Basement Tapes, Sheriff Mink initially made over 900 pages of documents, including the shooters' personal journals and school papers, available to the public (Schildkraut, 2012b). This figure later increased to over 25,000 pages of documents as more were released (Schildkraut, 2012b). Additional videos, including cafeteria surveillance footage from the day of the shooting, the gunmen's class documentary entitled "Hitmen for Hire," a video which foreshadows the attack on the school, and a separate video called "Rampart Range" that chronicled the pair using bowling pins for target practice with the guns later used in the attack, were released in phases following the publication of the Columbine Review Commission's (2001) report. While it originally was reported that the Basement Tapes were to remain sealed until 2026 (Schildkraut, 2012b), it later was uncovered that the videos (including any copies made) actually had been destroyed in 2011, along with other pieces of evidence, including the firearms used in the shooting and spent shell casings recovered at the scene (Prendergast, 2015).

THE VIRGINIA TECH SHOOTER'S MULTIMEDIA MANIFESTO

Like Columbine, the 2007 shooting at Virginia Tech was groundbreaking in respect to some elements of its coverage, such as the cell phone camera footage taken by a student, which was uploaded to CNN's website. Yet, it also was different for another reason. While people across the nation followed the story from their homes through various news outlets, from the initial attacks to President Bush's remarks to the nation later that day, a key piece of the puzzle was making its way from Blacksburg to New York City. During the two-hour break between the incident at West Ambler Johnston Hall and the shooting at Norris Hall, gunman Seung-Hui Cho mailed a package to NBC News. Two days later, on April 18, it was received by the station.

Inside the overnight mail envelope, which had arrived a day late due to it being incorrectly addressed, was the shooter's multimedia manifesto. An 1,800-word statement was among the items included in the bundle, totaling 23 pages (Associated Press, 2007; Kellner, 2008a). The news station also received 27 separate video clips equating to approximately 25 minutes of footage (Associated Press, 2007; Kellner, 2008a). An additional 43 still photographs of the shooter, posing in various positions with his firearms and a knife (which was not used in the attacks), also were included (Associated Press, 2007; Kellner, 2008a).

The content of the manifesto itself was believed to be the answer as to why the shootings had occurred. In both the written and video portions of the package, the shooter provided insight into what may have fueled his rage leading up to the attacks in excerpts such as this:

> You had a hundred billion chances and ways to have avoided today. But you decided to spill my blood. You forced me into a corner and gave me only one option. The decision was yours. Now you have blood on your hands that will never wash off. . . . You had everything you wanted. Your Mercedes wasn't enough, you brats. Your golden necklaces weren't enough, you snobs. Your trust fund wasn't enough. Your vodka and cognac weren't enough. All your debaucheries weren't enough. Those weren't enough to fulfill your hedonistic needs. You had everything. (CNN, 2007)

In addition to expressing his disdain for wealth and hedonism (and essentially modern mainstream American culture), the perpetrator also viewed the shootings as a spiritual or religious experience in which he sacrificed himself for those who similarly were oppressed (Schildkraut, 2012b). In the same vein, he also branded the Columbine shooters as martyrs who similarly surrendered themselves to a greater cause (Kellner, 2008a; Serazio, 2010).

Executives at NBC News were faced with a considerable dilemma: do they share the information with the public, thereby giving the shooter his 15 minutes of fame and possibly even motivating copycat shooters (e.g., Hoffman, 2007, which details a post made threatening to dwarf the Virginia Tech shootings and another threatening to kill 50 students at San Diego State University just days after the attack), or should this crucial evidence be withheld while people struggled to understand why the event had occurred? Ultimately, the network reached what they believed to be a compromise between these two polarizing options. After consulting their legal team and law enforcement working the shooting, they released just a fraction of the manifesto—2 minutes of video, 7 photographs, and 37 lines of text from the written material (Schildkraut, 2012b). Though NBC retained the exclusive rights to the portions released, other networks were able to rebroadcast the footage, branded with the network's logo, under the doctrine of fair use (Schildkraut, 2012b).

Mixed reactions were held by members of both the public and the media once the manifesto was released. Some believed that the network was insensitive for sharing the material, saying that it took focus away from the victims and placed it on the shooter (Associated Press, 2007; Carter, 2007). Others argued that it gave people a place to lay their anger and grief (Schildkraut, 2012b). NBC president Steve Capus defended the decision as he sat down days later with Oprah Winfrey, noting that "sometimes good journalism is bad public relations" (in Associated Press, 2007, para. 3). *Nightly News* anchor Brian Williams supported Capus's decision, pointing out that the information gleaned from the manifesto was too important to not share with the public (Schildkraut, 2012b). Others, even within the NBC organization, such as *Today* show anchor Matt Lauer, argued that the decision went against journalistic ethics (Carter, 2007). Still, the debate over airing the footage shows that the Virginia Tech shooter was successful in creating what Kellner (2003, 2008a, 2008b) calls a "media spectacle" (p. 37). As Capus ultimately summarized with regards to the package, "it's not every day we get a story like this. . . . It was extraordinary, and that's how we treated it" (in Carter, 2007, para. 10). While several other networks, such as ABC, CBS, and Fox, initially opted to air the shooter's manifesto, they ultimately pulled the footage from their news rotation within 24 hours of its initial release (Pérez-Peña, 2007). NBC also reduced their coverage of the manifesto, quickly limiting attention to the shooting to just 10 percent of airtime (Schildkraut, 2012b).

JOKELA HIGH SCHOOL AND THE "MANIFESTO OF A NATURAL SELECTOR"

The use of media manifestos has not been linked exclusively to mass shooters from the United States. Prior to the 2007 rampage at Jokela High School in Finland, Pekka-Eric Auvinen posted a number of videos on YouTube, which foreshadowed what would take place on November 7 (Lindgren, 2011). In fact, he was one of the first gunmen to actively use social media, particularly YouTube (which did not exist at the time of the Columbine shootings), to communicate his intentions and provide warning signs about the impending shooting (Oksanen et al., 2014; Raittila et al., 2010; Sumiala & Tikka, 2011a, 2011b). The Jokela shooter recognized the power of social media and understood that he could use its platforms to get his thoughts and ideas in front of a broad audience (Kiilakoski & Oksanen, 2011a; Serazio, 2010). He had a strong online presence that spanned across a number of different sites, including multiple accounts on YouTube and various profiles on Finnish social media sites, discussion groups, and web-based forums (Kiilakoski & Oksanen, 2011a, 2011b; Sumiala & Tikka, 2011a).

Unlike the Columbine and Virginia Tech perpetrators, who had to wait days or even years for their media manifestos to be made public, the Jokela shooter retained considerably more control over when his package was released (Kiilakoski & Oksanen, 2011b). In the days prior to the shooting, he uploaded photographs of his recently purchased gun, both on YouTube and his page on IRC-Galleria, Finland's largest online community (Kiilakoski & Oksanen, 2011a; Ministry of Justice, 2009; Sumiala & Tikka, 2011a, 2011b). Less than a half hour prior to his rampage (between 11:13 a.m. and 11:16 a.m.), he uploaded his multimedia package, which included his manifesto, entitled "Manifesto of a Natural Selector," videos, and still photographs, through RapidShare.com, a one-click web-based hosting service with several million users (Kiilakoski & Oksanen, 2011a, 2011b; Serazio, 2010; see also de Quetteville, 2007; Sumiala & Tikka, 2011a). At 11:28 a.m., he turned off his computer and headed to the school; the first shot was fired at 11:42 a.m. (Ministry of Justice, 2009; see also Kiilakoski & Oksanen, 2011b; Sumiala & Tikka, 2011b).

Within two hours of the shooting, a Finnish broadcasting company reported the existence of the gunman's YouTube video, *Jokela High School Massacre–11/7/2007*, and included a link to the page (Sumiala & Tikka, 2011a). In just over an hour (2:52 p.m.), a separate media outlet reported that the video had been watched 125,000 times, a figure which was updated to nearly 200,000 views within just 30 additional minutes (Sumiala & Tikka, 2011a). By 4:18 p.m., YouTube had closed the shooter's account and removed all related videos; more than a quarter of a million people, however, already had viewed the material (Kiilakoski & Oksanen, 2011b; Serazio, 2010; Sumiala & Tikka, 2011a). Within a week of the shooting, nearly a half-dozen media outlets in Finland either had provided links to these videos or hosted them directly, causing public backlash for how the organizations had handled the event (Ministry of Justice, 2009; Serazio, 2010). By the end of the investigation, Finnish law enforcement had seized a number of video clips made by the shooter (Kiilakoski & Oksanen, 2011b; Paton, 2012). While they released 46 of these, estimates suggest that there were numerous others, possibly as many as 150 (Kiilakoski & Oksanen, 2011b; Paton, 2012).

The Jokela shooter's videos also differed from those of the Columbine and Virginia Tech perpetrators in terms of their style and production. Unlike his predecessors, all of whom focused on themselves speaking into the camera, the Jokela shooter's videos mainly were void of any human faces (Paton, 2012). Instead, his productions were more akin to montages or video collages set to background music, or a "soundtrack," including songs from KMFDM, Marilyn Manson, Nine Inch Nails, and Rammstein, most of which were bands of choice for the Columbine shooters (Kiilakoski & Oksanen, 2011b; see also Paton, 2012; Schildkraut, 2012b; Sumiala & Tikka, 2011b). Strong color choices, such as red and black, were used to underscore the severity of his messages (de Quetteville, 2007; Sumiala & Tikka, 2011a, 2011b). He also published his videos in English as well as Finnish to appeal to the broadest audience (Serazio, 2010; Sumiala & Tikka, 2010, 2011a, 2011b).

Like the Seung-Hui Cho, the Jokela gunman held the Columbine shooters in high regard (Kiilakoski & Oksanen, 2011a; Paton, 2012; Serazio, 2010; see also de Quetteville, 2007; Lindberg, Oksanen, Sailas, & Kaltiala-Heino, 2012). In addition to using songs that were the favorites of one of the Columbine shooters, he incorporated images of the cafeteria surveillance footage from the day of the shooting into his own videos (Ministry of Justice, 2009; Paton, 2012). One of the gunman's videos, entitled *Just Testing My Gun*, included footage of him firing the weapon he later used in the shooting (Kiilakoski & Oksanen, 2011b; Ministry of Justice, 2009). This clip mimics, in part, the *Rampart Range* video produced by the Columbine shooters. The gunman also expressed happiness over the actions of the Virginia Tech perpetrator (Serazio, 2010). In his video *Jokela High School Massacre–11/7/2007*, he incorporated footage of his school and images of him pointing his gun at the camera (de Quetteville, 2007; Kiilakoski & Oksanen, 2011b), similar to stills found in the Virginia Tech shooter's manifesto.

There is comparability in the content between these videos and those coming from earlier shooters. These similarities, however, have more to do with the message itself rather than the presentation quality of the videos. Specifically, the content of the Jokela shooter's videos focused heavily on spreading his opinions (Paton, 2012). Like the Columbine shooters, the Jokela shooter wanted to kick start a revolution (Kiilakoski & Oksanen, 2011a, 2011b; see also Gibbs & Roche, 1999). Similar to the Virginia Tech shooter, he labeled his shooting as an act of political terrorism designed as retribution against the human race for how they had treated him, expressing his disdain for society while hoping to inspire others to follow in his path (Kiilakoski & Oksanen, 2011a). In the 10 months between Jokela and the September 23, 2008 Kauhajoki shooting, Finnish police reported that 86 similar threats of violence had been made, 34 of which resulted in criminal prosecutions (Ministry of Justice, 2009; see also Lindberg et al., 2012).

THE ISLA VISTA SHOOTER'S YOUTUBE MANIFESTO AND AUTOBIOGRAPHY

Like these other shooters before him, the Isla Vista gunman, Elliot Rodger, wanted to leave behind his own story. Less than 24 hours before his rampage, the shooter uploaded a series of videos to his YouTube channel (see Rodger, 2014a, 2014b, 2014c, 2014d, 2014e, 2014f). In each of these videos, he provides a glimpse into his version of reality, one filled with desperation mixed with arrogance. It is his final video, entitled *Elliot Rodger's Retribution*, that provides audiences insight into his detailed plan to exact revenge against those individuals he perceived as his enemies (Rodger, 2014f).

Filmed in his black BMW the evening before the attack (see Lovett & Nagourney, 2014), the shooter speaks directly into the camera lens as if he was addressing each person who would see the footage individually. He opens the video by declaring that

> [t]omorrow is the day of retribution. The day in which I will have my revenge against humanity, against all of you. (Rodger, 2014f, 0:16; see also Mozingo, 2014)

Over the next seven minutes, he delivers a carefully constructed message in which he explains how he will go to a sorority house on the campus of the University of California-Santa Barbara and kill every girl in there, before gunning down every person he sees in the Isla Vista community (Rodger, 2014f). He notes that since he was never shown any mercy, he will not give any to his victims (Rodger, 2014f). He further claims that he will punish all of the people who did not pay him any attention (Rodger, 2014f).

At the same time, the video also has undertones of declarations made by shooters before him. Like the Columbine gunmen, the Isla Vista shooter stresses how he is the alpha male, or what he calls "the superior one," who never was accepted by popular kids (Rodger, 2014f, 3:07). Like the Virginia Tech perpetrator, he expresses disdain for hedonism (Rodger, 2014f), though in other videos, he emphasizes his wealth in underscoring reasons females should not reject him (Rodger, 2014b). Similar to the Jokela shooter, he speaks of a hatred for humanity, which he calls a "disgusting, wretched, depraved species" (Rodger, 2014f, 5:23).

Similar to his final production, the shooter's other videos (all but one of which were uploaded on the same day but do not appear to have been filmed at the same time) paint the portrait of an inner turmoil between a guy who wants to be loved by a girl and a person who wants revenge because he was not. In several of the videos, he talks about how girls do not give him a chance, even remarking in some that he does not understand why and then listing all of the reasons why—including that he is magnificent and the ultimate gentleman—that they should date him (see Rodger, 2014b, 2014c, 2014e). He repeatedly notes how his life had been an injustice, a sad and depressing existence in which he had been left to rot (Rodger, 2014b, 2014c, 2014e). In one video (Rodger, 2014a), he walks through the park discussing how he must go alone because he has no one to share his spring break with. In another, he watches a couple kissing on the beach from his car and talks about how it makes him feel envious (Rodger, 2014d). Yet, in these same videos, he condemns other men, whom he views as inferior, for having what he wants and goes so far as to state that he is more deserving (Rodger, 2014b, 2014c).

In addition to his videos, many of which remain on his YouTube channel at the time of this writing (with the exception of *Elliot Rodger's Retribution*, which was removed from his profile yet reposted by others), the Isla Vista shooter also penned a detailed manifesto. Totaling over 106,000 words and 140 pages in length, *My Twisted World: The Story of Elliot Rodger* recounted each year of his life, in detail, and the failures that led up to the shooting (Rodger, n.d.). Like the video, the shooter's manifesto included detailed plans about the attack, including information indicating that he had been preparing for the massacre for several years (Rodger, n.d.; see also Duke, 2014; Nagourney, 2014). In fact, he originally had planned to carry it out the previous Halloween, but decided against it due to the increased police presence around Isla Vista; the shooting also was postponed several additional times as he healed from a fight (Rodger, n.d.; Nagourney, 2014). He emailed the document to a number of people, including his therapist, his parents, and childhood friends (Feldman, 2014; Mozingo, 2014; Nagourney, 2014). After reading the document, his parents alerted law enforcement in an attempt to prevent the shooting, but they were unsuccessful in stopping the attack (Feldman, 2014; Mozingo, 2014; Nagourney, 2014).

THE LURE OF A MEDIA PERSONA

For these and other mass shooters, there are a number of potential catalysts that spark their rampages. Newman and colleagues (2004) suggest that these shooters feel socially marginalized and detached from society (see also Dutton, White, & Fogarty, 2013; Leary, Kowalski, Smith, & Phillips, 2003).

Some (e.g., Kiilakoski & Oksanen, 2011a; Kimmel & Mahler, 2003; Leary et al., 2003; Tonso, 2009; Vossekuil et al., 2002) have speculated that this marginalization may be due to bullying of the perpetrators. It also may be attributed to what Kimmel and Mahler (2003, p. 1445) call "cultural marginalization"—the exclusion of individuals because they are different, due to their being shy, highly intelligent, artistic, nonathletic, nerdy, or weird (see also Consalvo, 2003; Dutton et al., 2013; Kalish & Kimmel, 2010; Ogle et al., 2003; Tonso, 2009).

As a result of such ostracism, whether real or perceived, the shooters seek to take a stand against their oppressors, termed the "revenge hypothesis" by Ogle, Eckman, and Leslie (2003, p. 16). These individuals will, as Dutton and colleagues (2013) suggest,

> [b]ecome and remain fixated and obsessed with rejection by what they see as an elite in-group whom they see as having unfairly achieved success. . . . They formulate plans to annihilate the transgressors, which they justify as vengeance for the transgressions made against them. (p. 548)

The locations of the shootings then become symbolic in the sense that they represent the community at large, which often is the focus of the retribution rather than targeting just a specific individual or group (Muschert, 2007a). Thus, these shootings and subsequent media manifestos are the product of aggrieved entitlement, which as Kalish and Kimmel (2010) note, is "a gendered [masculine] emotion, a fusion of that humiliating loss of manhood and the moral obligation and entitlement to get it back" (p. 454). As they further explain,

> Aggrieved entitlement inspires revenge against those who have wronged you; it is the compensation for humiliation. Humiliation is emasculation: humiliate someone and you take away his manhood. For many men, humiliation must be avenged, or you cease to be a man. (Kalish & Kimmel, 2010, p. 454)

For many of these shooters, media personas through their manifestos provide an outlet in which to reclaim their masculinity (see, generally, Consalvo, 2003; Kalish & Kimmel, 2010; Kimmel & Mahler, 2003; Muschert & Ragnedda, 2010; Tonso, 2009). A number of these shooters in fact were weak, timid, or shy in their everyday lives (Kiilakoski & Oksanen, 2011a). Their videos enable them to adopt a violent and aggressive identity (Kiilakoski & Oksanen, 2011a, 2011b; Paton, 2012), through which, as Paton (2012, p. 226) notes, they "become anti-heroic icons of modern times" (see also De Venanzi, 2012). As Consalvo (2003) further points out, the over-the-top theatrics displayed in the videos, and subsequently the shootings themselves, allow the gunmen to appear dominant, even if only for a day (see also Frymer, 2009; Kellner, 2008a).

A key component of the manifestos and related media personas of the shooters is the underlying cultural script (Carvalho, 2010; Larkin, 2009; Muschert & Ragnedda, 2010; Newman et al., 2004; Tonso, 2009). These performance stories allow the shooters to resolve some sort of a dilemma through acts of violence (Newman et al., 2004). A cultural script, as Newman and colleagues (2004) further explain, "provide[s] an image of what the shooters want to become and a template that links the method to the goal" (p. 230). Such lethal violence, coupled with the shooters' communication, allows them to convey some intended message to their audience (Muschert & Ragnedda, 2010).

A common theme throughout these manifestos that is expressed as a part of the cultural script is the idea of natural selection (de Quetteville, 2007; Kiilakoski & Oksanen, 2011a). This theme was emphasized by the Jokela shooter in his videos (de Quetteville, 2007; Kiilakoski & Oksanen, 2011a), as well as by the Columbine shooters (Schildkraut, 2012b), one of whom even wore the phrase on his shirt the day of the shooting (Larkin, 2007, 2009). Through natural selection, the shooters were able to decide who lived and who died, and essentially reach the godlike status they did not have in real life (Dutton et al., 2013; JCSO, 1999b; Tonso, 2009).

Additional ideas are conveyed through the cultural scripts woven through the shooters' media manifestos. Some shooters, such as the Jokela gunman, use their media personas to spread their anti-political views (Kiilakoski & Oksanen, 2011a, 2011b; see also Tonso, 2009, who notes that the Columbine shooters similarly expressed such opinions). Other perpetrators, such as the Virginia Tech shooter, anoint themselves as the voice of the oppressed (Carvalho, 2010; Schildkraut, 2012b; VTRP, 2007). Regardless of which cultural script shooters choose to employ in their virtual manifestos, the use of the media to disseminate their views gives them a global stage with no constraints or limitations (see, generally, Schildkraut, 2012b).

PROSUMERS AND MASS SHOOTER "FANDEMONIUM"

Beyond the videos made by the shooters themselves, another category of media users also exists that helps to spread these messages. Called "prosumers," these individuals create other videos, similar to mash-ups or montages, to form new material (Sumiala & Tikka, 2011a; see also Paton, 2012). These new videos may include clips from the shooters' original posts, news programs, documentaries, or interviews with law enforcement, among other sources (Paton, 2012; Sumiala & Tikka, 2011a). Technological advances and the ease of use of social media platforms make sharing the shooters' videos a simpler process. Users easily can edit digital documents retrieved from other sources and create new products to be shared (Paton, 2012; Sumiala & Tikka, 2011a). Another key characteristic of prosumers is that they emphasize participation in the process of communication with the shooters (Sumiala & Tikka, 2011a), even if that exchange takes place after the event. As such, many individuals comment back to the video clips that the shooters post (Lindgren, 2011).

At the same time, new videos or media documents need not be created in order to spread the shooters' messages. Instead, features built in to social media platforms allow users to repost or share the original record. Facebook, for example, utilizes a share feature that allows users to repost messages from other members (Osborne & Dredze, 2014). On the Twitter platform, users can re-share or "retweet" a post from any source, regardless of whether they are followers of the original messenger (Kwak et al., 2010). This essentially "recycles" the material, allowing it to have a considerably broader reach than just the original post (Sumiala & Tikka, 2011a). Kwak and colleagues (2010) have found that the retweeting process allows for a single message to reach 1,000 other Twitter users on average. Thus, the process of circulation helps just a few individuals get their messages out to a global audience (Kiilakoski & Oksanen, 2011b; Sumiala & Tikka, 2011a).

Beyond prosumers who generate new or share the original content from mass shooters, social media also has become a place where those who admire these perpetrators can interact (see, generally, Lindberg et al., 2012; Oksanen et al., 2014). Such communities have become a symbolic forum for individuals with shared interests, regardless of which country they live in (Oksanen et al., 2014). For these individuals, mass shooters have become unlikely heroes, objects of adoration, or even martyrs (Bondü, Cornell, & Scheithauer, 2011; Kiilakoski & Oksanen, 2011a; Larkin, 2009; Newman et al., 2004; Oksanen et al., 2014). These online communities allow such people to join together to show sympathy for the shooters or share their admiration (Ames, 2007; Oksanen et al., 2014, Paton, 2012). For example, within minutes of law enforcement releasing the name of the gunman following the June 17, 2015 shooting at a Charleston, South Carolina, church, a number of fan pages and discussion boards appeared on Facebook focused on the shooter, Dylann Roof. Some of these pages showed support for the shooter, while others expressed more hostile and punitive viewpoints.

These sites provide forums for conflicting or dissenting opinions as well (Oksanen et al., 2014). Some fan communities may be highly exclusive, requiring an access code to join (see Oksanen et al., 2014). Conversely, others are public forums where no membership is required. While some researchers (e.g., Paton, 2012) have suggested that these fan networks disband over time, others (see Oksanen et al., 2014) have found these communities to be sustained.

Online fan communities were particularly evident following the Columbine shooting (Fast, 2008; Larkin, 2009; Muschert & Larkin, 2007; Paton, 2012), though other perpetrators have garnered their own fan base (Oksanen et al., 2014). In a study of 113 YouTube profiles between April 2010 and June 2012, for example, Oksanen and colleagues (2014) found that nearly 90 percent of these biographies specifically emphasized—either in part or in whole—the Columbine shooting (see also Paton, 2012). Only two pre-Columbine events were referenced—the 1966 University of Texas and the 1998 Thurston High School shootings (Oksanen et al., 2014). Instead, aside from Columbine, most mentions related to post-1999 shootings, such as Virginia Tech and Jokela (Oksanen et al., 2014).

Each shooting has its own dedicated group of followers. One of the largest groups is the Columbiners, named after the 1999 attack (see, generally, Monroe, 2012), a term that only recently entered the discourse on mass shootings fandemonium (CBC, 2015). While these individuals are active across a number of social media sites, it is Tumblr, an online blogging community, that recently has been in the spotlight. A cursory examination of Tumblr using the search term "Columbiners" shows thousands of entries from a number of different individuals. (A similar hashtag is used on numerous posts on Twitter.) In early 2015, however, two individuals took their posts on the site further, stating that they were planning to shoot up a mall in Halifax, Nova Scotia, on Valentine's Day (Beaumont, 2015; CBC, 2015). The attack was foiled after a tip was called in to the authorities; two individuals were arrested, while a third committed suicide.

While some of the members of the Columbiners group advocate violence or aim to copy the shooting (Beaumont, 2015; CBC, 2015), others flock to the site for different reasons. Some share similar feelings, beyond the homicidal tendencies, with the shooters and can relate to them; others are suicidal or depressed and are looking for people to talk to (Beaumont, 2015). Some are fascinated by the criminology and science behind the shootings or the perpetrators (Beaumont, 2015). Still, there is another group of individuals active in posting about mass shooters online—those who are attracted to them (Monroe, 2012).

Some have likened the Columbiners' following of Eric Harris and Dylan Klebold to that of Justin Bieber and his "Beliebers," Taylor Swift's "Swifties," or One Direction's "Directioners" (CBC, 2015; Monroe, 2012). Numerous people, mainly teenage girls, post about being in love with the shooters and wanting to date them (Monroe, 2012). They discuss their physical and sexual attractiveness, known among psychologists as "hybristophilia" (a rare attraction to murderers—see Buxton, 2014; Monroe, 2012; "The sickening tweets," 2012). The Columbine shooters, however, are not the only perpetrators to have amassed such a following. Chardon, Ohio, school shooter T. J. Lane is the subject of a group following known as the "Laniacs" (Broderick, 2013; Romano, 2013). Similarly, Aurora movie theater shooter James Holmes is admired by his group of "Holmies" (Broderick, 2012; Monroe, 2012; "The sickening tweets," 2012). While Tumblr has been a main source of community for these groups, their reach also extends to other social media platforms, including Facebook and Twitter ("The sickening tweets," 2012).

It is important to note, however, that online fan communities also may have far greater implications. Such sites can act as a platform for like-minded individuals to join together to discuss their plans for similar attacks and provide support and reinforcement for one another (Oksanen et al., 2014; Patton et al., 2014). Several school shooters, including the Jokela gunman, found support in these types of communities (Kiilakoski & Oksanen, 2011a, 2011b). As Lindberg and colleagues (2012) point out, these forums tend to romanticize the idea of mass shootings for those individuals who share similar troubles or circumstances with the gunmen.

BEYOND THE HEADLINES: DO OTHERS KNOW PRIOR TO MASS SHOOTINGS?

As this chapter has illustrated, mass shooters leave behind a number of clues into their rampages via their media productions, a number of which are shared through prosumers and fans. This process, known as leakage (see Meloy & O'Toole, 2011; O'Toole, 2000), however, is not solely limited to the Internet. Leakage may occur via letters, diaries, emails, journals, and voice mails (Meloy & O'Toole, 2011). It also may take place by the sharing of intentions with other individuals, which a number of the shooters discussed in this book had done (see also Cullen, 2009).

Leakage has been common in a number of high profile mass shootings, including Columbine (Cullen, 2009; Gimpel, 2012) and Virginia Tech (Roy, 2009; VTRP, 2007). Other shooters also have provided clues of their impending attacks. It has been estimated, for example, that between 20 and 40 people knew about the 2005 Red Lake High School shooting before it happened (Associated Press, 2006a; Davey, 2005; Robertson, 2006; see also Meloy & O'Toole, 2011). In fact, several of the shooter's friends ultimately were indicted on conspiracy charges due to their participation in the leakage (Meloy & O'Toole, 2011).

Similarly, the Jokela gunman made a number of statements alluding to the rampage prior to the attack, raising such concern that friends explicitly tried to dissuade him from committing a school shooting (Kiilakoski & Oksanen,

2011a; Ministry of Justice, 2009; see also Lindberg et al., 2012). These friends also had seen the images he posted on IRC-Galleria (Kiilakoski & Oksanen, 2011a, 2011b). While he had not specifically confirmed that he would open fire on his school, he suggested that he had considered going on a killing spree at the country's parliament in response to the corruption by politicians (Kiilakoski & Oksanen, 2011a; Ministry of Justice, 2009). Thus, as Schildkraut, Elsass, and Muschert (in press) note, there were warning signs, despite the common misperception that these events came out of nowhere.

9

Mass Shootings
Today and Beyond

Myth: "It seems to happen almost every week now. A guy—and it seems to almost always be a guy—who shouldn't have a gun has one anyway, and uses it to shoot up a mall, a movie theater, a school, a church, a military camp—a generally public place that we would assume to be free from the threat of deadly violence."

—Surico, 2015

Statements such as the one that begins this chapter, which was published following the July 23, 2015 shooting at a Lafayette, Louisiana, movie theater (Surico, 2015), are detrimental to the development of workable, real-world approaches to dealing with mass shootings as they inflate the statistics regarding this phenomenon for the purpose of generating fear and hysteria with few goals beyond pushing a political agenda. This tactic readily is found in the media, across the political spectrum, and from organizations on opposing sides of the gun control–gun rights debate. Such methods are exceptionally detrimental to the search for realistic solutions to the issue of mass shootings—approaches that are intended to decrease the likelihood of attacks occurring or reduce their lethality when events do take place. Myths about this phenomenon, often created and disseminated by those valiantly claiming to be searching for answers, are at the very heart of our problem with truly addressing the issue of mass shootings.

WHY DOES THIS BOOK MATTER?

There are no perfect public policies or ideal set of laws that completely will rid us of the possibility of a mass shooting event occurring in our country. As Fox and DeLateur (2014) point out, "mass murder just may be a price we must pay for living in a society where personal freedom is so highly valued" (p. 141). That does not mean, however, that we should abandon the goals of reducing their frequency or their lethality when they do occur. Yet, in working toward these ends, we often collectively find ourselves lost in the fear that this phenomenon generates. In doing so, the realities of these types of events are forgone. At the outset of this book, we assert that in order to understand the problem, we first must know what the problem is; only once we truly appreciate the realities of any issue are we able to begin a valid search for solutions. This task is challenging given the complexities of this phenomenon as well as the strong emotions these types of events elicit. This book strives to provide that grounded base from which informed discussion can follow by presenting an unbiased look at the phenomenon of mass shootings in order to dispel common myths regarding these types of events.

Starting from a place of true understanding regarding the definition of mass shootings, as well as their history, prevalence, and statistics, we are able to begin a more research-focused, and therefore more productive, conversation. In doing so, we wipe away the emotional rhetoric and political agendas to get to the heart of the issue through the debunking of numerous myths about these attacks. The perpetuation of such fallacies does little more than give rise to fear in the general public, from which productive ideas about how to help prevent mass shootings and/or reduce their lethality when they do occur can never emerge. To this end, this book serves as an important first step in igniting candid, collaborative discussion across political lines about these types of events.

An open, cooperative idea exchange is vital for the development of strategies to increase safety; however, such a conversation must be as unbiased as possible. In order to achieve this, it is imperative that the discussion be based upon empirical findings from research conducted with rigorous methodology rather than conclusions colored by political agendas or driven by financial bottom lines. A focus on independent research, rather than findings produced by organizations with known agendas, will provide level ground upon which an interdisciplinary, multidimensional discussion about mass shootings can take place as trust is fostered. Ultimately, this affords us an opportunity to adopt new procedures as cutting edge research findings dictate. Collectively, we must resist the urge to draft laws and policies on the basis of fear, emotionality, and political agenda, instead making empirical evidence the cornerstone of our coordinated effort to combat the phenomenon of mass shootings.

AN END TO THE BLAME GAME

A goal of this book is to begin to put an end to the finger-pointing. When news of a mass shooting breaks, almost instantaneously we, as a society, are looking for someone (or something) to fault, and as was pointed out in Chapter 5, rarely is the shooter blamed. We instead tend to take issue with every person and place except for the one who pulled the trigger. This includes the tired and ill-conceived arguments of an incompetent approach to gun control, excessively restricted gun rights, a lack of access to mental health services, an overabundance of violence in the media, rampant bullying, illicit drug use, the shooters' dysfunctional families, and even the outrageous claim that victims of these tragedies partially are to blame because they were poorly prepared. In doing so, the nation most often finds itself in a stalemate, locked by pride and agenda in a fight that does nothing to deal with the actual problem.

While the same old debate over gun control versus gun rights or argument over who should be able to purchase violent video games continually is reignited, no real progress is being made to find realistic, workable solutions to the mass shooting problem, which would result in decreasing the loss of life either by helping to prevent these tragedies or by reducing their lethality. It is vital that our society begins to recognize that if the goal of reducing the likelihood of a mass shooting occurring is to be achieved, as well as saving lives when one does happen, we must begin to work together to search for realistic strategies. This means abandoning preconceived agendas for a more cooperative, collective approach to dealing with this phenomenon.

While we are not likely to ever comprehend exactly why mass shootings occur, a better understanding can be gained by holding a collaborative, constructive, and interdisciplinary discussion about the individual, community-level, and sociocultural attributes that impact this type of violence (Henry, 2000, 2009; Muschert, 2007a; Muschert, Henry, Bracy, & Peguero, 2014; Schildkraut & Muschert, 2013). This conversation, in order to be as productive as possible, must include a variety of viewpoints, including the media, academics, politicians, and the general public (Harris & Harris, 2012; Schildkraut & Muschert, 2013). Yet, in this exchange of ideas, society must deny the urge to divide itself based upon individual beliefs, figuratively drawing lines in the sand, as doing so is counterproductive. Instead, society must work together to truly address mass shootings.

THE MEDIA'S NECESSARY RESPONSIBILITY

It is imperative that empirical findings influence pubic agendas as to mass shootings, rather than the other way around. In this regard, the media are tasked with the vital role as secondary claims makers as they are instrumental in disseminating information about this phenomenon; however, that task carries great responsibility, as the media serves as the main source of information about crime for up to 95 percent of the general public (Graber, 1980; Surette, 1992). In order for the media to facilitate an honest, grounded discussion about mass shootings generally, it is crucial that they withstand the urge to package their stories in a way that incites fear and hysteria, as doing so distorts the general public's understanding of these types of events in a number of ways, including their prevalence and a person's risk of victimization. It is vital that the public is educated on the realities of mass shootings, thereby working to overcome the disproportionate fear that these rampages spur.

Furthermore, when the flames of fear are fueled by sensationalized reporting on the part of the media, a wide range of fallacies regarding shooters tend to be adopted. These inaccurate stereotypes are problematic as they may cause people to overlook warning signs in others who do not fit the erroneous profile of a mass shooter that has been created, or falsely label someone as such because he or she exhibits characteristics similar to those of a perpetrator. Additionally, security devices introduced in the wake of a rampage typically are developed without a basis of sound empirical findings, and therefore are not helpful. These tactics, often serving as news stories for media outlets, are little more than companies making money off the victimization of others by introducing devices that not only contribute to people's extreme fear over this statistically rare phenomenon but also seldom succeed at increasing safety.

The glorification of mass shootings by the media is undoubtedly problematic. It clearly has been found that news consumers express greater fear of crime than those who avoid the news media (e.g., Chiricos, Padgett, & Gertz, 2000; Kaminski, Koons-Witt, Thompson, & Weiss, 2010; Kupchik & Bracy, 2009), including in response to relatively rare events, such as mass violence. This may, in turn, aid in the development of moral panic, which has been found to exist with regard to mass shootings (Elsass, Schildkraut, & Stafford, 2014; Schildkraut, Elsass, & Stafford, 2015; see also Burns & Crawford, 1999; Springhall, 1999). The media's reporting and the general public's subsequent response to these types of events, as well as the attacks themselves, undoubtedly shape public policy with regard to a wide variety of topics including, among other issues, gun control legislation and funding for mental health services (Beale, 2006; Birkland & Lawrence, 2009; Hernandez, Schildkraut, & Elsass, 2015; Schildkraut & Hernandez, 2014; Soraghan, 2000). Such issues are significant for the entire country; thus, the media, which overwhelmingly inform people's understanding of mass shootings, has an important responsibility.

Moreover, misreporting, which often has plagued this area, is detrimental to the general public's understanding of the frequency of these types of events, as well as an individual's likelihood of victimization. Inaccurate and often irresponsible journalism fuels the adoption of myths about mass shootings, which this book focuses on dispelling, as they are damaging to the hope of cooperative discussion about strategies to deal with these types of events. Clearly, it is crucial that the media ensures accuracy in their coverage of mass shootings, as well as concentrate on the reporting of verified factual information, rather than jumping to conclusions with the hope of being the first one to break the news of an attack.

The most abhorrent mistake in the wake of a mass shooting is the lack of emphasis on the victims of these tragedies by the media, politicians, pundits, and the general public alike. In the midst of all of the inaccurate reporting and generation of myths, the most important topic—those who lost their lives—often largely is left out of the conversation. This pattern begins with the media's choice of how much attention to give individual events. Some events, like Columbine, Aurora, and Sandy Hook, garner enormous media attention while others, such as the shootings at Northern Illinois University and a mall in Clackamas, Oregon, receive very little coverage (Schildkraut, 2014; see also Muschert & Carr, 2006). In prioritizing some mass shootings over others through the amount of time and space the media allow each attack to have, the victims of the deemphasized events basically are forgotten.

Even within the coverage of an individual mass shooting—especially with regard to those events that are highly salient—some victims receive much more attention than others. Research focusing on how the victims of mass shootings are framed in the media has uncovered patterns with regard to who gets highlighted in the coverage of an event (e.g., Muschert, 2007b; Schildkraut, 2012a). Essentially, victims are prioritized by which stories will sell. Among the victims of the Columbine shooting, for example, Cassie Bernall most often is covered while Kyle Velasquez largely is ignored, though both were murdered in the school's library (Muschert, 2007b). In the massacre at Virginia Tech, students Emily Hilscher and Ryan Clark and Professor Liviu Librescu are the most prominently featured victims, with little attention given to the other victims (Schildkraut, 2012a).

Not only do victims get lost in the back and forth of the mass shootings discourse, but some are forgotten completely, making them nothing more than a number. In doing so, these overlooked victims lose their identities as they are simply reported as an aggregate victim count (see Schildkraut, 2014). For example, while the *New York Times* mentioned each Virginia Tech victim at least once, in the *New York Post*, 18 of the 25 student victims received no coverage (Schildkraut, 2012a). Furthermore, these patterns appear to hold when examining the media's coverage of other events, including the shootings at Aurora, Tucson, and Sandy Hook. The media's focus on only certain victims of these tragedies is a travesty. Every life matters, and in the case of mass shootings, each victim is equally important and represents a heartbreaking loss.

As time moves on after a mass shooting, the media also should concentrate on creating a forum for grounded, cooperative discourse about the phenomenon more generally, rather than supplying an outlet for primary claims makers pushing their agendas on the general public. The media has the ability and the responsibility to provide a medium for honest discussion on what realistically can be done about mass shootings, as well as disseminate the findings of empirical research about these types of events. In doing so, the media is facilitating the creation of a more informed general public.

WHERE DO WE GO FROM HERE?

Schildkraut, Elsass, and Muschert (in press) point out that mass shootings have left an undeniable mark on American culture as they elicit strong emotions of shock and horror through direct and indirect victimization. As such, it is vital that we continue to research the phenomenon of mass shootings. Still, what will it take for true change to happen? Clearly, the answer lies in a more meaningful discourse about these types of events (Schildkraut et al., in press; see also Henry, 2000, 2009; Muschert, 2007a, 2010; Muschert et al., 2014; Schildkraut & Muschert, 2013). As news of a mass shooting breaks, the focus of our discussion about this phenomenon seems to center on only the short-term goal of comforting a grieving country (Schildkraut et al., in press). This overwhelmingly results in knee-jerk, "feel good" legislation based upon agenda and rhetoric rather than empirical research, which does little more than to provide a false sense of security to the general public. This type of legislation is wholly ineffective as it does not deter potential mass shooters, reduce lethality when an attack does take place, or increase public safety.

To look for a "quick fix" to the problem of mass shootings is an incompetent approach that fails to acknowledge the sophistication and multidimensionality of the issue (Schildkraut et al., in press). The media, politicians, and even researchers have a tendency to treat each shooting as somewhat fundamentally different—most often due to the type of location (e.g., school, workplace, public space) where an attack takes place. This is a mistake, however, as the reality is that there exists a certain commonality among these events. This realization has caused some researchers to begin to call for studies that recognize this (e.g., Harris & Harris, 2012). To facilitate the implementation of more effective preventative measures, we must investigate this phenomenon across time and space—connecting the dots in order to see where improvement is really needed. This approach is more likely to result in the creation of responsible, well-informed legislation, as well as the better enforcement of existing laws and policies that meet the needs identified (Schildkraut et al., in press). Furthermore, empirical findings should be used not only as a foundation for law and public policy but also for informing crisis-training techniques, first-responder action plans, security devices, and emergency procedures that aspire to reduce lethality in the case of an attack.

While there is no way to completely negate the risk of a mass shooting event occurring in the future, we can take steps to reduce the threat; however, this only can be achieved through open, collaborative, constructive discourse and cooperation. It is time for our society to choose to learn from these events rather than to allow them to fade into history without any real steps being made to decrease their future likelihood and increase public safety. At present, by refusing to engage in a realistic, responsible, and communal dialogue about this phenomenon, we are allowing the victims of these tragedies to die in vain. If we are to be successful, it is necessary for public policies and statutes, as well as training techniques and security adaptations, to be empirically informed.

It is time that we, as a nation, denounce the personal and political agendas, and alternatively call for unbiased scientific research to be the foundation of a discussion about mass shootings. We all agree that the loss of even one life to a mass shooter is too great, but still find ourselves locked in a fight over topics such as gun control while ignoring the bigger picture. Statutes, policies, and procedures drafted for the purpose of helping to prevent mass shootings and reduce their lethality when they do occur that are based upon inaccurate stereotypes, uninformed political agenda, inflated fear, and raw emotion cannot be successful. We must band together to work toward realistic change, which only can be achieved through the desertion of political agenda and pride.

Bibliography

Abcarian, R., & Fausset, R. (2010, February 13). Three killed in shooting at Alabama campus. *Los Angeles Times*. Retrieved from http://articles.latimes.com/2010/feb/13/nation/la-na-alabama-shooting13-2010feb13

Aboudi, S. (2015, January 14). Al Qaeda claims French attack, derides Paris rally. *Reuters*. Retrieved from http://www.reuters.com/article/2015/01/14/us-france-shooting-aqap-idUSKBN0KN0VO20150114

Addington, L.A. (2009). Cops and cameras: Public security as a policy response to Columbine. *American Behavioral Scientist, 52*(10), 1426–1446.

The age of mass murder: Speck's rampage ushered in a bloody new era for America. (1991, December 6). *Houston Chronicle*. p. 11. Retrieved from http://infoweb.newsbank.com.libproxy.txstate.edu/resources/doc/nb/news/0ED7B159AA21102C?p=NewsBank

Agence France-Presse. (1992, July 2). Sacked French worker kills six. *Independent*. Retrieved from http://www.independent.co.uk/news/world/sacked-french-worker-kills-six-1530596.html

Agence France-Presse. (2013, August 21). Egypt gunman kills 15 in family dispute. *Fox News*. Retrieved from http://www.foxnews.com/world/2013/08/21/egypt-gunman-kills-15-in-family-dispute/

Ahmad, M. (2004, November 29). Slaughter in stress zone. *Telegraph India*. Retrieved from http://www.telegraphindia.com/1041129/asp/frontpage/story_4062751.asp

ALERRT. (n.d.). *About*. Retrieved from http://alerrt.org/About

Alfano, S. (2006, September 14). Police: Montreal gunman killed himself. *CBS News*. Retrieved from http://www.cbsnews.com/news/police-montreal-gunman-killed-himself/

ALICE Training Institute. (n.d.a). *Active shooter – definition*. Retrieved from http://www.alicetraining.com/active-shooter/

ALICE Training Institute. (n.d.b). *About us*. Retrieved from http://www
.alicetraining.com/about-us/

Allen, E., Levenson, M., & Ryan, A. (2015, April 15). Boston marks two years since
Boston Marathon bombings. *Boston Globe*. Retrieved from http://www
.bostonglobe.com/metro/2015/04/15/boston-marks-two-years-since-boston
-marathon-bombings/Wr4vLyFqh9opMPfGSTxOvL/story.html

Allens in Roanoke jail: Prison services omitted to comply with no-visitor rule. (1912,
March 18). *New York Times*. p. 3. Retrieved from http://query.nytimes.com/
mem/archive-free/pdf?
res=9C0CE1DC1F31E233A2575BC1A9659C946396D6CF

AllPolitics. (1999, April 22). Poll: More parents worried about school safety. *CNN*.
Retrieved from http://www.cnn.com/ALLPOLITICS/stories/1999/04/22/
school.violence.poll/

Al-Mahdi, K. (2009, March 5). Yemen mosque attacker executed. *Arab News*.
Retrieved from http://www.arabnews.com/node/321659

Almasy, S. (2014, January 26). Cops: Mall gunman expressed 'general unhappiness'
in journal. *CNN*. Retrieved from http://www.cnn.com/2014/01/26/us/
maryland-mall-shooting/

Almasy, S., O'Neill, A., Weisfeldt, S., & Cabrera, A. (2015, August 8). James
Holmes sentenced to life in prison for Colorado movie theater murders. *CNN*.
Retrieved from http://www.cnn.com/2015/08/07/us/james-holmes-movie
-theater-shooting-jury/

Altheide, D.L. (2009). The Columbine shooting and the discourse of fear. *American
Behavioral Scientist, 52*(10), 1354–1370.

Altimari, D. (2015, January 12). Sandy Hook families sue Newtown, schools, citing
lax security. *Hartford Courant*. Retrieved from http://www.courant.com/news/
connecticut/hc-sandy-hook-town-lawsuit-20150112-story.html

American Academy of Child & Adolescent Psychiatry. (2008). *Children and guns*.
Washington, DC: American Academy of Child & Adolescent Psychiatry.
Retrieved from http://www.aacap.org/aacap/Policy_Statements/2013/
Children_and_Guns.aspx

Ames, M. (2007). *Going postal: Rage, murder, and rebellion in America*. London:
Snowbooks.

Amichai, R. (2009, August 1). Gunman kills 2 at Tel Aviv club for gay youths.
Reuters. Retrieved from http://www.reuters.com/article/2009/08/01/us-israel
-shooting-idUSTRE5701V520090801

Andersen, I., Krekling, D.V., Sandvik, S., Helljesen, V., Hirsti, K., & Zondag, M.
(2012, July 3). 57 henrettet med hodeskudd på Utøya [57 executed with head-
shots on Utøya]. *NRK*. Retrieved from http://www.nrk.no/norge/57-henrettet
-med-hodeskudd-pa-utoya-1.8025218

Anderson, C. (2012, December 23). Murder in a small Kiwi school. *Stuff*. Retrieved
from http://www.stuff.co.nz/national/8112416/Murder-in-a-small-Kiwi-school

Anderson, C.A. (2004). An update on the effects of playing violent video games.
Journal of Adolescence, 27(1), 113–122.

Anderson, M., Kaufman, J., Simon, T.R., Barrios, L., Paulozzi, L., Ryan, G., Hammond, R., Modzeleski, W., Feucht, T., & Potter, L. (2001). School-assisted violent deaths in the United States, 1994–1999. *Journal of the American Medical Association, 286*(21), 2695–2702.

Angry principal kills 4 in school; Wounds two and himself in attack on board and aides in South Pasadena. (1940, May 7). *New York Times*, p. 1. Retrieved from http://query.nytimes.com/mem/archive/pdf?res=9B00EED91F3CE533A25754 C0A9639C946193D6CF

Applebome, P. (1986, August 21). Mail carrier kills 14 in post office, then himself. *New York Times*. Retrieved from http://www.nytimes.com/1986/08/21/us/ mail-carrier-kills-14-in-post-office-then-himself.html

Applebome, P., & Stetler, B. (2012, December 16). Media spotlight seen as a blessing, or a curse, in a grieving town. *New York Times*. Retrieved from http://www .nytimes.com/2012/12/17/business/media/newtown-has-mixed-feelings-about-the -media-horde-in-its-midst.html?ref=media&_r=0

Ariosto, D. (2012, August 26). Police: All Empire State shooting victims were wounded by officers. *CNN*. Retrieved from http://www.cnn.com/2012/08/25/ justice/new-york-empire-state-shooting/

Armed Police Working Group. (2011). *Operation bridge: Peer review into the response of Cumbria Constabulary following the actions of Derrick Bird on 2nd June 2010*. Cumbria, UK: Armed Police Working Group. Retrieved from http://www .cumbria.police.uk/Admin/uploads/attachment/files/News_Files/Inquest/ Running_Orders/ACC_Chestermans_report.pdf

Around the world. (1997, April 2). *Seattle Times*. Retrieved from http://community. seattletimes.nwsource.com/archive/?date=19970402&slug=2531929

Askar, J.G. (2012, December 17). TV coverage of Sandy Hook shootings draws heavy criticism: Reporting considered invasive, exploitative and sensationalized. *Desert News*. Retrieved from http://www.deseretnews.com/article/865568947/ In-context-where-TV-coverage-of-Sandy-Hook-shootings-fell-short.html?pg=all

Assault Weapons Ban of 2013, H.R. 437, 113th Cong., 1st Sess. (2013).

Associated Press. (1956, May 5). Boy kills teacher, wounds 2 others. *The Milwaukee Sentinel*. Retrieved from https://news.google.com/newspapers?id=QX FQAAAAIBAJ&sjid=8Q8EAAAAIBAJ&pg=5966,2070614&dq=prevatte&hl=en

Associated Press. (1966a, August 6). Sniper indicated readiness to die; made feeling known in note written before rampage. *New York Times*. p. 18. Retrieved from http://query.nytimes.com/mem/archive-free/pdf?res=9905E1DB163CE43BBC 4E53DFBE66838D679EDE

Associated Press. (1966b, November 13). Youth, 18, slays 4 woman and child in beauty school. *New York Times*. pp. 1, 51. Retrieved from http://query.nytimes .com/mem/archive-free/pdf?res=9A07E4D8133CE53BBC4B52DFB767838D 679EDE

Associated Press. (1975a, May 29). Teen-ager takes own life after killing 2, wounding 13. *Bulletin*. p. 20. Retrieved from https://news.google.de/newspapers?id= eTYVAAAAIBAJ&sjid=8vcDAAAAIBAJ&pg=1363,432029&dq=&hl=de

Associated Press. (1975b, September 24). Charges filed in shooting. *Spokane Daily Chronicle.* p. 19. Retrieved from https://news.google.com/newspapers?id=pFVOAAAAIBAJ&sjid=yPgDAAAAIBAJ&pg=3249,2241230&hl=en

Associated Press. (1979, January 29). Sniping suspect had a grim goal. *The Milwaukee Journal.* Retrieved from https://news.google.com/newspapers?id=Q1waAAAAIBAJ&sjid=mykEAAAAIBAJ&pg=5169,5587238&dq=brenda+spencer&hl=en

Associated Press. (1983, June 4). Gunman kills 5 in school. *The Spokesman-Review.* p. 3. Retrieved from https://news.google.com/newspapers?id=YNURAAAAIBAJ&sjid=1O4DAAAAIBAJ&pg=7147,1879619&dq=eppstein&hl=en

Associated Press. (1984, June 30). 6 die in Dallas club as enraged man fires wildly. *New York Times.* Retrieved from http://www.nytimes.com/1984/06/30/us/6-die-in-dallas-club-as-enraged-man-fires-wildly.html

Associated Press. (1989a, September 15). Worker on disability leave kills 7, then himself, in printing plant. *New York Times.* Retrieved from http://www.nytimes.com/1989/09/15/us/worker-on-disability-leave-kills-7-then-himself-in-printing-plant.html

Associated Press. (1989b, December 7). Montreal gunman kills 14 women and himself. *New York Times.* Retrieved from http://www.nytimes.com/1989/12/07/world/montreal-gunman-kills-14-women-and-himself.html

Associated Press. (1991a, June 19). Student shoots three outside his school. *AP News Archive.* Retrieved from http://www.apnewsarchive.com/1991/Student-Shoots-Three-Outside-His-School/id-9a37235e1f46bbf7d2e0acc5415db1b8

Associated Press. (1991b, October 24). Killeen recordings released by police. *The Press-Courier.* Retrieved from https://news.google.com/newspapers?id=RIdLAAAAIBAJ&sjid=2CMNAAAAIBAJ&pg=2979,5254738&hl=en

Associated Press. (1992, March 10). Killer hangs himself in cell. *The Free Lance-Star.* p. A4. Retrieved from https://news.google.com/newspapers?nid=1298&dat=19920310&id=MuBLAAAAIBAJ&sjid=VYsDAAAAIBAJ&pg=5738,1315582&hl=en

Associated Press. (1996a, April 29). Australian gunman kills at least 32. *New York Times.* Retrieved from http://www.nytimes.com/1996/04/29/world/australia-gunman-kills-at-least-32.html

Associated Press. (1996b, April 30). Australian gunman called a loner with a mental history. *New York Times.* Retrieved from http://www.nytimes.com/1996/04/30/world/australia-gunman-called-a-loner-with-a-mental-history.html

Associated Press. (2002a, July 31). Gunman kills 8 in Beirut office. *Fox News.* Retrieved from http://www.foxnews.com/story/2002/07/31/gunman-kills-8-in-beirut-office.html

Associated Press. (2002b, August 21). Columbine killing suit is settled. *Los Angeles Times.* Retrieved from http://articles.latimes.com/2002/aug/21/nation/na-columbine21

Associated Press. (2003a, February 1). Families Columbine school shooting victims settle lawsuits over gun sales. *Sioux City Journal.* Retrieved from http://siouxcityjournal.com/news/local/families-columbine-school-shooting-victims-settle

-lawsuits-over-gun-sale/article_9f275821-1a75-5753-8004-21d69948a962
.html

Associated Press. (2003b, June 6). Pupil opens fire at school. *News 24.* Retrieved
from http://www.news24.com/World/News/Pupil-opens-fire-at-school-20030606

Associated Press. (2005, December 15). Nepalese soldier kills 11 civilians. *USA
Today.* Retrieved from http://usatoday30.usatoday.com/news/world/2005-12
-15-nepal-civilians_x.htm

Associated Press. (2006a, February 8). Prosecutor discusses school shooting with Red
Lake officials. *Farmers Independent.* Retrieved from https://news.google.com/
newspapers?nid=1027&dat=20060208&id=5EplAAAAIBAJ&sjid=vJMNAAA
AIBAJ&pg=2118,5968450&hl=en

Associated Press. (2006b, March 14). Two hurt in Reno middle school shooting. *Fox
News.* Retrieved from http://www.foxnews.com/story/2006/03/14/two-hurt-in
-reno-middle-school-shooting/

Associated Press. (2006c, April 4). Judge rules Michigan video game law is unconsti-
tutional. *USA Today.* Retrieved from http://usatoday30.usatoday.com/tech/
gaming/2006-04-04-michigan-law_x.htm

Associated Press. (2006d, May 24). Sniper accomplice says mentor had extortion and
terror plan. *New York Times.* Retrieved from http://www.nytimes.com/2006/05/
24/us/24malvo.html?_r=0

Associated Press. (2006e, September 15). Police say Montreal gunman killed himself.
USA Today. Retrieved from http://usatoday30.usatoday.com/news/world/2006
-09-14-canada-shooting_x.htm

Associated Press. (2007, April 24). NBC exec: Airing Cho video 'good journalism.'
NBC News: Today. Retrieved from http://today.msnbc.msn.com/id/18295682/
ns/today-entertainment/t/nbc-execairing-cho-video-good-journalism/#.Tj8ANs
0RGqk

Associated Press. (2009, July 11). James W. Von Brunn: Holocaust Museum shooting suspect is white supremacist. *Huffington Post.* Retrieved from http://
www.huffingtonpost.com/2009/06/10/james-w-von-brunn-holocau_n_21
3864.html

Associated Press. (2011, April 9). 7 killed, 15 wounded in Dutch mall shooting. *USA
Today.* Retrieved from http://usatoday30.usatoday.com/news/nation/2011-04
-09-dutch-mall-shooting_N.htm

Associated Press. (2012, September 28). Minnesota: Shooting toll rises to six.
New York Times. Retrieved from http://www.nytimes.com/2012/09/29/us/
minnesota-shooting-toll-rises-to-six.html

Associated Press. (2013a, June 23). China shooting spree ends with six dead. *Guardian.* Retrieved from http://www.theguardian.com/world/2013/jun/23/six-die
-china-shooting-spree

Associated Press. (2013b, December 6). 20 years later: Long Island Rail Road shooting remembered as day killer Colin Ferguson went off the rails. *New York Daily
News.* Retrieved from http://www.nydailynews.com/new-york/lirr-bloodbath
-remembered-20-years-article-1.1539603

Associated Press. (2014a, February 27). Gun-sniffing dogs will patrol Tampa Bay schools. *Ocala Star Banner.* Retrieved from http://www.ocala.com/article/20140227/WIRE/140229722

Associated Press. (2014b, April 3). Gunman kills 3, wounds 16 at Fort Hood army base. *New York Times.* Retrieved from http://www.nytimes.com/aponline/2014/04/02/us/ap-us-fort-hood.html

Associated Press. (2014c, June 10). Company creates bulletproof blanked to protect kids in a shooting. *New York Post.* Retrieved from http://nypost.com/2014/06/10/company-creates-bulletproof-blanket-to-protect-children-from-handguns/

Associated Press. (2014d, September 2014). Michigan starts confidential school safety hotline. *WNDU 16.* Retrieved from http://www.wndu.com/home/headlines/Michigan-starts-confidential-school-safety-hotline-276989771.html

Associated Press. (2015, April 15). Jury seated in James Holmes trial in Colorado. *CBS News.* Retrieved from http://www.cbsnews.com/news/jury-seated-in-trial-of-colorado-movie-theater-shooter-james-holmes/

Australian Associated Press. (2004, June 17). Killer sent to psych hospital. *Sydney Morning Herald.* Retrieved from http://www.smh.com.au/articles/2004/06/17/1087245033577.html

Australian Associated Press. (2007, December 6). Melbourne remembers Queen St massacre. *Age.* Retrieved from http://www.theage.com.au/news/National/Melbourne-remembers-Queen-St-massacre/2007/12/06/1196812912743.html

Authorities say drunk policeman kills 7 in El Salvador. (2000, June 3). *Star-News.* Retrieved from https://news.google.com/newspapers?id=qLlOAAAAIBAJ&sjid=7h4EAAAAIBAJ&pg=3383,965429&dq=&hl=en

Autopsy reveals Lörrach woman smothered son. (2010, September 21). *The Local.* Retrieved from http://www.thelocal.de/20100921/29971

Axelrod v. Cinemark Holdings, Inc., 65 F.Supp.3d 1093 (2014).

Baker, P., Cooper, H., & Mazzetti, M. (2011, May 1). Bin Laden is dead, Obama says. *New York Times.* Retrieved from http://www.nytimes.com/2011/05/02/world/asia/osama-bin-laden-is-killed.html

Baldassare, M., Bonner, D., Petek, S., & Shrestha, J. (2013). *PPIC Statewide survey: Californians and their government.* San Francisco, CA: Public Policy Institute of California.

Balingit, M. (2015, July 24). Teachers, doing what they were trained to do, likely helped save lives during La. Movie theater shooting. *Washington Post.* Retrieved from http://www.washingtonpost.com/news/local/wp/2015/07/24/teachers-doing-what-they-were-trained-to-do-likely-helped-save-lives-during-la-movie-theater-shooting/

Barak, G. (1994). Media, society, and criminology. In G. Barak (Ed.), *Media, process, and the social construction of crime: Studies in newsmaking criminology* (pp. 3–45). New York: Garland Publishing, Inc.

Barnes, J. (2014, September 25). State urges better security at schools, but funds scarce. *Boston Globe.* Retrieved from http://www.bostonglobe.com/metro/

regionals/south/2014/09/24/state-urges-better-security-schools-but-money
-short-retrofit-existing-buildings/OOdfSBPmdKmV94OBqanCPM/story.html

Barrineau, T. (2014, December 5). Building safer schools after Sandy Hook: An architect's view. *US Glass News Network*. Retrieved from http://www.usglassmag.com/2014/12/building-safer-schools-after-sandy-hook-an-architects-view/

Barron, J. (1987, April 25). Suspect in Florida shootings: Tormented and tormenting. *New York Times*. Retrieved from http://www.nytimes.com/1987/04/25/us/suspect-in-florida-shootings-tormented-and-tormenting.html

Barron, J. (2012, December 15). Nation reels after gunman massacres 20 children at school in Connecticut. *New York Times*. Retrieved from http://www.nytimes.com/2012/12/15/nyregion/shooting-reported-at-connecticut-elementary-school.html

Barry, D. (2011, January 15). Looking behind the mug-shot grin. *New York Times*. Retrieved from http://www.nytimes.com/2011/01/16/us/16loughner.html

Barry, C.L., McGinty, E.E., Vernick, J.S., & Webster, D.W. (2013). After Newtown – public opinion on gun policy and mental illness. *New England Journal of Medicine, 368*(12), 1077–1081.

BBC News. (2000, June 24). Eleven killed in Bogota disco. *BBC News*. Retrieved from http://news.bbc.co.uk/2/hi/americas/804343.stm

BBC News. (2001, September 27). Gunman kills 14 in Swiss assembly. *BBC News*. Retrieved from http://news.bbc.co.uk/2/hi/europe/1566321.stm

BBC News. (2002, March 27). Eight dead in Paris shooting. *BBC News*. Retrieved from http://news.bbc.co.uk/2/hi/europe/1895751.stm

BBC News. (2004, September 29). Argentine boy shoots classmates. *BBC News*. Retrieved from http://news.bbc.co.uk/2/hi/americas/3697678.stm

BBC News. (2005, June 28). Man held over Italy killing spree. *BBC News*. Retrieved from http://news.bbc.co.uk/2/hi/europe/4628065.stm

BBC News. (2007, April 30). U.S. college faulted over massacre. *BBC News*. Retrieved from http://news.bbc.co.uk/2/hi/6969842.stm

BBC News. (2009a, March 12). How German school shooting unfolded. *BBC News*. Retrieved from http://news.bbc.co.uk/2/hi/europe/7937554.stm

BBC News. (2009b, April 30). Survivor remembers shooting spree. *BBC News*. Retrieved from http://news.bbc.co.uk/2/hi/uk_news/england/tyne/8026315.stm

BBC News. (2009c, April 30). Baku gun attack 'leaves 12 dead.' *BBC News*. Retrieved from http://news.bbc.co.uk/2/hi/europe/8026194.stm

BBC News. (2010, June 3). As it happened: Cumbria shootings. *BBC News*. Retrieved from http://www.bbc.com/news/10216179

BBC News. (2011, July 23). Norway police say 85 killed in island youth camp attack. *BBC News*. Retrieved from http://www.bbc.com/news/world-europe-14259356

BBC News. (2012, November 7). Moscow shootings: 'Spurned lover' kills five. *BBC News*. Retrieved from http://www.bbc.com/news/world-europe-20242875

BBC News. (2015, January 14). Charlie Hebdo attack: Three days of terror. *BBC News*. Retrieved from http://www.bbc.com/news/world-europe-30708237

Beale, S.S. (2006). The news media's influence on criminal justice policy: How market-driven news promotes punitiveness. *William and Mary Law Review, 48* (2), 397–481.

Bearak, B. (1987, April 25). 6 dead and 14 hurt in rampage: Florida shooting suspect 'meanest man on block.' *Los Angeles Times*. Retrieved from http://articles.latimes.com/1987-04-25/news/mn-990_1_palm-bay-police

Beauchamp, Z. (2013, September 17). What mass shootings tell us about America. *Think Progress*. Retrieved from http://thinkprogress.org/justice/2013/09/17/2626991/mass-shootings-says-america/

Beaumont, H. (2015, February 24). *Inside the world of Columbine-obsessed Tumblr bloggers*. Retrieved from http://www.vice.com/read/speaking-to-columbiners-about-depression-suicide-and-the-halifax-shooting-plot-232

Belkin, L. (1999, October 31). Parents blaming parents. *New York Times*. Retrieved from http://www.nytimes.com/1999/10/31/magazine/parents-blaming-parents.html

Belkin, L. (2009, April 20). Do we blame the Columbine parents? *New York Times*. Retrieved from http://parenting.blogs.nytimes.com/2009/04/20/do-we-blame-the-columbine-parents/?_r=0

Bell, C. (2012, May 10). Marilyn Manson thinks he's the most blamed person 'in the history of music.' *Huffington Post*. Retrieved from http://www.huffingtonpost.com/2012/05/10/marilyn-manson-born-villain-most-blamed-person_n_1507130.html

Bell, M. (2012, December 14). Newtown school shooting: Sandy Hook Elementary. *Washington Post*. Retrieved from http://www.washingtonpost.com/blogs/liveblog/wp/2012/12/14/newtown-school-shooting-sandy-hook-elementary/

Berger, J. (2011, January 9). Born on Sept. 11, claimed by a new horror. *New York Times*. Retrieved from http://www.nytimes.com/2011/01/10/us/10green.html

Berger, M. (1949, September 7). Veteran kills 12 in mad rampage on Camden street. *New York Times*. pp. 1, 3. Retrieved from http://query.nytimes.com/mem/archive-free/pdf?res=9A01E1D7113BE23BBC4F53DFBF668382659EDE

Bergquist, G. (2014). Columbia schools will get armed security staff. *KRCG 13*. Retrieved from http://www.connectmidmissouri.com/news/story.aspx?id=1133411#.VZXR3flVikp

Berkowitz, D. (1987). TV news sources and news channels: A study in agenda-building. *Journalism Quarterly, 64*(2), 508–513.

Bernard, T. (1999). Juvenile crime and the transformation of juvenile justice: Is there a juvenile crime wave? *Justice Quarterly, 16*(2), 337–356.

Beronio, K., Po, R., Skopec, L., & Glied, S. (2013). *Affordable Care Act will expand mental health and substance use disorder benefits and parity protections for 62 million Americans*. Washington, DC: U.S. Department of Health & Human Services, Office of the Assistant Secretary for Planning and Evaluation. Retrieved from http://aspe.hhs.gov/health/reports/2013/mental/rb_mental.pdf

Berserk man kills 7. (1962, January 27). *Palm Beach Post.* p. 14. Retrieved from https://news.google.de/newspapers?id=aE4tAAAAIBAJ&sjid=js0FAAAAIBAJ&pg=3522,4967992&dq=&hl=de

Beslan bell tolls for 186 children and 148 adults murdered in 2004 terror attack. (2012, September 3). *Russia Today.* Retrieved from https://www.rt.com/news/beslan-tragedy-russia-commemorate-195/

Best, J. (1987). Rhetoric in claims-making: Constructing the missing children problem. *Social Problems, 34*(2), 101–121.

Best, J. (1989). Secondary claims-making: Claims about threats to children on network news. *Perspectives on Social Problems, 1*, 259–282.

Best, J. (1990). *Threatened children.* Chicago, IL: University of Chicago Press.

Best, J. (2006). The media exaggerate the school-shooting problem. In S. Hunnicutt (Ed.), *School shootings* (pp. 18–27). Farmington Hills, MI: Greenhaven Press.

Best, J. (2013, June 16). *How should we classify the Sandy Hook killings?* Retrieved from http://reason.com/archives/2013/06/16/the-politics-of-gun-violence.

Bidgood, J. (2014, December 7). Military-style technology finds way into school district safety measures. *New York Times.* Retrieved from http://www.nytimes.com/2014/12/08/education/military-style-technology-finds-way-into-school-district-safety-measures.html?_r=2

Bilco. (n.d.). *The Barracuda Intruder Defense System.* Retrieved from http://www.bilco.com/Barracuda-Intruder-Defense-System.html

Bindel, J. (2012, December 3). The Montreal massacre: Canada's feminists remembered. *Guardian.* Retrieved from http://www.theguardian.com/world/2012/dec/03/montreal-massacre-canadas-feminists-remember

Birkland, T.A., & Lawrence, R.G. (2009). Media framing and policy change after Columbine. *American Behavioral Scientist, 52*(10), 1405–1425.

Bjelopera, J.P., Bagalman, E., Caldwell, S.W., Finklea, K.M., & McCallion, G. (2013). *Public mass shootings in the United States: Selected implications for federal public health and safety policy.* Washington, DC: Congressional Research Service. Retrieved from http://fas.org/sgp/crs/misc/R43004.pdf

Blair, J.P., Nichols, T., Burns, D., and Curnett, J. (2013). *Active shooter events and response.* Boca Raton, FL: CRC Press Taylor & Francis Group.

Blair, J.P., & Schweit, K.W. (2014). *A study of active shooter incidents, 2000–2013.* Washington, DC: U.S. Department of Justice, Federal Bureau of Investigation. Retrieved from http://www.fbi.gov/news/stories/2014/september/fbi-releases-study-on-active-shooter-incidents/pdfs/a-study-of-active-shooter-incidents-in-the-u.s.-between-2000-and-2013

BluePoint Alert Solutions. (n.d.). *How it works.* Retrieved from http://www.bluepointalert.com/howitworks.html

Bluepoint Alert's school safety solution is 2014 "new product of the year." (2014, December 2). *Kane County Connects.* Retrieved from http://kanecountyconnects.com/2014/12/bluepoint-alerts-school-safety-solution-is-2014-new-product-of-the-year/

Blumenthal, M. (2012, July 24). Gun control polls show longterm decline in support, despite Columbine bump. *Huffington Post*. Retrieved from http://www.huffingtonpost.com/2012/07/20/gun-control-polls-aurora-shooting_n_1690169.html

Bodyguard Blanket. (n.d.). *Specifications/regulations*. Retrieved from http://bodyguardblanket.com/pages/bgspecs.html

Boesveld, S., & Cross, A. (2012, July 21). Friend made 'heroic' attempt to save aspiring sportscaster Jessica Ghawi in chaotic Aurora theatre. *National Post*. Retrieved from http://news.nationalpost.com/news/friend-made-heroic-attempt-to-save-aspiring-sportscaster-after-gunman-opened-fire-in-aurora-theatre

Bondü, R., Cornell, D.G., & Scheithauer, H. (2011). Student homicidal violence in schools: An international problem. *New Directions for Youth Development, 2011* (129), 13–30.

Bonnie, R.J., Reinhard, J.S., Hamilton, P., & McGarvey, E.L. (2009). Mental health system transformation after the Virginia Tech tragedy. *Health Affairs, 28*(3), 793–804.

Borders, W. (1966, August 27). Killer in New Haven slays 5, wounds 2. *New York Times*. pp. 1, 28. Retrieved from http://query.nytimes.com/mem/archive-free/pdf?res=9A06EFDA123CE53BBC4F51DFBE66838D679EDE

Borum, R., Cornell, D., Modzeleski, W., & Jimerson, S. (2010). What can be done about school shootings? A review of the evidence. *Educational Researcher, 39*(1), 27–37.

Botelho, G., & Sterling, J. (2013, September 26). FBI: Navy Yard shooter 'delusional,' said 'low frequency attacks' drove him to kill. *CNN*. Retrieved from http://www.cnn.com/2013/09/25/us/washington-navy-yard-investigation/

Bovsun, M. (2010, August 15). Mailman massacre: 14 die after Patrick Sherrill 'goes postal' in 1986 shootings. *New York Daily News*. Retrieved from http://www.nydailynews.com/news/crime/mailman-massacre-14-die-patrick-sherrill-postal-1986-shootings-article-1.204101

BoxOffice.com. (n.d.). *Box office – Natural born killers*. Retrieved from http://www.boxoffice.com/statistics/movies/natural-born-killers-1994

Boy kills teacher in 'wild jealousy.' (1919, March 28). *The Washington Times*. p. 9. Retrieved from http://chroniclingamerica.loc.gov/lccn/sn84026749/1919-03-28/ed-1/seq-9/#words=Warner&date1=1919&sort=date&sort=date&sort=date&sort=date&date2=1922&searchType=basic&state=District+of+Columbia&rows=20&proxtext=warner&y=18&x=26&dateFilterType=yearRange&page=3&page=5&page=6&index=2

Boy shot by teacher is dead. (1903, February 28). *New York Times*. p. 1. Retrieved from http://timesmachine.nytimes.com/timesmachine/1903/02/28/101975628.html?pageNumber=1

Brady Campaign Press Release. (2011, January 7). One million mental health records now in Brady background check system. *BradyCampaign.org*. Retrieved from http://bradycampaign.org/media/press/view/1336/

Brady Campaign Press Release. (2014, September 16). Brady Center sues online sellers of ammunition and equipment used in Aurora movie theater massacre. *BradyCampaign.org*. Retrieved from http://www.bradycampaign.org/press-room/brady-center-sues-online-sellers-of-ammunition-and-equipment-used-in-aurora-movie-theater

Braun, J., & Gillespie, T. (2011). Hosting the public discourse, hosting the public: When online news and social media converge. *Journalism Practice, 5*(4), 383–398.

Brennan, A. (2012, December 20). The list: Despite emotions, little happens legislatively after mass shootings. *CNN Politics*. Retrieved from http://www.cnn.com/2012/12/20/politics/legislation-after-mass-shootings/index.html

Broache, A. (2006, November 28). Court rejects Illinois video game law. *CNet*. Retrieved from http://www.cnet.com/news/court-rejects-illinois-video-game-law/

Brockett, M. (1997, February 10). It was 'a nice, quiet little place' until one man started shooting. *Independent*. Retrieved from http://www.independent.co.uk/news/world/it-was-a-nice-quiet-little-place-until-one-man-started-shooting-1277932.html

Broderick, R. (2012, July 31). A guide to the dark world of James Holmes internet fandom. *BuzzFeed News*. Retrieved from http://www.buzzfeed.com/ryanhatesthis/a-guide-to-the-dark-world-of-the-james-holmes-inte#.cjk5PmX99

Broderick, R. (2013, March 20). Of course there's an online fandom for Ohio shooter T.J. Lane. *BuzzFeed News*. Retrieved from http://www.buzzfeed.com/ryanhatesthis/of-course-theres-an-online-fandom-for-the-ohio-shooter-tj-la#.mmnN5Vrxx

Brooks, D. (2004, May 15). Columbine: Parents of a killer. *New York Times*. Retrieved from http://www.nytimes.com/2004/05/15/opinion/columbine-parents-of-a-killer.html

Brooks, D. (2007, April 19). The mortality line. New York Times. Retrieved from http://select.nytimes.com/2007/04/19/opinion/19brooks.html?hp

Brown, B., & Merritt, R. (2002). *No easy answers: The truth behind death at Columbine*. New York: Lantern Books.

Brown v. Entertainment Merchants Association, 131 S. Ct. 2729 (2011).

Brumfield, B. (2014, May 4). Police: Woman's gut feeling thwarts planned school massacre, family murder. *CNN*. Retrieved from http://www.cnn.com/2014/05/02/justice/minnesota-attack-thwarted/

Bruzda, N. (2015, January 11). Security chief establishes crisis response team at VO-Tech. *Herald-Standard*. Retrieved from http://www.heraldstandard.com/education/news/security-chief-establishes-crisis-response-team-at-vo-tech/article_7bc2ee74-7696-5038-9b86-a9021a509e6d.html

Buell, S. (2014, October 24). Arlington to adopt ALIC school crisis training. *The Arlington Advocate*. Retrieved from http://arlington.wickedlocal.com/article/20141024/NEWS/141027551

BulletBlocker. (n.d.). BulletBlocker NIG IIIA bulletproof survival pack and safety kit. Retrieved from http://www.bulletblocker.com/busakit.html

Burgos, N.P. (2005, January 22). Massacre leaves Kalibo folk asking why. *Philippine Daily Inquirer.* p. A16. Retrieved from https://news.google.de/newspapers? id=QFg1AAAAIBAJ&sjid=kCUMAAAAIBAJ&pg=3348,9018695&dq=&hl=de

Burns, R., & Crawford, C. (1999). School shootings, the media, and public fear: Ingredients for a moral panic. *Crime, Law & Social Change, 32*(2), 147–168.

Bush, G.W. (2001, September). *Address to the nation on the terrorist attacks.* Speech presented at the Oval Office, Washington, DC. Retrieved from http://www .presidency.ucsb.edu/ws/index.php?pid=58057

Buxton, R. (2014, November 20). Explaining hybistophilia: Why some people are sexually attracted to serial killers. *Huffington Post Live.* Retrieved from http:// www.huffingtonpost.com/2014/11/20/hybristophilia-serial-killers_n_6194386 .html

Bwire, J. (2015, May 22). UPDF officer kills four, injures seven. *Daily Monitor.* Retrieved from http://www.monitor.co.ug/News/National/UPDF-officer-kills -four-injures-seven/-/688334/2726086/-/gcmr5az/-/index.html

CA Assem. Bill 1179. (2005). 2005–2006 Reg. Sess.

Cable news in brief. (1928, May 30). *Argus.* p. 19. Retrieved from http://trove.nla .gov.au/ndp/del/article/3946636

California mass shooter identified as 22-year-old Elliot Rodger: NY Times. (2014, May 24). *Reuters.* Retrieved from http://www.reuters.com/article/2014/05/24/ us-usa-shooting-california-identificatio-idUSBREA4N0D520140524

Campbell, B. (2012, June 11). Update: Murder charges dismissed after Shell ruled incompetent for trial. *Johnson City Press.* Retrieved from http://www.johnson citypress.com/article/100776/update-murder-charges-dismissed-after-shell -ruled-incompetent-for-trial

Canadian Press. (1972a, August 29). Gunman on rampage kills six people in remote lake area of B.C. interior. *Ottawa Citizen.* p. 1. Retrieved from https://news .google.de/newspapers? id=L70yAAAAIBAJ&sjid=He0FAAAAIBAJ&pg=5253,4901077&dq=&hl=de

Canadian Press. (1972b, August 31). Suspect, 27, charged in B.C. killing spree. *Montreal Gazette.* p. 8. Retrieved from https://news.google.de/newspapers? id=HQsyAAAAIBAJ&sjid=w6EFAAAAIBAJ&pg=2529,7458891&dq=&hl=de

Canadian Press. (1972c, September 30). Slayer confined to hospital. *Lethbridge Herald.* p. 1. Retrieved from http://newspaperarchive.com/ca/alberta/lethbridge/ lethbridge-herald/1972/09-30/

Canadian Press. (1974, October 8). Confessed killer 'insane.' *Calgary Herald.* p. 64. Retrieved from https://news.google.com/newspapers?id=OHBkAAAAIBA J&sjid=mH0NAAAAIBAJ&hl=de&pg=1076,3787333

Caniglia, J. (2012, March 6). T.J. Lane, accused in Ohio shooting, described as quiet, smart, no outcast. *Cleveland.com.* Retrieved from http://blog.cleveland .com/metro/2012/03/lake_academy_students_recall_q.html

Carlson, D.K. (2002, January 22). The blame game: Youth and media violence. *Gallup News Service.* Retrieved from http://www.gallup.com/poll/5626/Blame -Game-Youth-Media-Violence.aspx

Carlson, D.K., & Simmons, W.W. (2001, March 6). Majority of parents think a school shooting could occur in their community. *Gallup.* Retrieved from http://www.gallup.com/poll/1936/Majority-Parents-Think-School-Shooting -Could-Occur-Their-Community.aspx

Carroll, L., & O'Connor, M. (2014, June 13). Have there been 74 school shootings since Sandy Hook? A closer look at a tricky statistic. *Politifact.* Retrieved from http://www.politifact.com/truth-o-meter/statements/2014/jun/13/everytown -gun-safety/have-there-been-74-school-shootings-sandy-hook-clo/

Carter, B. (2007, April 20). NBC News defends its use of material sent by the killer. *New York Times.* Retrieved from http://www.nytimes.com/2007/04/20/us/ 20nbc.html

Carvalho, E.J. (2010). The poetics of a school shooter: Decoding political significance in Cho Seung-Hui's multimedia manifesto. *The Review of Education, Pedagogy, and Cultural Studies, 32*(4–5), 403–430.

Castaldo v. Stone, 192 F.Supp.2d 1124 (2001).

CBC. (2014a, May 8). Denis Lortie: 30 years after the National Assembly shooting. *Huffington Post Canada.* Retrieved from http://www.huffingtonpost.ca/2014/ 05/09/denis-lortie-quebec-assembly-shooting-video_n_5286614.html

CBC. (2014b, December 17). Eaton Centre shooting: Christopher Husbands guilty of 2nd-degree murder. *CBC News.* Retrieved from http://www.cbc.ca/news/ canada/toronto/eaton-centre-shooting-christopher-husbands-guilty-of-2nd -degree-murder-1.2876874

CBC. (2015, April 18). Halifax shooting plot: Who are the 'Columbiners'? *Huffington Post Canada.* Retrieved from http://www.huffingtonpost.ca/2015/02/17/ halifax-shooting-plot-columbiners_n_6696498.html

CBS News. (2008, May 30). Shooting rampage kills 8 in Yemen mosque. *CBS News.* Retrieved from http://www.cbsnews.com/news/shooting-rampage-kills-8-in -yemen-mosque/

CBS News. (2012a, February 27). 1 dead in Ohio shooting; suspect detained. *CBS News.* Retrieved from http://www.cbsnews.com/news/1-dead-in-ohio-school -shooting-suspect-detained/

CBS News. (2012b, November 7). Jilted lover allegedly kills five in Moscow office. *CBS News.* Retrieved from http://www.cbsnews.com/news/jilted-lover -allegedly-kills-five-in-moscow-office/

CBS News. (2014, May 26). *Timeline of murder spree in Isla Vista.* Retrieved from http://www.cbsnews.com/news/timeline-of-murder-spree-in-isla-vista/

Centers for Disease Control. (2006). School associated violent deaths. Retrieved from http://www.cdc.gov/ncipc/sch-shooting.htm

Centers for Disease Control. (2014). *School-assisted violent death study.* Retrieved from http://www.cdc.gov/ViolencePrevention/youthviolence/schoolviolence/SAVD.html

Central Intelligence Agency. (n.d.). *The World Factbook*. Retrieved from https://www.cia.gov/library/publications/the-world-factbook/rankorder/2119rank.html

Chasmar, J. (2014, May 25). Michael Moore: 'Guns don't kill people – Americans kill people.' *The Washington Times*. Retrieved from http://www.washingtontimes.com/news/2014/may/25/michael-moore-guns-dont-kill-people-americans-kill/

Chermak, S.M. (1994). Body count news: How crime is presented in the news media. *Justice Quarterly, 11*(4), 561–582.

Chermak, S.M. (1995). *Victims in the news: Crime and the American news media*. Boulder, CO: Westview Press.

Chermak, S.M. (1998). Predicting story crime salience: The effects of crime, victim, and defendant characteristics. *Journal of Criminal Justice, 26*(1), 61–70.

Chester, G. (1993). *Berserk! Terrifying true stories of notorious mass murders and the deranged killers who committed them*. New York: St. Martin's Press.

Chin, P. (1991, November 4). A Texas massacre. *People*. Retrieved from http://www.people.com/people/archive/article/0,,20111193,00.html

Chiricos, T., Padgett, K., & Gertz, M. (2000). Fear, TV news, and the reality of crime. *Criminology, 38*(3), 755–785.

Chyi, H.I., & McCombs, M.E. (2004). Media salience and the process of framing: Coverage of the Columbine school shootings. *Journalism and Mass Communication Quarterly, 81*(1), 22–35.

Ciokajlo, M. (2002, January 4). Elgin spree killer gets death. *Chicago Tribune*. Retrieved from http://articles.chicagotribune.com/2002-01-04/news/0201040237_1_penalty-sentenced-bar-employees

Clark, A. (2015, January 13). Should school security guards carry guns? Questions arises at public forum on safety. *NJ.com*. Retrieved from http://www.nj.com/education/2015/01/school_security_task_force.html

Clark, M.D. (2014, October 19). Is concealed carry coming to a school near you? *Cincinnati Enquirer*. Retrieved from http://www.cincinnati.com/story/news/2014/10/19/concealed-carry-coming-school-near/17591717/

Cloud, J. (2011, January 15). The troubled life of Jared Loughner. *Time*. Retrieved from http://content.time.com/time/magazine/article/0,9171,2042358,00.html

Cloud, J. (2014, October 2). The bulletproof classroom: Armored whiteboards defend against school shootings. *Bloomberg Business*. Retrieved from http://www.bloomberg.com/bw/articles/2014-10-02/hardwires-armored-whiteboards-defend-against-school-shootings

Clouston, E., & Boseley, S. (2013, March 14). From the archive, 14 March 1996: Sixteen children killed in Dunblane massacre. *Guardian*. Retrieved from http://www.theguardian.com/theguardian/2013/mar/14/dunblane-massacre-scotland-killing

CNN. (1996, April 29). Gunman kills at least 34 in Australia. *CNN*. Retrieved from http://www.cnn.com/WORLD/9604/29/australia.shooting/index.html

CNN. (1997, February 9). New Zealand massacre suspect charged with murder. *CNN International*. Retrieved from http://edition.cnn.com/WORLD/9702/09/new.zealand.update/

CNN. (1999, May 26). Parents of Harris, Klebold to be sued in Columbine shootings. *CNN*. Retrieved from http://www.cnn.com/US/9905/26/columbine.lawsuit.02/

CNN. (2001, April 19). Columbine families reach $2.5 million in shooting settlements. *CNN*. Retrieved from http://edition.cnn.com/2001/LAW/04/19/columbine.settlements/

CNN. (2007, April 18). *Killer's manifesto: 'You forced me into a corner.'* Retrieved from http://www.cnn.com/2007/US/04/18/vtech.shooting/index.html

CNN Library. (2014). *DC area sniper fast facts*. Retrieved from http://www.cnn.com/2013/11/04/us/dc-area-sniper-fast-facts/

CNN Library. (2015a). *September 11th fast facts*. Retrieved from http://www.cnn.com/2013/07/27/us/september-11-anniversary-fast-facts/

CNN Library. (2015b). *Columbine High School shooting fast facts*. Retrieved from http://www.cnn.com/2013/09/18/us/columbine-high-school-shootings-fast-facts/

CNN Newsroom. (2014, August 19). Mass shooting prevented through the power of social media. *WHSV.com*. Retrieved from http://www.whsv.com/home/headlines/Mass-Shooting-Prevented-Through-the-Power-of-Social-Media-271941321.html

CNN Staff. (2013, March 12). Judge enters not guilty plea for accused theater shooter. *CNN*. Retrieved from http://www.cnn.com/2013/03/12/justice/colorado-theater-shooting/

Coburn-Griffis, S. (2014, December 17). Elida schools to consider armed presence. *The Delphos Herald*. Retrieved from http://www.delphosherald.com/Content/News/News/Article/Elida-schools-to-consider-an-armed-presence/191/1183/189855

Coffman, K. (2012, October 21). James Holmes, accused Colorado gunman, saw 3 mental health experts prior to deadly shooting. *Huffington Post*. Retrieved from http://www.huffingtonpost.com/2012/08/21/james-holmes-mental-health-colorado_n_1820450.html

Cohen, B.C. (1963). *The press and foreign policy*. Princeton, NJ: Princeton University Press.

Cohen, S. (1972). *Folk devils and moral panics: The creations of the Mods and the Rockers*. London: MacGibbon & Kee.

Cohen, L.E., & Felson, M.K. (1979). Social change and crime rate trends: A routine activities approach. *American Sociological Review, 44*(4), 588–608.

Colli, G. (2013, August 27). Sandy Hook: The first 15 minutes. *NBC Connecticut*. Retrieved from http://www.nbcconnecticut.com/troubleshooters/Sandy-Hook-The-First-15-Minutes-221260161.html

Colli, G. (2014, November 19). Redefining school security. *NBC Connecticut*. Retrieved from http://www.nbcconnecticut.com/troubleshooters/Redefining-School-Security-283136861.html

Columbine Review Commission. (2001). *The Report of Governor Bill Owens' Columbine Review Commission*. Denver, CO: State of Colorado. Retrieved from http://trac.state.co.us/Documents/Reports%20and%20Publications/Columbine_2001_Governor_Review_Commission.pdf

Connelly, M. (1999, August 26). Public supports stricter gun control laws. *New York Times*. Retrieved from http://partners.nytimes.com/library/national/082699poll-watch.html.

Connor, T. (2013, August 21). Bulletproof school supplies get low grades from safety experts. *NBC News*. Retrieved from http://www.nbcnews.com/news/other/bulletproof-school-supplies-get-low-grades-safety-experts-f6C10963127

Consalvo, M. (2003). The monsters next door: Media construction of boys and masculinity. *Feminist Media Studies*, *3*(1), 27–45.

Corella, H. (2013, March 27). Tucson shooting: No mental health treatment for Loughner before Giffords rampage. *Arizona Daily Star*. Retrieved from http://tucson.com/news/local/crime/tucson-shooting-no-mental-health-treatment-for-loughner-before-giffords/article_70b5b03c-96f4-11e2-b7dc-0019bb2963f4.html

Corliss, R. (2007, April 19). The movie that motivated Cho? *Time*. Retrieved from http://content.time.com/time/arts/article/0,8599,1612724,00.html

Cosgrove, B. (2014, May 4). Behind the picture: 'Dewey defeats Truman' and the politics of memory. *Time*. Retrieved from http://time.com/3879744/dewey-defeats-truman-the-story-behind-a-classic-political-photo/

Coultan, M., Wright, G., & Gawenda, M. (2007, April 18). Jealous boyfriend guns down 32. *Brisbane Times*. Retrieved from http://www.brisbanetimes.com.au/news/national/jealous-boyfriend-kills-32/2007/04/18/1176696865676.html

Cowan, J. (2007, August 9). Hoddle Street killer won't be forgotten. *Australian Broadcasting Corporation (ABC) News*. Retrieved from http://www.abc.net.au/news/2007-08-09/hoddle-street-killer-wont-be-forgotten/635402

Cratty, C. (2011, March 4). Alleged Tucson gunman indicted on 49 charges in shooting. *CNN*. Retrieved from http://www.cnn.com/2011/CRIME/03/04/arizona.loughner/

Creason, N., Walmer, D., & Vaughn, J. (2014). Pass or fail: Armed teachers, intruder training for security at Midstate schools. *Sentinel*. Retrieved from http://cumberlink.com/news/local/education/pass-or-fail-armed-teachers-intruder-training-options-for-security/article_e808d26a-469b-11e4-8dfe-f745cca640b0.html

Crepeau-Hobson, M.F., Filaccio, M., & Gottfried, L. (2005). Violence prevention after Columbine. *Children & Schools*, *27*(3), 157–165.

Criminally careless: An unloaded needle gun and its work. (1883, February 16). *Omaha Daily Bee*. p. 8. Retrieved from http://chroniclingamerica.loc.gov/lccn/sn99021999/1883-02-16/ed-1/seq-8/

Cser, A. (2008, September 23). Gunman kills 10, self in Finnish school shooting. *Reuters*. Retrieved from http://www.reuters.com/article/2008/09/23/us-finland-shooting-news-idUSTRE48M92I20080923

Cullen, D. (2009). *Columbine*. New York: Twelve.

Daly, K. (2014, October 15). Intruder drill works to improve safety on Miguel Hidalgo Elementary School campus. *Imperial Valley Press*. Retrieved from http://www.ivpressonline.com/news/local/education/intruder-drill-works-to -improve-safety-on-miguel-hidalgo-elementary/article_75116aca-3041-50d2 -bf21-603b2ebb2570.html

D'Amico, D. (2015, January 15). Armed officers should be in schools, security panel told. *Press of Atlantic City*. Retrieved from http://www.pressofatlanticcity.com/ education/armed-officers-should-be-in-schools-security-panel-told/article_329 cecc2-9d08-11e4-9b9d-ab151ef247df.html

D'Angelo, J. (2001, March 22). Marilyn Manson bows out of Denver Ozzfest date. *MTV News*. Retrieved from http://www.mtv.com/news/1442018/marilyn -manson-bows-out-of-denver-ozzfest-date/

Dao, J. (2012, July 23). Aurora gunman's arsenal: Shotgun, semiautomatic rifle, and, at the end, a pistol. *New York Times*. Retrieved from http://www.nytimes.com/ 2012/07/24/us/aurora-gunmans-lethal-arsenal.html.

D.A.R.E. (2014, October 9). Wayne-Westland backs OK2SAY school safety hotline. *Dare.com*. Retrieved from http://www.dare.org/wayne-westland-backs-ok2say -school-safety-hotline/

DaSilva, S. (2015, January 7). Safety matters: Beekmantown holds active shooter training. *MyChampionValley.com*. Retrieved from http://www.mychamplain valley.com/story/d/story/safety-matters-beekmantown-holds-active-shooter-tr/ 64466/R4xTfj8540in8GHg1f14vg

Davey, M. (2005, April 3). Inquiry on school attack may include 20 students. *New York Times*. Retrieved from http://www.nytimes.com/2005/04/03/us/inquiry -on-school-attack-may-include-20-students.html

Davis, M. (2014, December 5). Robbinsville township, school district reach agreement on security camera access for police. *Trenton Times*. Retrieved from http://www.nj.com/mercer/index.ssf/2014/12/robbinsville_township_and_school _district_agree_on_security_camera_access_for_police.html

DC mass shooting prompts surprising gun control reactions. (2013, September 20). *Rasmussen Reports*. Retrieved from http://www.rasmussenreports.com/ public_content/listicles/dc_mass_shooting_prompts_surprising_gun_control _reactions

De Avila, J., & King, K. (2015, August 3). Claim in Newtown massacre settled for $1.5 million. *Wall Street Journal*. Retrieved from http://www.wsj.com/articles/ claim-in-newtown-massacre-settled-for-1-5-million-1438649374

De Benedetti, C. (2015, June 18). Newark adds ShotSpotter gunfire detection system to high school campus. *Contra Costa Times News*. Retrieved from http:// www.contracostatimes.com/breaking-news/ci_28340279/newark-adds-shotspotter -gunfire-detection-system-high-school

de Quetteville, H. (2007, November 7). Biography of a teen killer. *Telegraph*. Retrieved from http://www.telegraph.co.uk/news/worldnews/1568631/ Biography-of-a-teen-killer.html

De Venanzi, A. (2012). School shootings in the USA: Popular culture as risk, teen marginality, and violence against peers. *Crime Media Culture, 8*(3), 261–278.

Deacon, D. (2007). Yesterday's papers and today's technology: Digital newspaper archives and 'push button' content analysis. *European Journal of Communications, 22*(1), 5–25.

Dean, C.W., Brame, R., & Piquero, A.R. (1996). Criminal propensities, discrete groups of offenders, and persistence in crime. *Criminology, 34*(4), 547–574.

Death toll in Yemen mosque shooting rises to nine. (2003, July 31). *Middle East Online*. Retrieved from http://www.middle-east-online.com/english/?id=6609

DeNinno, N. (2012, December 14). Celebrities react to Sandy Hook Elementary shooting in Newtown, Connecticut on Twitter. *International Business Times*. Retrieved from http://www.ibtimes.com/celebrities-react-sandy-hook -elementary-shooting-newtown-connecticut-twitter-938601

Deputy hailed as hero after school shooting. (2006, September 6). *WRAL*. Retrieved from http://www.wral.com/news/local/story/1057911/

Desperate nation tries getting on board with mass shootings. (2013, September 17). *The Onion*. Retrieved from http://www.theonion.com/articles/desperate -nation-tries-getting-on-board-with-mass,33894/

Dewan, S. (2008, July 28). Hatred said to motivate Tenn. Shooter. *New York Times*. Retrieved from http://www.nytimes.com/2008/07/28/us/28shooting.html

Dewey, C. (2012, December 20). Sales of kids' bulletproof backpacks soar. *Washington Post*. Retrieved from http://www.washingtonpost.com/business/economy/ sales-of-kids-bullet-proof-backpacks-soar/2012/12/20/6cba668a-4a1e-11e2-820e -17eefac2f939_story.html

Dietz, P.E. (1986). Mass, serial, and sensational homicides. *Bulletin of the New York Academy of Medicine, 62*(5), 477–490.

Do, T.T. (2014, September 25). School safety requires early intervention, advocate says. *CBC News*. Retrieved from http://www.cbc.ca/news/school-safety -requires-early-intervention-against-violence-advocate-says-1.2776584

Dobrin, A. (2001). The risk of offending on homicide victimization: A case control study. *Journal of Research in Crime & Delinquency, 38*(2), 154–173.

Doherty, C. (2015, January 9). A public opinion trend that matters: Priorities for gun policy. *Pew Research Center: FactTank*. Retrieved from http://www .pewresearch.org/fact-tank/2015/01/09/a-public-opinion-trend-that-matters -priorities-for-gun-policy/.

Donohue, E., Schiraldi, V., & Ziedenberg, J. (1998, July). *School house hype: School shootings and the real risks kids face in America*. Washington, DC: Justice Policy Institute. Retrieved from http://www.justicepolicy.org/uploads/justicepolicy/ documents/98-07_rep_schoolhousehype_jj.pdf

Driehaus, B. (2008, June 25). Man in Kentucky kills 5 co-workers. *New York Times*. Retrieved from http://www.nytimes.com/2008/06/25/us/26kentuckycnd.html

Duke, A. (2012, November 8). Loughner sentenced to life for Arizona shootings. *CNN*. Retrieved from http://www.cnn.com/2012/11/08/justice/arizona -loughner-sentencing/

Duke, A. (2014, May 27). Timeline to 'retribution': Isla Vista attacks planned over years. *CNN*. Retrieved from http://www.cnn.com/2014/05/26/justice/california-elliot-rodger-timeline/

Dutton, D.G., White, K.R., & Fogarty, D. (2013). Paranoid thinking in mass shooters. *Aggression and Violent Behavior, 18*(5), 548–553.

Duwe, G. (2000). Body-count journalism: The presentation of mass murder in the news media. *Homicide Studies, 4*(4), 364–399.

Duwe, G. (2004). The patterns and prevalence of mass murder in twentieth-century America. *Justice Quarterly, 21*(4), 729–761.

Duwe, G. (2005). A circle of distortion: The social construction of mass murder in the United States. *Western Criminology Review, 6*(1), 59–78.

Dwyer, D., & Hochmuth, A. (2013, July 1). 101 California shooting: 20 years later. *NBC Bay Area*. Retrieved from http://www.nbcbayarea.com/news/local/101-California-Shooting-20-Years-Later-213705691.html

Eagleman, D. (2011, July/August). The brain on trial. *The Atlantic, 7*, 112–123. Retrieved from http://www.eaglemanlab.net/papers/Eagleman%20Atlantic%20The%20Brain%20on%20Trial.pdf

Eckersley, T. (2014, October 22). Safe schools week: Three things we can do right now to better secure our schools. *Fox News*. Retrieved from http://www.foxnews.com/opinion/2014/10/22/safe-schools-week-three-things-can-do-right-now-to-better-secure-our-schools.html

Edmiston, J., & O'Toole, M. (2012, June 16). What was behind Eaton Centre shooting that left two dead? *National Post*. Retrieved from http://news.nationalpost.com/news/what-was-behind-eaton-centre-shooting-that-left-two-dead

Egyptian who shot 7 is dead. (1986, January 8). *New York Times*. Retrieved from http://www.nytimes.com/1986/01/08/world/egyptian-who-shot-7-is-dead.html

Ehrenfreund, M., & Goldfarb, Z.A. (2015, June 18). 11 essential facts about guns and mass shootings in the United States. *Washington Post*. Retrieved from http://www.washingtonpost.com/blogs/wonkblog/wp/2015/06/18/11-essential-facts-about-guns-and-mass-shootings-in-the-united-states/

Eliason, S. (2009). Murder-suicide: A review of the recent literature. *Journal of the American Academy of Psychiatry & Law, 37*(3), 371–376.

Eliseev, A., & Cherney, C. (2006, April 5). Jealousy sparked bloody massacre in Kagiso. *IOL News*. Retrieved from http://www.iol.co.za/news/south-africa/jealousy-sparked-bloody-massacre-in-kagiso-1.272120#.VYxeHflVhBc

Elliott, D. (2013, June 5). James Holmes, Aurora shooting suspect, to get mental evaluation. *Huffington Post*. Retrieved from http://www.huffingtonpost.com/2013/06/05/theater-shooting-suspect-_0_n_3389524.html

Elliott, R. (2015). The real school safety debate: Why legislative responses should focus on schools and not on guns. *Arizona Law Review, 57*(2), 523–550.

Ellsworth, M.J. (1991). *The Bath School disaster*. Bath, MI: Bath School Museum Committee.

Elsass, H.J., Schildkraut, J., & Stafford, M.C. (2014). Breaking news of social problems: Examining media effects and panic over school shootings. *Criminology, Criminal Justice, Law & Society, 15*(2), 31–42.

Emery, A. (2014, December 2). Explicit 'afterschool' app responsible for heightened security at Flushing High School after gun threat. *MLive*. Retrieved from http://www.mlive.com/news/flint/index.ssf/2014/12/explicit_afterschool_app_respo.html

Enos, J.F. (2014, September 25). Hamilton-Wenham school safety plans constantly evaluated. *The Hamilton-Wenham Chronicle*. Retrieved from http://wenham.wickedlocal.com/article/20140925/NEWS/140927625/12425/NEWS

Entman, R.M. (2007). Framing bias: Media in the distribution of power. *Journal of Communication, 57*(1), 163-173.

Erlanger, S. (2002, July 8). Erfurt journal: After a school massacre, a sadness without end. *New York Times*. Retrieved from http://www.nytimes.com/2002/07/08/world/erfurt-journal-after-a-school-massacre-a-sadness-without-end.html

Esterbrook, J. (2002, March 26). French gunman jumps to his death. *CBS News*. Retrieved from http://www.cbsnews.com/news/french-gunman-jumps-to-his-death/

Evers files bill to allow designees to carry guns on local school grounds. *NorthEscambia.com*. Retrieved from http://www.northescambia.com/2014/12/evers-files-bill-to-allow-designees-to-carry-guns-on-local-school-grounds

Everytown for Gun Safety. (2014). *Analysis of school shootings: December 15, 2012– December 9, 2014*. Retrieved from http://everytown.org/documents/2014/10/analysis-of-school-shootings.pdf

Faison, S. (1993, December 8). Gunman kills 5 on L.I.R.R. train; 19 are wounded. *New York Times*. Retrieved from http://www.nytimes.com/1993/12/08/nyregion/gunman-kills-5-on-lirr-train-19-are-wounded.html

Falk, G. (1990). *Murder: An analysis of its forms, conditions, and causes*. Jefferson, NC: McFarland.

Fallahi, C.R., Austad, C.S., Fallon, M., & Leishman, L. (2009). A survey of the perceptions of the Virginia Tech tragedy. *Journal of School Violence, 8*(2), 120–135.

Farrington, D.P. (1986). Age and crime. In M. Tonry & N. Morris (Eds.), *Crime and justice: An annual review of research, vol. 7* (pp. 189–250). Chicago, IL: Chicago University Press.

Fast, J. (2008). *Ceremonial violence: A psychological explanation of school shootings*. New York: Overlook Press.

Fast, J., & Fanelli, R. (2003). The tennis ball bomb incident or the safety plan as "shelf document." *Journal of School Violence, 2*(3), 53–71.

Father blames LSD for shooting outburst by son. (1971, November 14). *New York Times*. p. 73. Retrieved from http://query.nytimes.com/mem/archive-free/pdf?res=9D07E7D9163DEF34BC4C52DFB767838A669EDE

Federal Bureau of Investigation. (2014). *Crime in the United States, 2013: Annual Uniform Crime Report*. Washington, DC: U.S. Department of Justice. Retrieved from https://www.fbi.gov/about-us/cjis/ucr/crime-in-the-u.s/2013/crime-in-the-u.s.-2013

Federal Bureau of Investigation. (n.d.). *Video: Run. Hide. Fight. Surviving an active shooter event*. Retrieved from https://www.fbi.gov/about-us/cirg/active-shooter -and-mass-casualty-incidents/run-hide-fight-video

Federal Emergency Management Agency (FEMA). (2013). *Guide for developing high-quality emergency operations plans for houses of worship*. Washington, DC: FEMA. Retrieved from https://www.whitehouse.gov/sites/default/files/docs/ developing_eops_for_houses_of_worship_final.pdf

Feijo, S. (2014, September 26). Cambridge boasts 'integrated strong support net-work' for school safety. *The Cambridge Chronicle & Tab*. Retrieved from http://cambridge.wickedlocal.com/article/20140926/NEWS/140927524

Feinblatt, J. (2014, December 13). The number of school shootings since Sandy Hook is higher than you think. *MSNBC*. Retrieved from http://www.msnbc .com/msnbc/the-number-school-shootings-sandy-hook-higher-you-think

Feldman, D. (2014, May 26). Father blames government 'idiots' as California town mourns killings. *Reuters*. Retrieved from http://news.yahoo.com/california -gunman-manifesto-said-police-nearly-thwarted-plot-004327059.html

Ferguson, C. (2014, November 7). Parents complain school safety drill too scary for students. *Eyewitness News*. Retrieved from http://www.bakersfieldnow.com/news/ local/Parents-concerned-over-school-active-shooter-drill-281867601.html

Ferguson, C.J. (2008). The school shooting/violent video game link: Causal relation-ship or moral panic? *Journal of Investigative Psychology and Offender Profiling, 5* (1), 25–37.

Ferguson, C.J. (2011). 'Video games are like smoking and lung cancer' and other urban legends in the violent video game debate. *The Journal of Education, Community and Values, 11*, 53–58.

Ferguson, C.J. (2014). Violent video games, mass shootings, and the Supreme Court: Lessons for the legal community in the wake of recent free speech cases and mass shootings. *New Criminal Law Review, 17*(4), 553–586.

Ferguson, C.J., & Olson, C.K. (2014). Video game violence use among "vulnerable" populations: The impact of violent games on delinquency and bullying among children with clinically elevated depression or attention deficit symptoms. *Journal of Youth Adolescence, 43*(1), 127–136.

Fernandez, M., & Blinder, A. (2014, April 8). At Fort Hood, wrestling with label of terrorism. *New York Times*. Retrieved from http://www.nytimes.com/2014/04/ 09/us/at-fort-hood-wrestling-with-label-of-terrorism.html

Fernandez, M., & Montgomery, D. (2015, June 2). Texas lawmakers pass a bill allowing guns at colleges. *New York Times*. Retrieved from http://www.nytimes .com/2015/06/03/us/texas-lawmakers-approve-bill-allowing-guns-on-campus .html?_r=0

Fick, J., & Lyons, J. (2011, April 8). Rio shooter kills at least 12 young students. *Wall Street Journal*. Retrieved from http://www.wsj.com/articles/SB10001424 052748704630004576248600469362440

Fiel, Sr., P.V. (2015, January 1). Panic button. *Security Today*. Retrieved from https:// security-today.com/articles/2015/01/01/panic-button.aspx

Fired into a group of children. (1891, April 10). *New York Times.* p. 2. Retrieved from http://query.nytimes.com/mem/archive-free/pdf?res=9E00EFDE163A E533A25753C1A9629C94609ED7CF

First victory for Newtown families in wrongful death suit against gun maker. (2015, October 1). *CBS New York.* Retrieved from http://newyork.cbslocal.com/2015/ 10/01/newtown-shooting-lawsuit-remington/

5 killed in Serb village. (1930, April 27). *New York Times.* p. 2. Retrieved from http://timesmachine.nytimes.com/timesmachine/1930/04/27/96110381.html? pageNumber=2

Flashes. (1922, February 17). *The Daily Ardmoreite.* p. 1. Retrieved from http:// chroniclingamerica.loc.gov/lccn/sn85042303/1922-02-17/ed-1/seq-1/

Flashes from the wire. (1900, September 17). *The Quebec Daily Telegraph.* p. 4. Retrieved from https://news.google.de/newspapers?id=t4ofAAAAIBAJ&sji d=1tIEAAAAIBAJ&pg=3700,2352965&dq=&hl=de

Fleming v. Stone, No. 00-CV-884 (2006).

Floyd Allen must pay death penalty: Jury finds Virginia court house assassin guilty of first degree murder. (1912, May 18). *New York Times.* p. 3. Retrieved from http://query.nytimes.com/mem/archive-free/pdf?res=9F0DEEDB153CE633A2 575BC1A9639C946396D6CF

Fluvoxamine. (n.d.). Retrieved from http://www.ncbi.nlm.nih.gov/pubmedhealth/ PMHT0010372/?report=details

Follman, M., Pan, D., & Aronsen, G. (2013, February 27). A guide to mass shootings in America. *Mother Jones.* Retrieved from http://www.motherjones.com/ politics/2012/07/mass-shootings-map

Forbes-Mewett, H., McCulloch, J., & Nyland, C. (2015). *International students and crime.* New York: Palgrave Macmillan.

Forman, E. (2014, November 7). Danvers students to learn lockdown procedures. *The Salem News.* Retrieved from http://www.salemnews.com/news/local_news/ danvers-students-to-learn-lockdown-procedures/article_b4a04ae4-72ab-521d -a52a-4a139b5453f7.html

Former soldier kills 15 in rampage. (1997, May 23). *Vindicator.* Retrieved from https://news.google.com/newspapers?id=SoJKAAAAIBAJ&sjid=oYYMAAAAIB AJ&hl=de&pg=4906,4620046&dq=

45 years later, UT tower shooting rampage still remembered. (2011, August 1). *KHOU.com.* Retrieved from http://www.khou.com/story/news/2014/07/17/ 11513472/

Foster, A. (2007). After Va. Tech, campuses rush to add alert systems. *The Chronicle of Higher Education, 54*(6), 1.

Fourteen persons wounded: A shotgun fired into a colored school exhibition. (1891, March 31). *Daily Alta California.* p. 1. Retrieved from http://cdnc.ucr.edu/ cgi-bin/cdnc?a=d&d=DAC18910331.2.6&e=————en—20—1— txIN————

Fox, C., & Harding, D. (2005). School shootings as organizational deviance. *Sociology of Education, 78*(1), 69–97.

Fox, J.A., & DeLateur, M.J. (2014). Mass shootings in America: Moving beyond Newtown. *Homicide Studies, 18*(1), 125–145.

Fox, J.A., & Levin, J. (1994a). *Overkill: Mass and serial killing exposed.* New York, NY: Plenum.

Fox, J.A., & Levin, J. (1994b). Firing back: The growing threat of workplace homicide. *The Annals of the American Academy of Political & Social Sciences, 536,* 126–130.

Fox, J.A., & Levin, J. (1998). Multiple homicide: Patterns of serial and mass murder. *Crime and Justice, 23,* 407–455.

Fox, J.A., & Levin, J. (2014). *Extreme killing: Understanding serial and mass murder.* Thousand Oaks, CA: Sage.

Fox, J.A., & Savage, J. (2009). Mass murder goes to college: An examination of changes on college campuses following Virginia Tech. *American Behavioral Scientist, 52*(10), 1465–1485.

Fox, J.A., & Zawitz, M.W. (2007). *Homicide trends in the United States.* Washington, DC: Bureau of Justice Statistics.

Fox, L. (2013, December 10). Sandy Hook anniversary leads White House to invest $100 million in mental health system. *U.S. News and World Report.* Retrieved from http://www.usnews.com/news/articles/2013/12/10/sandy-hook -anniversary-leads-white-house-to-invest-100-million-in-mental-health-system

Francis, C. (2011, July 9). Raurimu killer back in custody. *Dominion Post.* Retrieved from http://www.stuff.co.nz/dominion-post/news/5259161/Raurimu-killer -back-in-custody

Frankel, T.C. (2014, October 27). Can a wave of new inventions stop school shootings? *Washington Post.* Retrieved from http://www.washingtonpost.com/news/ storyline/wp/2014/10/27/in-wake-of-school-shootings-a-flood-of-inventions -and-the-question-is-this-one-the-answer/

Franscell, R. (2011). *Delivered from evil: True stories of ordinary people who faced monstrous mass killers and survived.* Beverly, MA: Fair Winds Press.

Free safety tip line available to schools. (2014, December 15). *Athens Messenger.* Retrieved from http://www.athensmessenger.com/news/free-safety-tip-line -available-to-schools/article_e3b4a4bd-66a4-5e04-99a7-36e9dcceda30.html

Frequency. (n.d.). Retrieved from http://www.merriam-webster.com/dictionary/ frequency

Friedman, R.A. (2014, May 27). Why can't doctors identify killers? *New York Times.* Retrieved from http://www.nytimes.com/2014/05/28/opinion/why-cant -doctors-identify-killers.html

Friedson, M., & Sharkey, P. (2015). Violence and neighborhood disadvantage after the crime decline. *The Annals of the American Academy of Political & Social Science, 660,* 341–358.

Frosch, D. (2015, June 16). James Holmes's psychiatrist testifies in Colorado theater shooting trial. *Wall Street Journal.* Retrieved from http://www.wsj.com/articles/ james-holmess-psychiatrist-testifies-in-colorado-theater-shooting-trial-143448 4324

Frosch, D., & Johnson, K. (2012, July 20). Gunman kills 12 in Colorado, reviving gun debate. *New York Times*. Retrieved from http://www.nytimes.com/2012/07/21/us/shooting-at-colorado-theater-showing-batman-movie.html?ref=michaelsschmidt

Frost, E. (2014, November 24). Time for 'heinous' school metal detectors to go, officials say. *DNAinfo*. Retrieved from http://www.dnainfo.com/new-york/20141124/upper-west-side/time-for-heinous-school-metal-detectors-go-officials-say

Fry, J. (2014, November 24). *Boston explosions a reminder of how breaking news reporting is changing*. Retrieved from http://www.poynter.org/news/mediawire/210471/boston-explosions-a-reminder-of-how-breaking-news-reporting-is-changing/

Frymer, B. (2009). The media spectacle of Columbine: Alienated youth as an object of fear. *American Behavioral Scientist, 52*(10), 1387–1404.

Fu, C.L. (1994, September 21). Police identify gunman as member of Chinese army. *Seattle Times*. Retrieved from http://community.seattletimes.nwsource.com/archive/?date=19940921&slug=1931725

Fuchs, E. (2013, November 25). Sandy Hook report reveals why cops feared there were more shooters. *Business Insider*. Retrieved from http://www.businessinsider.com/why-people-thought-there-were-more-sandy-hook-shooters-2013-11

Funk, J.B., Balducci, H.B., Pasold, T., & Baumgardner, J. (2004). Violence exposure in real-life, video games, television, movies, and the internet: Is there desensitization? *Journal of Adolescence, 27*(1), 23–29.

Gans, H.J. (1979). *Deciding what's news: A study of CBS Evening News, NBC Nightly News, Newsweek, and Time*. New York, NY: Pantheon Books.

Garcia, C.A. (2003). School safety technology in America: Current use and perceived effectiveness. *Criminal Justice Policy Review, 14*(1), 30–54.

Garofoli, J. (2007, April 20). New-media culture challenges limits of journalism ethics. Retrieved from http://articles.sfgate.com/2007-04-20/news/17242016_1_new-media-traditional-media-traditional-news-sources/3

Gaudiosi, J. (2011, July 28). Expert calls blaming video games on tragic massacres like Oslo and Columbine racist. *Forbes*. Retrieved from http://www.forbes.com/sites/johngaudiosi/2011/07/28/expert-calls-blaming-video-games-on-tragic-massacres-like-oslo-and-columbine-racist/

General summary. (1880, July 30). *Burlington Weekly Free Press*. p. 2. Retrieved from http://chroniclingamerica.loc.gov/lccn/sn86072143/1880-07-30/ed-1/seq-2/

Gentile, C.L. (2015, January 8). Falmouth drafts emergency plans for schools. *The Enterprise*. Retrieved from http://www.capenews.net/falmouth/news/falmouth-drafts-emergency-plans-for-schools/article_e8e713ea-97a9-11e4-a0db-57d588f8f469.html

Gentile, D.A., Lynch, P.L., Linder, J.R., & Walsh, D.A. (2004). The effects of violent video game habits on adolescent hostility, aggressive behaviors, and school performance. *Journal of Adolescence, 27*(1), 5–22.

Georgia killer's note shows a troubled man. (1999, July 30). *CNN*. Retrieved from http://www.cnn.com/US/9907/30/atlanta.shooting.06/

Gest, T. (2001). *Crime and politics: Big government's erratic campaign for law and order.* New York: Oxford University Press.

Gibbs, N., & Roche, T. (1999, December 20). *The Columbine tapes.* Retrieved from http://www.time.com/time/magazine/article/0,9171,992873,00.html

Gieber, W. (1964). News is what newspapermen make it. In L.A. Dexter & D.M. White (Eds.), *People, society, and mass communications* (pp. 173–191). New York: Free Press.

Gillespie, M. (1999, April 30). Americans have very mixed opinions about blame for Littleton shootings. *Gallup News.* Retrieved from http://www.gallup.com/poll/3889/americans-very-mixed-opinions-about-blame-littleton-shootings.aspx

Gillespie, M. (2000, April 20). One in three say it is very likely that Columbine-type shootings could happen in their community. *Gallup.* Retrieved from http://www.gallup.com/poll/2980/One-Three-Say-Very-Likely-ColumbineType-Shootings-Could.aspx

Gilmer, M. (2012, December 14). The fast and the frivolous: How media bungled the Sandy Hook shootings. *Chicago Sun Times.* Retrieved from http://blogs.suntimes.com/news/2012/12/the_fast_and_the_frivolous_how_media_bungled_the_sandy_hook_shootings.html

Gimpel, D.M. (2012). *Columbine shootings.* Minneapolis, MN: ABDO Publishing Company.

Gjovaag, L. (2014, October 3). New safety/security plans presented to school board. *Daily Sun News.* Retrieved from http://www.dailysunnews.com/news/2014/oct/31/new-safetysecurity-plans-presented-school-board/

Glickman, A. (2009, January 5). Demolition of Mercaz Harav terrorist's home authorized. *YNet News.* Retrieved from http://www.ynetnews.com/articles/0,7340,L-3650679,00.html

Glum, J. (2015, April 15). Virginia Tech shooting anniversary: How the 2007 massacre changed safety on college campuses. *International Business Times.* Retrieved from http://www.ibtimes.com/virginia-tech-shooting-anniversary-how-2007-massacre-changed-safety-college-campuses-1883642

Goldberg, C. (2000, December 27). 7 die in rampage at company; Co-worker of victims arrested. *New York Times.* Retrieved from http://www.nytimes.com/2000/12/27/us/7-die-in-rampage-at-company-co-worker-of-victims-arrested.html

Goldman, R. (2011, March 9). Jared Loughner pleads not guilty to 49 charges, including murder. *ABC News.* Retrieved from http://abcnews.go.com/US/jared-loughner-suspected-tucson-arizona-shooter-pleads-not-guilty/story?id=13097807

Goode, E., & Ben-Yehuda, N. (1994). Moral panics: Culture, politics, and social construction. *Annual Review of Sociology, 20,* 149–171.

Goodman, B. (2005, November 9). Assistant principal is fatally shot in Tennessee; Student is held. *New York Times.* Retrieved from http://www.nytimes.com/2005/11/09/national/09shooting.html

Goss, K.A. (2015). Defying the odds on gun regulation: The passage of bipartisan mental health laws across the states. *American Journal of Orthopsychiatry, 85*(3), 203–210.

Governor's committee and consultants report on the Charles J. Whitman catastrophe. (1966). Retrieved from http://alt.cimedia.com/statesman/specialreports/whitman/findings.pdf

Gow, G.A., McGee, T., Townsend, D., Anderson, P., & Varnhagen, S. (2009). Communication technology, emergency alerts, and campus safety. *Technology and Society Magazine, IEEE, 28*(2), 34–41.

Graber, D.A. (1980). *Crime news and the public.* Chicago, IL: University of Chicago Press.

Graber, D.A. (2006). *Mass media and American politics* (7th ed.). Washington, DC: CQ Press.

Graff, T. (2014, December 12). Education committee advances school security initiatives. *Casper Star Tribune.* Retrieved from http://trib.com/news/local/education/education-committee-advances-school-security-initiatives/article_7d7cd4f7-6636-51d5-8508-151d24e56b6d.html

Graham, M. (2011, June 29). Judge rules prison can forcibly medicate Loughner. *Reuters.* Retrieved from http://www.reuters.com/article/2011/06/30/us-shooting-loughner-medication-idUSTRE75S85P20110630

Graham, D., & Schimroszik, N. (2010, September 19). Woman opens fire in German town, four killed. *Reuters.* Retrieved from http://uk.reuters.com/article/2010/09/19/uk-germany-shooting-idUKTRE68I1SP20100919

Graham, J., Shirm, S., Liggin, R., Aitken, M.E., & Dick, R. (2006). Mass-casualty events at schools: A national preparedness survey. *Pediatrics, 117*(1), 8–15.

Greenblatt, M. (2012, September 30). TSA lets loaded guns past security, on to planes. *ABCNews.* Retrieved from http://abcnews.go.com/US/tsa-lets-loaded-guns-past-security-planes/story?id=17358872

Grossfeld, M. (2015, January 16). Proposed bill about concealed carry in school. *KFYR-TV 5.* Retrieved from http://www.kfyrtv.com/news/headlines/KFYR-Proposed-Bill-About-Concealed-Carry-in-School-288784331.html

Gruenewald, J., Pizarro, J., & Chermak, S. (2009). Race, gender, and the newsworthiness of homicide incidents. *Journal of Criminal Justice, 37*(3), 262–272.

Gulum, M.S., & Murray, S.L. (2009). Evaluation of the effectiveness of a mass emergency notification system. *Proceedings of the Human Factors and Ergonomics Society Annual Meeting, 53*(18): 1466–1470.

Gunman's life sentence in Tasmania killings. (1996, November 22). *New York Times.* Retrieved from http://www.nytimes.com/1996/11/22/world/gunman-s-life-sentence-in-tasmania-killings.html

Gun Show Loophole Closing Act of 2011, H.R. 591, 112th Cong., 1st Sess. (2011).

Gun Show Loophole Closing Act of 2013, H.R. 141, 113th Cong., 1st Sess. (2013).

Gupta, P. (2014, September 2). "I am Adam Lanza's mother" writer Liza Long: I'm not scared of my son anymore. *Salon.* Retrieved from http://www.salon.com/2014/09/02/i_am_adam_lanzas_mother_writer_liza_long_im_not_scared_of_my_son_anymore/

Hack, C. (2012, December 17). Former Jersey Journal reporter helped clear up misidentification of Connecticut school gunman. *The Jersey Journal.* Retrieved from

http://www.nj.com/jjournal-news/index.ssf/2012/12/confusion_about_killers
_name_i.html

Haddow, G., & Haddow, K.S. (2014). *Disaster communications in a changing media world*. Waltham, MA: Elsevier.

Haeck, T. (2014, November 5). State schools chief says metal detectors not a practical response to threats. *KIRO Radio*. Retrieved from http://mynorthwest.com/
11/2638292/State-schools-chief-says-metal-detectors-not-a-practical-response
-to-threats

Haider-Markel, D.P., & Joslyn, M.R. (2001). Gun policy, opinion, tragedy, and blame attribution: The conditional influence of issue frames. *Journal of Politics*, *63*(2), 520–543.

Halbfinger, D.M. (2003, July 16). National briefing: South: Mississippi: Death toll rises in plant shooting. *New York Times*. Retrieved from http://www.nytimes
.com/2003/07/16/us/national-briefing-south-mississippi-death-toll-rises-in
-plant-shooting.html

Halbfinger, D.M., & Hart, A. (2003, July 9). Man kills 5 co-workers at plant and himself. *New York Times*. Retrieved from http://www.nytimes.com/2003/07/
09/us/man-kills-5-co-workers-at-plant-and-himself.html

Halbig, W.W. (2000). Breaking the code of silence: A school security expert says student silence is our worst enemy. *American School Board Journal, 183*(3), 34–35.

Halligan, T. (2009). Safety systems: Technologies, programs help colleges react in emergencies. *Community College Journal, 79*(6), 16–18.

Halsey III, A. (2015, June 3). Why the TSA catches your water bottle, but guns and bombs get through. *Washington Post*. Retrieved from http://www.washingtonpost
.com/local/trafficandcommuting/why-the-tsa-catches-your-water-bottle-but-guns
-and-bombs-get-through/2015/06/03/7e0596fc-0a07-11e5-95fd-d580f1c5d44e
_story.html

Hamblen, M. (2008, April 15). Va. Tech tragedy led other schools to embrace emergency communications. *ComputerWorld, 42*, 20. Retrieved from http://www
.computerworld.com/article/2536720/mobile-wireless/va—tech-tragedy-led
-other-schools-to-embrace-emergency-communications.html

Hamilton, W.L. (1999, May 6). How suburban design is failing teenagers. *New York Times*. Retrieved from http://www.nytimes.com/1999/05/06/garden/how
-suburban-design-is-failing-teen-agers.html

Hanson, L.T. (2002). Psst! Janie's got a gun: Anonymous tips and Fourth Amendment search and seizure rights in schools. *Georgia Law Review, 37*(1), 267–394.

Harmon, A. (2012, December 18). Fearing a stigma for people with autism. New York Times. Retrieved from http://www.nytimes.com/2012/12/18/health/
fearing-a-stigma-for-people-with-autism.html

Harris, C., & Kiefer, M. (2011, May 25). Judge finds Jared Loughner incompetent to stand trial. *Arizona Republic*. Retrieved from http://www.azcentral.com/
news/articles/2011/05/25/20110525gabriel-giffords-shot-jared-loughner
-competncy-hearing.html

Harris, J.M., & Harris, R.B. (2012). Rampage violence requires a new type of research. *American Journal of Public Health, 102*(6), 1054–1057.

Harte, T. (2014, November 26). Weapons in our schools – Part 3: Technologically secure. *WNDU 16.* Retrieved from http://www.wndu.com/home/headlines/Weapons-in-Our-Schools-Part-3-Technologically-secure-284020331.html

Hasham, A. (2015, April 16). Eaton Centre shooter Christopher Husbands sentenced to 30 years without parole. *Toronto Star.* Retrieved from http://www.thestar.com/news/crime/2015/04/16/eaton-centre-shooter-christopher-husbands-sentenced-to-30-years-without-parole.html

Hayes, H. (2014, October 13). Cranberry schools prepare for the worst with active shooter training. *CBS Pittsburgh.* Retrieved from http://pittsburgh.cbslocal.com/2014/10/13/cranberry-schools-prepare-for-the-worst-with-active-shooter-training/

Hayes, T.C. (1991, October 17). Gunman kills 22 and himself in Texas cafeteria. *New York Times.* Retrieved from http://www.nytimes.com/1991/10/17/us/gunman-kills-22-and-himself-in-texas-cafeteria.html

Hayes, R., & Hayes, R. (2014). Agent-based simulation of mass shootings: Determining how to limit the scale of a tragedy. *Journal of Artificial Societies & Social Simulation, 17*(2), 5. Retrieved from http://jasss.soc.surrey.ac.uk/17/2/5.html

Healy, J. (2013, May 13). Mental evaluations endorse insanity plea in Colorado shootings, defense says. *New York Times.* Retrieved from http://www.nytimes.com/2013/05/14/us/james-holmes-aurora-shooting-suspect-enters-insanity-plea.html

Healy, M. (2015, June 19). It's not just a perception: Mass shootings have become more frequent, data show. *Los Angeles Times.* Retrieved from http://www.latimes.com/science/sciencenow/la-sci-sn-mass-shootings-more-frequent-data-20150618-story.html

Heath, L., & Gilbert, K. (1996). Mass media and fear of crime. *American Behavioral Scientist, 39*(4), 379–386.

Heilbrun, K., Dvoskin, J., & Heilbrun, A. (2009). Toward preventing future tragedies: Mass killings on college campuses, public health, and threat/risk assessment. *Psychological Injury and Law, 2*(2), 93–99.

Henderson, B. (2012, December 18). Connecticut school massacre: Adam Lanza 'spent hours playing Call of Duty.' *Telegraph.* Retrieved from http://www.telegraph.co.uk/news/worldnews/northamerica/usa/9752141/Connecticut-school-massacre-Adam-Lanza-spent-hours-playing-Call-Of-Duty.html

Henry, S. (2000). What is school violence? An integrated definition. *Annals of the American Academy of Political and Social Science, 567,* 16–29.

Henry, S. (2009). School violence beyond Columbine: A complex problem in need of an interdisciplinary analysis. *American Behavioral Scientist, 52*(9), 1246–1265.

Hermida, A. (2010). Twittering the news: The emergence of ambient journalism. *Journalism Practice, 4*(3), 297–308.

Hernandez, T.C., Schildkraut, J., & Elsass, H.J. (2015). *The Sandy Hook Elementary School shooting and changes in mental health legislation: A review of the evidence.* Manuscript submitted for publication (original copy on file with authors).

Herring, K., & Jacobson, L. (2015, June 22). Is Barack Obama correct that mass killings don't happen in other countries? *Politifact.* Retrieved from http://www .politifact.com/truth-o-meter/statements/2015/jun/22/barack-obama/barack -obama-correct-mass-killings-dont-happen-oth/

Hesse, J.M. (2015, June 23). Why are so many mass shootings committed by young white men? *Vice.* Retrieved from http://www.vice.com/read/why-are-so-many -mass-shootings-committed-by-young-white-men-623

Hirschi, T., & Gottfredson, M. (1983). Age and the explanation of crime. *American Journal of Sociology, 89*(3), 552–584.

Hoddle Street massacre. (n.d.). Retrieved from http://ergo.slv.vic.gov.au/explore -history/rebels-outlaws/city-criminals/hoddle-street-massacre

Hoffman, A. (2007, April 20). School threats sweep country. Retrieved from http:// www.washingtonpost.com/wpdyn/content/article/2007/04/19/AR2007041900 918.html

Holusha, J. (2006, October 2). Students killed by gunman at Amish schoolhouse. *New York Times.* Retrieved from http://www.nytimes.com/2006/10/02/us/ 03amishcnd.html

Hooper, J. (2002, April 29). Killer's secret behind revenge attack. *Guardian.* Retrieved from http://www.theguardian.com/world/2002/apr/29/schools .education

Hughes, A.L., & Palen, L. (2009). *Twitter adoption and use in mass convergence and emergency events.* Paper presented at the Sixth International ISCRAM Conference, Gothenburg, Sweden. Retrieved from http://www.researchgate .net/publication/215500880_Twitter_adoption_and_use_in_mass_convergence _and_emergency_events/file/d912f5112a31de0455.pdf

Hunt, T. (2014, November 15). Flashback: The Aramoana massacre. *Stuff.* Retrieved from http://www.stuff.co.nz/national/crime/63230292/Flashback-The -Aramoana-massacre

Injured Columbine student settles suit vs. sheriff's officials. (2004, March 3). *Orlando Sentinel.* Retrieved from http://articles.orlandosentinel.com/2004-03 -03/news/0403030245_1_ireland-columbine-lawsuit-against-sheriff

Insane chemist tries to murder. (1919, August 9). *Sausalito News.* p. 2. Retrieved from http://cdnc.ucr.edu/cgi-bin/cdnc?a=d&d=SN19190809.2.24&e=———— en–20-SN-1–txt-txIN-sausalito————

Ireland v. Jefferson County Sheriff's Department, 193 F.Supp.2d 1201 (2002).

IRIN. (1999, November 8). Burundi: Soldier sentenced to death. *IRIN.* Retrieved from http://www.irinnews.org/report/10343/burundi-soldier-sentenced-to -death

Italian killer slain by police. (1956, July 4). *Saskatoon Star-Phoenix.* p. 11. Retrieved from https://news.google.com/newspapers?id=PL9kAAAAIBAJ&sjid=Dm 8NAAAAIBAJ&pg=3135,192217&hl=en

Italian runs amok. (1900, September 15). *New York Times.* p. 6. Retrieved from http://timesmachine.nytimes.com/timesmachine/1900/09/15/105751037.html ?pageNumber=6

Jaccarino, M. (2013, September 12). 'Training simulation:' Mass killers often share obsession with violent video games. *Fox News.* Retrieved from http://www .foxnews.com/tech/2013/09/12/training-simulation-mass-killers-often-share -obsession-with-violent-video-games/

James Holmes, Colorado shooting suspect, saw psychiatrist who specializes in schizophrenia: What is it? (2012, July 30). *Huffington Post.* Retrieved from http:// www.huffingtonpost.com/2012/07/30/james-holmes-schizophrenia-mental -health_n_1720163.html

James v. Meow Media, Inc., 300 F. 3d 683 (2002).

Janicek, K. (2015, February 24). 9 dead including gunmen in Czech restaurant shooting. *Associated Press.* Retrieved from http://bigstory.ap.org/article/ 168fb416b841447d870ccc9890198bbc/mayor-8-dead-czech-restaurant -shooting

Jankowski, P. (2011, October 16). Survivors reflect on Oct. 16, 1991, Luby's shooting. *Killeen Daily Herald.* Retrieved from http://kdhnews.com/news/survivors -reflect-on-oct-luby-s-shooting/article_e2660bfc-d24a-5566-a65f-a67a9fe6365b .html

Janowitz, M. (1975). Professional models in journalism: The gatekeeper and the advocate. *Journalism Quarterly, 52*(4), 618–626.

Jany, L. (2012, December 18). 911 Sandy Hook call shows early confusion. *Danbury News Times.* Retrieved from http://www.newstimes.com/policereports/article/ 911-Sandy-Hook-call-shows-early-confusion-4127274.php

Jealousy causes crime. (1913, January 18). *San Francisco Call.* p. 1. Retrieved from http://cdnc.ucr.edu/cgi-bin/cdnc?a=d&d=SFC19130118.2.12&e=———— en–20–1–txt-txIN————

Jefferson County Sheriff's Office. (1999a). *Columbine documents.* Golden, CO: Jefferson County Sheriff's Office Records Unit. Retrieved from http://www .schoolshooters.info/PL/Original_Documents_files/JCSO%20Pages%2010, 001%20-%2010,937.pdf

Jefferson County Sheriff's Office. (1999b). *Columbine documents.* Golden, CO: Jefferson County Sheriff's Office Records Unit. Retrieved from http://www .schoolshooters.info/PL/Original_Documents_files/JCSO%2025,923%20 -%2026,859.pdf

Jewkes, Y.E. (2004). *Media & crime: Key approaches to criminology.* Los Angeles, CA: Sage Publications.

Jilted man kills 10, himself in shooting spree. (2002, February 11). *Dawn.* Retrieved from http://www.dawn.com/news/20340/jilted-man-kills-10-himself-in -shooting-spree

Johansson, B. (2015, July 7). Aurora theater shooting trial day 44: Schizophrenia expert continues testimony. *Aurora Sentinel.* Retrieved from http://www

.aurorasentinel.com/breaking-news/aurora-theater-shooting-trial-day-44
-schizophrenia-expert-continues-testimony/

Johnson, K. (2014, November 3). Schools test gunfire-locator system. *USA Today.*
Retrieved from http://www.usatoday.com/story/news/nation/2014/11/03/
school-shooter-technology/18176599/?utm_source=feedblitz&utm_medium
=FeedBlitzRss&utm_campaign=usatoday-newstopstories

Johnson, M. (2014, December 30). VAS implementing ALICE safety plan. *Vernon
County Broadcaster.* Retrieved from http://lacrossetribune.com/vernonbroad
caster/news/local/vas-implementing-alice-safety-plan/article_dbe8a8ad-8fa9-56
53-bce4-8f75f6104771.html

Johnson, S. (2011, October 3). Dark meaning of bubble-gum Pumped Up Kicks is
tough to chew. *Chicago Tribune.* Retrieved from http://articles.chicagotribune
.com/2011-10-03/entertainment/ct-ent-1004-foster-lyrics-20111004_1_school
-shooting-pop-music-song

Johnson, K., & Frosch, D. (2007, December 11). Police tie Colorado church shootings to one gunman. *New York Times.* Retrieved from http://www.nytimes.com/
2007/12/11/us/11churches.html

Johnson, K., & Kovaleski, S.F. (2012, December 12). Series of turning points limited death toll at Oregon mall. *New York Times.* Retrieved from http://www
.nytimes.com/2012/12/13/us/oregon-mall-closed-after-deadly-shooting.html

Johnson, M.A., & Rascon, J. (2015, July 16). Aurora theater trial: James Holmes
found guilty of murder. *NBC News.* Retrieved from http://www.nbcnews.com/
news/us-news/aurora-theater-trial-jury-reaches-verdict-n393391

Johnstone, J., Hawkins, D., & Michener, A. (1994). Homicide reporting in Chicago
dailies. *Journalism Quarterly, 71*(4), 860–872.

Jojola, J. (2014, February 19). James Holmes to face second mental exam. *USA Today.* Retrieved from http://www.usatoday.com/story/news/nation/2014/02/19/
colorado-theater-suspect-james-holmes-new-mental-exam/5621295/

Jones, L. (2005, November 5). Return to Aramoana. *New Zealand Herald.* Retrieved
from http://www.nzherald.co.nz/nz/news/article.cfm?c_id=1&objectid=10
353715

Jones, T. (n.d.). Dewey defeats Truman. *Chicago Tribune.* Retrieved from http://
www.chicagotribune.com/news/nationworld/politics/chi-chicagodays-dewey
defeats-story-story.html

Jones, B.J., McFalls, J.A., & Gallagher, B.J. (1989). Toward a unified model
for social problems theory. *Journal for the Theory of Social Behavior, 19*(3),
337–356.

Joshi, M. (2009, August 25). Man kills six in Tehran over family dispute. *TopNews.*
Retrieved from http://www.topnews.in/man-kills-six-tehran-over-family
-dispute-2205944

Judge dismisses all but one lawsuit from Columbine attack. (2001, November 28).
New York Times. Retrieved from http://www.nytimes.com/2001/11/28/us/
judge-dismisses-all-but-one-lawsuit-from-columbine-attack.html

Kain, E. (2012, November 24). 'Black Ops 2' tops 11M units sold in first week, no signs of Call of Duty fatigue yet. *Forbes*. Retrieved from http://www.forbes .com/sites/erikkain/2012/11/24/black-ops-2-tops-11m-units-sold-in-first-week -no-signs-of-call-of-duty-fatigue-yet/

Kalin, C. (2015, January 14). Schools ask students to be armed with canned food in case of school shooting. *CNS News*. Retrieved from http://www.cnsnews.com/ blog/curtis-kalin/schools-ask-students-be-armed-canned-food-case-school -shooting

Kalish, R., & Kimmel, M. (2010). Suicide by mass murder: Masculinity, aggrieved entitlement, and rampage school shootings. *Health Sociology Review, 19*(4), 451–464.

Kaminski, R.J., Koons-Witt, B.A., Thompson, N.S., & Weiss, D. (2010). The impacts of Virginia Tech and Northern Illinois University shootings on the fear of crime on campus. *Journal of Criminal Justice, 38*(1), 88–98.

Karam, Z. (2004, January 17). Lebanon executes three convicted murderers despite international protests. *Lebanon Wire*. Retrieved from http://www.lebanonwire .com/0401/04011701LW.asp

Karugaba, M., & Bekunda, C. (2009, May 4). Army apologises over pub shooting. *New Vision*. Retrieved from http://www.newvision.co.ug/D/8/13/680188

Kass, J. (2012, July 27). Five myths about mass shootings. *Washington Post*. Retrieved from https://www.washingtonpost.com/opinions/five-myths-about-mass -shootings/2012/07/27/gJQAcpB8DX_story.html

Kelleher, M. (1997). *Flashpoint: The American mass murderer*. Westport, CT: Praeger.

Kellner, D. (2003). *Media spectacle*. London: Routledge.

Kellner, D. (2008a). *Guys and guns amok: Domestic terrorism and school shootings from the Oklahoma City bombing to the Virginia Tech massacre*. Boulder, CO: Paradigm Publishers.

Kellner, D. (2008b). Media spectacle and the "Massacre at Virginia Tech." In B. Agger & T.W. Luke (Eds.), *There is a gunman on campus* (pp. 29–54). Lanham, MD: Rowman & Littlefield Publishers, Inc.

Kenber, B. (2013, August 28). Nidal Hasan sentenced to death for Fort Hood shooting rampage. *Washington Post*. Retrieved from http://www.washingtonpost.com/ world/national-security/nidal-hasan-sentenced-to-death-for-fort-hood-shooting -rampage/2013/08/28/aad28de2-0ffa-11e3-bdf6-e4fc677d94a1_story.html

Kennedy, S. (2014, November 27). Sarasota lawmaker files bill allowing armed 'safety designee' in schools. *Bradenton Herald*. Retrieved from http://www .bradenton.com/2014/11/27/5499090_sarasota-lawmaker-files-bill-allowing .html?rh=1

Kenyan police officer kills 10 revellers during shooting spree in three bars. (2010, November 7). *The Daily Mail*. Retrieved from http://www.dailymail.co.uk/ news/article-1327431/Kenyan-police-officer-kills-10-revellers-shooting-spree -bars.html?ito=feeds-newsxml

Kepner, R. (2010). Efficiency of the emergency alert system. (Unpublished doctoral dissertation). Washington State University, Pullman, Washington.

Kiefer, M. (2012, August 7). Loughner found competent, pleads guilty in mass shooting. *Arizona Republic*. Retrieved from http://www.azcentral.com/news/articles/2012/08/07/20120807tucson-shooting-loughner-court-hearing.html

Kifner, J. (1970, May 5). 4 Kent State students killed by troops; 8 hurt as shooting follows reported sniping at rally. *New York Times*. pp. 1, 17. Retrieved from http://query.nytimes.com/mem/archive-free/pdf?res=9C03E7DB133EE034BC4D53DFB366838B669EDE

Kiilakoski, T., & Oksanen, A. (2011a). Cultural and peer influences on homicidal violence: A Finnish perspective. *New Directions for Youth Development, 2011* (129), 31–42.

Kiilakoski, T., & Oksanen, A. (2011b). Soundtrack of the school shootings: Cultural script, music and male rage. *Young, 19*(3), 247–269.

Killer at nightclub gets life in prison. (1995, June 29). *Herald-Journal*. p. A9. Retrieved from https://news.google.com/newspapers?nid=1876&dat=19950629&id=77UeAAAAIBAJ&sjid=ZM8EAAAAIBAJ&pg=1684,2867731&hl=en

Killer released on 20-year anniversary of murders. (2014, June 11). *Radio Sweden*. Retrieved from http://sverigesradio.se/sida/artikel.aspx?programid=2054&artikel=5886157

Killings recall Unruh rampage; he slew 13 strangers in Camden. (1966, August 2). *New York Times*. p. 15. Retrieved from http://query.nytimes.com/mem/archive-free/pdf?res=950CEFD71F3DE43BBC4A53DFBE66838D679EDE

Kills five, wounds 20, and is himself slain. (1915, March 7). *New York Times*. pp. 1, 13. Retrieved from http://query.nytimes.com/mem/archive-free/pdf?res=9F04E6DE153BE233A25754C0A9659C946496D6CF

Kills 3, wounds 17, in a classroom. (1913, June 21). *New York Times*. p. 4. Retrieved from http://query.nytimes.com/mem/archive-free/pdf?res=9506E3DF153FE633A25752C2A9609C946296D6CF

Kimmel, M., & Leek, C. (2012, December 23). The unbearable whiteness of suicide-by-mass-murder. *Huffington Post*. Retrieved from http://www.huffingtonpost.com/michael-kimmel/the-unbearable-whiteness-_2_b_2350931.html

Kimmel, M.S., & Mahler, M. (2003). Adolescent masculinity, homophobia, and violence: Random school shootings, 1982–2001. *American Behavioral Scientist, 46*(10), 1439–1458.

Kinsey, T. (2014, December 3). New bill would allow armed volunteers on school campuses. *News 13*. Retrieved from http://mynews13.com/content/news/cfnews13/news/article.html/content/news/articles/bn9/2014/12/3/bill_armed_volunteer.html

Kittle, R. (2014, October 15). SC school safety task force: more lockdown drills, officers needed. *WBTW News 13*. Retrieved from http://wbtw.com/2014/10/15/sc-school-safety-task-force-more-lockdown-drills-officers-needed/

Klebold, S. (2009, November). "I will never know why." *O Magazine*. Retrieved from http://www.oprah.com/world/Susan-Klebolds-O-Magazine-Essay-I-Will-Never-Know-Why

Kleck, G. (2009). Mass shootings in schools: The worst possible case for gun control. *American Behavioral Scientist, 52*(10), 1447–1464.

Kluger, J. (2014, May 25). Why mass killers are always male. *Time*. Retrieved from http://time.com/114128/elliott-rodgers-ucsb-santa-barbara-shooter/

Kondolojy, A. (2012, December 17). *Friday night cable ratings: 'Gold Rush' wins night + Sandy Hook news coverage, 'Jungle Gold', 'Duck Dynasty', 'Friday Night Smackdown' & more*. Retrieved from http://tvbythenumbers.zap2it.com/2012/12/17/friday-cable-ratings-gold-rush-wins-night-sandy-hook-news-coverage-jungle -gold-duck-dynasty-friday-night-smackdown-more/162164/

Krajicek, D.J. (1998). *Scooped! Media miss real story on crime while chasing sex, sleaze, and celebrities*. New York, NY: Columbia University Press.

Kuby, R.L., & Kunstler, W.M. (1995). So crazy he thinks he is sane: The Colin Ferguson trial and the competency standard. *Cornell Journal of Law & Public Policy, 5*(1), 19–26.

Kupchik, A., & Bracy, N.L. (2009). The news media on school crime and violence. *Youth Violence and Juvenile Justice, 7*(2), 136–155.

Kuruvilla, C., & Chinese, V. (2013, November 29). Families of Newtown victims say Adam Lanza's mom shares blame for raising a murderer. *New York Daily News*. Retrieved from http://www.nydailynews.com/news/national/newtown -families-blame-adam-lanza-mom-raising-murderer-article-1.1531903

Kwak, H., Lee, C., Park, H., & Moon, S. (2010). *What is Twitter, a social network or news media?* Paper presented at the International World Wide Web Conference, Raleigh, NC. Retrieved from http://product.ubion.co.kr/upload2012022014 2222731/ccres00056/db/_2250_1/embedded/2010-www-twitter.pdf

Kwaru, M.I. (2002, July 16). Nigeria: Soldier to die for Kaduna shootings. *Daily Trust*. Retrieved from http://allafrica.com/stories/200207160721.html

Lacey, M. (2011a, May 25). Suspect in shooting of Giffords ruled unfit for trial. *New York Times*. Retrieved from http://www.nytimes.com/2011/05/26/us/ 26loughner.html

Lacey, M. (2011b, September 28). Tucson shooting suspect to have more treatment. *New York Times*. Retrieved from http://www.nytimes.com/2011/09/29/us/ loughner-makes-court-appearance.html

Lacey, M., & Herszenhorn, D.M. (2011, January 8). In attack's wake, political repercussions. *New York Times*. Retrieved from http://www.nytimes.com/2011/01/ 09/us/politics/09giffords.html

Langman, P. (2009). Rampage school shooters: A typology. *Aggression and Violent Behavior, 14*(1), 79–86.

Lankford, A. (2015). Mass shooters in the USA, 1966–2010: Differences between attackers who live and die. *Justice Quarterly, 32*(2), 360–379.

Larkin, R.W. (2007). *Comprehending Columbine*. Philadelphia, PA: Temple University Press.

Larkin, R.W. (2009). The Columbine legacy: Rampage shootings as political acts. *American Behavioral Scientist, 52*(9), 1309–1326.

Las víctimas de la taberna del San Jorge [Victims of the tavern of San Jorge]. (2000, June 25). *El Tiempo*. Retrieved from http://www.eltiempo.com/archivo/documento/MAM-1243524

Latimer, D. (2008). Text messaging as emergency communication superstar? Nt so gr8. *Educause Review, 43*(3), 84–85.

Laughing, an Australian admits killing 35. (1996, November 7). *New York Times*. Retrieved from http://www.nytimes.com/1996/11/07/world/laughing-an -australian-admits-killing-35.html

Lavergne, G.M. (1997). *A sniper in town: The Charles Whitman mass murders*. Denton: University of North Texas Press.

Lawrence, R.G., & Birkland, T.A. (2004). Guns, Hollywood, and school safety: Defining the school-shooting problem across public arenas. *Social Science Quarterly, 85*(5), 1193–1207.

Lea, L. (2015, February 17). Nurses get medical training for school shootings. *News 4 San Antonio*. Retrieved from http://news4sanantonio.com/m/news/features/ health-news/stories/Nurses-get-medical-training-for-school-shootings-85404 .shtml#.VZOVAPlViko

Leary, M.R., Kowalski, R.M., Smith, L., & Phillips, S. (2003). Teasing, rejection, and violence: Case studies of the school shootings. *Aggressive Behavior, 29*(3), 202–214.

Leger, D.L., Welch, W.M., & Bacon, J. (2013, September 17). Shooting rampage at Navy Yard in D.C. leaves 13 dead. *USA Today*. Retrieved from http://www .usatoday.com/story/news/nation/2013/09/16/navy-yard-shooting/2819543/

Lemonick, M.D. (2002, May 6). Germany's Columbine. *Time*. Retrieved from http://faculty.vassar.edu/jeschnei/G230/G230-Time-GsErfurt-060502 .pdf

Leon Capraro. (n.d.). Retrieved from http://monumentaustralia.org.au/themes/ people/crime/display/30559-leon-capraro-

Levin, J., & Fox, J.A. (1996). A psycho-social analysis of mass murder. In T. O'Reilly-Fleming (Ed.), *Serial and mass murder: Theory, research, and policy* (pp. 55–76). Toronto, Canada: Canadian Scholar's Press.

Levin, J., & Madfis, E. (2009). Mass murder at school and cumulative strain: A sequential model. *American Behavioral Scientist, 52*(9), 1227–1245.

Levkulich, J. (2014, November 26). 'Panic button' provides instant response at schools. *WYTV 33 News*. Retrieved from http://wytv.com/2014/11/26/panic -button-provides-instant-response-at-schools/

Levulis, J. (2015, January 15). 'Dented, but not broken' glass innovator hopes to pre-vent tragedy. *Northeast Public Radio*. Retrieved from http://wamc.org/post/ dented-not-broken-glass-innovator-hopes-prevent-tragedy#stream/0

Lewin, T. (1999, May 2). Terror in Littleton: The teenage culture; Arizona high school provides glimpse inside cliques' divisive webs. New York Times. Retrieved from http://www.nytimes.com/1999/05/02/us/terror-littleton-teen-age-culture -arizona-high-school-provides-glimpse-inside.html?pagewanted=all&src=pm

Lewis, M., & Lyall, S. (2012, August 24). Norway mass killer gets the maximum: 21 years. *New York Times.* Retrieved from http://www.nytimes.com/2012/08/25/world/europe/anders-behring-breivik-murder-trial.html?_r=0

Lewis, Scarlett, Administratrix of the Estate of J et al v. The Town of Newtown et al, No. DBD-CV15-6016722-S (Conn. Super. Ct., filed Jan. 21, 2015).

Lichtblau, E. (2013, January 12). Makers of violent video games marshal support to fend off regulation. New York Times. Retrieved from http://www.nytimes.com/2013/01/12/us/politics/makers-of-violent-video-games-marshal-support-to-fend-off-regulation.html?_r=0

Lindberg, N., Oksanen, A., Sailas, E., & Kaltiala-Heino, R. (2012). Adolescents expressing school massacre threats online: Something to be extremely worried about? *Child and Adolescent Psychiatry and Mental Health, 6*(1), 39–46.

Lindgren, S. (2011). YouTube gunmen? Mapping participatory media discourse on school shooting videos. *Media, Culture & Society, 33*(1), 123–136.

Lindsey, R. (1976, July 13). Seven killed, two injured as gunman sprays shots at college in California. *New York Times.* p. 16. Retrieved from http://query.nytimes.com/mem/archive-free/pdf?res=9D00E5DF153FE334BC4B52DFB166838D669EDE

Lindsey, R. (1988, February 18). Love that turned to hate is linked to the killing of 7. *New York Times.* Retrieved from http://www.nytimes.com/1988/02/18/us/love-that-turned-to-hate-is-linked-to-the-killing-of-7.html

Lipschultz, J.H., & Hilt, M.L. (2011). Local television coverage of a mall shooting: Separating facts from fiction in breaking news. *Electronic News, 5*(4), 197–214.

Long, L. (2012, December 15). I am Adam Lanza's mother. *The Blue Review.* Retrieved from http://thebluereview.org/i-am-adam-lanzas-mother/

Lorenzi, R. (2012, December 20). Mass shootings have long history. *Discovery News.* Retrieved from http://news.discovery.com/history/mass-shootings-history-121220.htm

Lott, J.R. (2014, October 12). The FBI's bogus report on mass shootings. *New York Post.* Retrieved from http://nypost.com/2014/10/12/the-fbis-bogus-report-on-mass-shootings/

Loughman, M. (2014, September 26). School security: Lincoln schools work together to stay safe. *The Lincoln Journal.* Retrieved from http://lincoln.wickedlocal.com/article/20140926/NEWS/140927110/12426/NEWS

Louisson, S. (1997, February 11). Mental patient held in N.Z. massacre. *The Moscow Times.* Retrieved from http://www.themoscowtimes.com/news/article/tmt/312043.html

Lovett, L.L. (2012, December 21). Opinion: Female mass shooter can teach us about Adam Lanza. *CNN.* Retrieved from http://inamerica.blogs.cnn.com/2012/12/21/opinion-female-mass-shooter-can-teach-us-about-adam-lanza/

Lovett, I., & Nagourney, A. (2014, May 24). Video rant, then deadly rampage in California town. *New York Times.* Retrieved from http://www.nytimes.com/2014/05/25/us/california-drive-by-shooting.html?_r=1

Lutz, A. (2012, December 14). Why mass shootings have become more common in the U.S. *Business Insider*. Retrieved from http://www.businessinsider.com/why-shootings-have-become-more-common-2012-12

Lyman, R. (2002, July 5). An attack where security is probably the world's tightest. *New York Times*. Retrieved from http://www.nytimes.com/2002/07/05/us/an-attack-where-security-is-probably-the-world-s-tightest.html

MacCormack, Z. (2013, July 2). Massacre postings on Facebook have New Braunfels man locked up. *San Antonio Express News*. Retrieved from http://www.mysanantonio.com/news/local/article/Massacre-postings-have-man-locked-up-4643607.php

Madfis, E. (2014). *The risk of school rampage: Assessing and preventing threats of school violence*. New York: Palgrave Macmillan.

Madison, L. (2011, January 20). Poll: Americans remain split on gun control. *CBS News*. Retrieved from http://www.cbsnews.com/news/poll-americans-remain-split-on-gun-control/

Madman shoots, kills; Captured. (1912, September 29). *The Spokesman Review*. p. 2. Retrieved from https://news.google.com/newspapers?id=TuFVAAAAIBAJ&sjid=ZeADAAAAIBAJ&pg=5274,5564728&dq=&hl=en

Mad teacher kills 15 and wounds 16. (1913, September 6). *New York Times*. p. 2. Retrieved from http://timesmachine.nytimes.com/timesmachine/1913/09/06/100573620.html?pageNumber=2

Maguire, B., Sandage, D., & Weatherby, G.A. (1999). Crime stories as television news: A content analysis of national big city and small town newscasts. *Journal of Criminal Justice and Popular Culture, 7*(1), 1–14.

Maguire, B., Weatherby, G.A., & Mathers, R.A. (2002). Network news coverage of school shootings. *The Social Science Journal, 39*(3), 465–470.

Maher, B.A., & Spitzer, M. (1993). Delusions. In C.G. Costello (Ed.), *Symptoms of schizophrenia* (pp. 92–120). New York: John Wiley & Sons, Inc.

Malphurs, J.E., & Cohen, D. (2002). A newspaper surveillance study of homicide-suicide in the USA. *American Journal of Forensic Medical Pathology, 23*(2), 142–148.

Maniac amok. (1928, May 23). *The Canberra Times*. p. 1. Retrieved from http://trove.nla.gov.au/ndp/del/article/1231457

Man runs amok. (1934, June 22). *Straits Times*. p. 11. Retrieved from http://eresources.nlb.gov.sg/newspapers/Digitised/Article/straitstimes19340622.2.38.aspx

Man who slew 15 insane. (1914, February 5). *New York Times*. p. 4. Retrieved from http://timesmachine.nytimes.com/timesmachine/1914/02/05/100298308.html?pageNumber=4

Marcelo, P. (2014, November 11). School demonstrates 'active shooter' system. *Yahoo News*. Retrieved from http://news.yahoo.com/massachusetts-school-demos-active-shooter-system-212941341.html

Marilyn Manson. (n.d.). Retrieved from http://cookingvinyl.com/artists/marilyn-manson/

Mark, R. (2008, April 16). After Virginia Tech, alert systems proliferate. *eWeek, 25* (13). Retrieved from http://www.eweek.com/c/a/Messaging-and-Collaboration/ After-Virginia-Tech-Alert-Systems-Proliferate

Markey, P.M., French, J.E., & Markey, C.N. (2015). Violent movies and severe acts of violence: Sensationalism versus science. *Human Communication Research, 41*(2), 155–173.

Markey, P.M., Markey, C.N., & French, J.E. (2014). Violent video games and real-world violence: Rhetoric versus data. *Psychology of Popular Media Culture.* Retrieved from http://id-libre.org/projet-autoblog/autoblogs/wwwpsyetgeek com_b5b05cdb291029679998f4bbf13bf6d0c1b27186/media/bb7b64e0 .ppmc_-_vvgs_and_real-world_violence2.pdf

Martin, C. (2014, December 27). Out of tragedy, a protective glass for schools. *New York Times.* Retrieved from http://www.nytimes.com/2014/12/28/technology/ out-of-tragedy-a-protective-glass-for-schools.html?_r=0

Martin, D. (1984, May 9). Soldier in Quebec opens fire at legislature, killing three. *New York Times.* Retrieved from http://www.nytimes.com/1984/05/09/world/ soldier-in-quebec-opens-fire-at-legislature-killing-three.html

Martin, M.L. (2008). Lessons learned from the Virginia Tech tragedy. *Journal of Collective Bargaining in the Academy, 0*(3), 1–8.

Martin, M.L., & Snyder, A.E. (2011). Recent devastating tragedies: Lessons learned. *Journal of Race & Policy, 7*(1), 98–110.

Martinez, M. (2012, December 15). Slain Connecticut principal remembered as energetic, positive, passionate. *CNN.* Retrieved from http://www.cnn.com/ 2012/12/14/us/connecticut-shooting-school-principal/index.html

Mass. Officials to hold safe schools summit in Holyoke. (2014, November 16). *WCVB 5.* Retrieved from http://www.wcvb.com/news/mass-officials-to-hold -safe-school-summit-in-holyoke/29750252

Massacre at police station tied to bribes. (1997, June 12). *Nation.* Retrieved from https://news.google.com/newspapers? nid=sszUF3NjhM4C&dat=19970612&printsec=frontpage&hl=en

Massacre gunman's deadly infatuation with Emily. (2007, April 17). *London Evening Standard.* Retrieved from http://www.standard.co.uk/news/massacre-gunmans -deadly-infatuation-with-emily-7238319.html

Massacre toll rises to 16 as two more victims die. (1987, August 22). *The Glasgow Herald.* p. 3. Retrieved from https://news.google.com/newspapers?nid=2507 &dat=19870822&id=-RI1AAAAIBAJ&sjid=yKULAAAAIBAJ&pg=4112,522 2288&hl=en

Mastrodicasa, J. (2008). Technology use in campus crisis. *New Directions for Student Services, 2008*(124), 37–53.

Mauer, M. (2001). The causes and consequences of prison growth in the United States. *Punishment & Society, 3*(1), 9–20.

Mayors against Illegal Guns. (2013). *Analysis of recent mass shootings.* Retrieved from http://libcloud.s3.amazonaws.com/9/56/4/1242/1/analysis-of-recent-mass -shootings.pdf.

Mayr, A., & Machin, D. (2012). *The language of crime and deviance: An introduction to critical linguistic analysis in media and popular culture.* London: Continuum International Publishing Group.

McCarter, M. (2014, September 29). Schools, cities have 'responsibility' for safety, Battle says, supporting monitoring of social media. *Huntsville Times.* Retrieved from http://www.al.com/news/huntsville/index.ssf/2014/09/battle_on_schools .html

McClanahan, M. (2015, June 19). Safety in a mass shooting situation. *WIAT.* Retrieved from http://wiat.com/2015/06/19/safety-in-a-mass-shooting -situation/

McCombs, M.E. (1997). Building consensus: The news media's agenda-setting roles. *Political Communication, 14*(4), 433–443.

McCombs, M.E., & Shaw, D.L. (1972). The agenda-setting function of the mass media. *The Public Opinion Quarterly, 36*(2), 176–187.

McCormack, D. (2012, December 14). Murdered principal's haunting pictures of Sandy Hook children practicing their evacuation drill – just days before massacre. *Daily Mail.* Retrieved from http://www.dailymail.co.uk/news/article -2248426/Connecticut-massacre-Heart-breaking-pictures-Sandy-Hook -Elementary-School-just-days-shooting.html

McCoy, L. (2015, January 22). Trumball schools dial into state tip line for threat alerts. *WFMJ.com.* Retrieved from http://www.wfmj.com/story/27872209/ trumbull-schools-dial-into-state-tip-line-for-threat-alerts

McCracken, H. (2014, February 4). Facebook turns 10: What if it had never been invented? *Time.* Retrieved from http://time.com/4004/facebook-anniversary/

McDowall, K. (2012, August 1). Remembering the UT tower shooting, 46 years later. *Alcade.* Retrieved from http://alcalde.texasexes.org/2012/08/ remembering-the-ut-tower-shooting-46-years-later/

McElvaine, R.S. (1993). *The Great Depression: America, 1929–1941.* New York, NY: Three Rivers Press.

McFadden, R.D. (1974, December 31). 3 killed and 9 wounded by an upstate sniper, 18. *New York Times.* pp. 45, 48. Retrieved from http://query.nytimes .com/mem/archive-free/pdf?res=9904E2D81F38EF3ABC4950DFB467838F6 69EDE

McFadden, R.D. (2007, December 10). 2 fatal shootings at Colorado religious sites. *New York Times.* Retrieved from http://www.nytimes.com/2007/12/10/us/ 10shooting.html

McFadden, R.D. (2009, November 5). Army doctor held in Ft. Hood rampage. *New York Times.* Retrieved from http://www.nytimes.com/2009/11/06/us/ 06forthood.html

McGinty, E.E., Webster, D.W., Vernick, J.S., & Barry, C.L. (2013). Public opinion on proposals to strengthen U.S. gun laws: Findings from a 2013 survey. In D.W. Webster & J.S. Vernick (Eds.), *Reducing gun violence in America: Informing policy with evidence and analysis* (pp. 239–258). Baltimore, MD: The Johns Hopkins University Press.

McKay, J. (2014, September 30). Intentions to action: Tips for creating a culture of preparedness. *Emergency Management.* Retrieved from http://www.emergency mgmt.com/training/Tips-for-Creating-Culture-Preparedness.html

McKinley, J.C. (2005, August 2). 17 are killed in 2 incidents, fueling Mexicans' fears of violence. *New York Times.* Retrieved from http://www.nytimes.com/2005/08/02/world/americas/17-are-killed-in-2-incidents-fueling-mexicans-fears-of-violence.html

McKinley, J.C. (2009, November 6). She ran to gunfire, and ended it. *New York Times.* Retrieved from http://www.nytimes.com/2009/11/07/us/07police.html

McKinney, R. (2014, October 21). Policy to allow school security officials to carry guns back on table. *Columbia Daily Tribune.* Retrieved from http://www.columbiatribune.com/news/education/policy-to-allow-school-security-officials-to-carry-guns-back/article_05dbca59-5ace-58c8-9047-592f44e88581.html

Medina, J., & Lovett, I. (2013, November 1). Security agent is killed at Los Angeles International Airport. *New York Times.* Retrieved from http://www.nytimes.com/2013/11/02/us/shots-fired-at-airport-in-los-angeles.html?_r=0

Mehtiyeva, A. (2009, April 30). "Loner" shoots 13 dead at Azerbaijan college. *Reuters.* Retrieved from http://www.reuters.com/article/2009/04/30/us-azerbaijan-shooting-idUSTRE53T1NF20090430?feedType=RSS&feedName=topNews&rpc=22&sp=true

Meloy, J.R., & O'Toole, M.E. (2011). The concept of leakage in threat assessment. *Behavioral Sciences and the Law, 29*(4), 513–527.

Michel, P. (2009). *40 ans d'affaires criminelles, 1969–2009* [40 criminal cases, 1969–2009]. Raleigh, NC: Lulu.com.

Milford, P., & Dolmetsch, C. (2014, December 15). Sandy Hook families blame Bushmaster in suit for shooting. *Bloomberg Business.* Retrieved from http://www.bloomberg.com/news/articles/2014-12-15/sandy-hook-families-sue-bushmaster-over-school-shooting

Miller, E. (2013, November 25). Miller: What would have prevented Lanza from mass murder at Sandy Hook? *The Washington Times.* Retrieved from http://www.washingtontimes.com/news/2013/nov/25/adam-lanza-shooting-sandy-hook-elementary-school-n/?page=all

Mingus, W., & Zopf, B. (2010). White means never having to say you're sorry: The racial project in explaining mass shootings. *Social Thought & Research, 31*(1), 57–77.

Ministry of Justice. (2009). *Jokela school shooting on 7 November 2007: Report of the investigation commission.* Helsinki: Finland: Ministry of Justice, Finland. Retrieved from https://schoolshooters.info/sites/default/files/Jokela%20School%20Shooting%20Official%20Report.pdf

Mink, T. (2006). *Sheriff Ted Mink's statement regarding Columbine tapes.* Golden, CO: Jefferson County Sheriff's Office. Retrieved from http://www.co.jefferson.co.us/jeffco/news_uploads/sheriff_statement_061906.pdf

Mitchell, J. (2014, October 16). Columbine visit underscores need for response plan. *eMissourian.* Retrieved from http://www.emissourian.com/local_news/

county/columbine-visit-underscores-need-for-response-plan/article_8dcf2405
-d997-5a76-9a35-c275a906bec1.html

Modern sporting rifle facts. (n.d.). *National Shooting Sports Foundation*. Retrieved from http://www.nssf.org/msr/facts.cfm

Monroe, R. (2012, October 5). *The killer crush: The horror of teen girls, from Columbiners to Beliebers*. Retrieved from http://www.theawl.com/2012/10/the-killer-crush-from-columbiners-to-beliebers

Montgomery, D., Fernandez, M., & Southall, A. (2014, April 2). Iraq veteran at Fort Hood kills 3 and himself in rampage. *New York Times*. Retrieved from http://www.nytimes.com/2014/04/03/us/gunshots-reported-at-fort-hood.html

The Montreal massacre. (2007, February 9). *Ottawa Citizen*. Retrieved from http://www.canada.com/ottawacitizen/features/rapidfire/story.html?id=bd7367a7-1f49-4c5d-949d-7e5a85941b40

Morello, C., Hermann, P., & Williams, C. (2013, September 16). At least 13 dead in Navy Yard shooting; possible suspect at large. *Washington Post*. Retrieved from http://www.washingtonpost.com/local/police-search-for-active-shooter-on-grounds-of-washington-navy-yard-in-southeast-dc/2013/09/16/b1d72b9a-1ecb-11e3-b7d1-7153ad47b549_story.html

Morton, R.J., & Hilts, M.A. (Eds.). (2006). *Serial murder: Multi-disciplinary perspectives for investigators*. Washington, DC: National Center for the Analysis of Violent Crime (NCAVC).

Mozingo, J. (2014, May 25). Frantic parents of shooting suspect raced to Isla Vista during rampage. *Los Angeles Times*. Retrieved from http://www.latimes.com/local/lanow/la-me-ln-frantic-parents-isla-vista-shootings-20140525-story.html

Mukherjee, S. (2013, December 15). One year after Sandy Hook, progress on mental health care is real, but slow. *Think Progress*. Retrieved from http://thinkprogress.org/health/2013/12/15/3047611/mental-health-progress-year-sandy-hook/

Murphy, P., Ketchell, M., & Heasley, A. (2002, October 22). Two die as gunman attacks his own class. *Sydney Morning Herald*. Retrieved from http://www.smh.com.au/articles/2002/10/21/1034561446759.html

Muschert, G.W. (2002). Media and massacre: The social construction of the Columbine story. (Unpublished doctoral dissertation). University of Colorado at Boulder, Boulder, CO.

Muschert, G.W. (2007a). Research in school shootings. *Sociology Compass, 1*(1), 60–80.

Muschert, G.W. (2007b). The Columbine victims and the myth of the juvenile superpredator. *Youth Violence and Juvenile Justice, 5*(4), 351–366.

Muschert, G.W. (2009). Frame-changing in the media coverage of a school shooting: The rise of Columbine as a national concern. *The Social Science Journal, 46*(1), 164–170.

Muschert, G.W. (2010). School shootings. In M. Herzog-Evans (Ed.), *Transnational criminology manual, volume 2* (pp. 73–89). Nijmegen, Netherlands: Wolf Legal Publishing.

Muschert, G.W., & Carr, D. (2006). Media salience and frame changing across events: Coverage of nine school shootings, 1997–2001. *Journalism and Mass Communication Quarterly, 83*(4), 747–766.

Muschert, G.W., Henry, S., Bracy, N.L., and Peguero, A.A. (Eds.). (2014). Responding to school violence: Confronting the Columbine effect. Boulder, CO: Lynne Rienner.

Muschert, G.W., & Larkin, R.W. (2007). The Columbine High School shootings. In S. Chermak & F.Y. Bailey (Eds.), *Crimes and trials of the century* (pp. 253–266). Westport, CT: Praeger.

Muschert, G.W., & Ragnedda, M. (2010). Media and violence control: The framing of school shootings. In W. Heitmeyer, H.G. Haupt, S. Malthaner, & A. Kirschner (Eds.), *The control of violence in modern society: Multidisciplinary perspectives, from school shootings to ethnic violence* (pp. 345–361). New York: Springer Publishing.

Nagourney, A. (2014, May 25). Parents' nightmare: Futile race to stop killings. *New York Times*. Retrieved from http://www.nytimes.com/2014/05/26/us/parents-nightmare-failed-race-to-stop-killings.html

Najteži zločini u Slavoniji [The worst crimes in Slavonia]. (2006, November 12). *Jutarnji*. Retrieved from http://www.jutarnji.hr/najtezi-zlocini-u-slavoniji/161908/

National Alliance on Mental Illness. (2013). *State legislation report 2013: Trends, themes & best practices in state mental health legislation.* Retrieved from http://www.nami.org/Content/NavigationMenu/State_Advocacy/Tools_for_Leaders/2013StateLegislationReportFinal.pdf

National Association of Students Against Violence Everywhere. (n.d.). *National youth violence prevention week.* Retrieved from http://nationalsave.org/what-we-do/save-events/national-youth-violence-prevention-week/

National Post Staff. (2012, June 4). Toronto Eaton Centre suspect Christopher Husbands was on house arrest at time of shooting. *National Post.* Retrieved from http://news.nationalpost.com/toronto/toronto-eaton-centre-suspect-christopher-husbands-was-on-house-arrest-at-time-of-shooting

Nelson, K. (2014, June 12). 'Bulletproof' blanket isn't as promising as it seems. *Mashable.* Retrieved from http://mashable.com/2014/06/12/bulletproof-blanket/

Nevel, J. (2014, October 6). Committee to review security, metal detectors in Springfield public schools. *The State Journal-Register.* Retrieved from http://www.sj-r.com/article/20141006/NEWS/141009659

Newcomb, A. (2012, December 15). 22 kids slashed in China elementary school knife attack. *ABC News.* Retrieved from http://abcnews.go.com/blogs/headlines/2012/12/22-kids-slashed-in-china-elementary-school-knife-attack/

Newman, K.S. (2006). School shootings are a serious problem. In S. Hunnicutt (Ed.), *School shootings* (pp. 10–17). Farmington Hills, MI: Greenhaven Press.

Newman, K.S., & Fox, C. (2009). Repeat tragedy: Rampage shootings in American high school and college settings, 2002–2008. *American Behavioral Scientist, 52*(9), 1286–1308.

Newman, K.S., Fox, C., Harding, D.J., Mehta, J., and Roth, W. (2004). *Rampage: The social roots of school shootings.* New York: Basic Books.

Newport, F. (1999, May 13). Public continues to believe a variety of factors caused Littleton. *Gallup News Service.* Retrieved from http://www.gallup.com/poll/3856/Public-Continues-Believe-Variety-Factors-Caused-Littleton.aspx

Newport, F. (2012, December 19). To stop shootings, Americans focus on police, mental health. *Gallup News Service.* Retrieved from http://www.gallup.com/poll/159422/stop-shootings-americans-focus-police-mental-health.aspx

The News Tribune. (2014, October 28). In Marysville, the most mysterious school shooting. *Bellingham Herald.* Retrieved from http://www.bellinghamherald.com/2014/10/28/3937394/in-marysville-the-most-mysterious.html

New York City Police Department (NYPD). (2010). *Active shooter: Recommendations and analysis for risk mitigation.* New York: NYPD. Retrieved from http://www.nyc.gov/html/nypd/downloads/pdf/counterterrorism/ActiveShooter.pdf

Ngo, E. (2011, September 1). 9/11 memorial honors unborn babies. *Newsday.* Retrieved from http://www.newsday.com/911-anniversary/9-11-memorial-honors-unborn-babies-1.3138677

NICS Improvement Amendments Act of 2007, H.R. 2640, 110th Cong., 1st Sess. (2007).

Nine dead after Finland school shooting. (2007, November 8). *Age.* Retrieved from http://www.theage.com.au/news/world/nine-dead-after-high-school-massacre/2007/11/08/1194329351154.html?page=fullpage#contentSwap1

Nizza, M. (2007, July 5). Tying Columbine to video games. *New York Times.* Retrieved from http://thelede.blogs.nytimes.com/2007/07/05/tieing-columbine-to-video-games/?_r=0

Noe, G. (2013). *Lessons from the Century 16 theatre shooting* [PDF document]. Retrieved from https://www.google.com/url?sa=t&rct=j&q=&esrc=s&source=web&cd=14&cad=rja&uact=8&ved=0CDEQFjADOApqFQoTCLTE9d6xgMcCFYGBDQodHqcAzQ&url=http%3A%2F%2Ficma.org%2FDocuments%2FDocument%2FDocument%2F305481&ei=Yc24VfSPIIGDNp7OgugM&usg=AFQjCNETsLCPtI7R9x18VeQbZ83O1KmF5w&sig2=VooqkGgRGkZ_PJJ6B7NFNQ&bvm=bv.98717601,d.eXY

Northern Illinois University. (2008). *Report of the February 14, 2008 shootings at Northern Illinois University.* DeKalb: Northern Illinois University. Retrieved from http://www.niu.edu/feb14report/Feb14report.pdf

Nott, R. (2014, September 29). School safety summit updates parents on SFPS emergency protocols. *Santa Fe New Mexican.* Retrieved from http://www.santafenewmexican.com/news/education/school-safety-summit-updates-parents-on-sfps-emergency-protocols/article_a0e0a22d-06d7-52aa-90f6-b184695147f8.html

NYSAFE Act Gun Reform. (n.d.). Retrieved from https://www.governor.ny.gov/nysafeact/gunreform.

Obama on Charleston: 'This does not happen in other advanced countries.' (2015, June 18). *Guardian.* Retrieved from http://www.theguardian.com/us-news/

2015/jun/18/obama-on-charleston-ive-had-to-make-statements-like-this-too -many-times

Ochsenbein, G. (2011, September 27). Zug shooting spree leaves lasting memories. *SWI*. Retrieved from http://www.swissinfo.ch/eng/zug-shooting-spree-leaves -lasting-memories/31163938

Ogle, J.P., Eckman, M., & Leslie, C.A. (2003). Appearance cues and the shootings at Columbine High: Construction of a social problem in the print media. *Sociological Inquiry, 73*(1), 1–27.

O'Keefe, E. (2014, December 5). Carolyn McCarthy, public face of the gun control movement, is leaving Congress. *Washington Post*. Retrieved from http://www .washingtonpost.com/politics/carolyn-mccarthy-public-face-of-the-gun-control -movement-is-leaving-congress/2014/12/05/b15eb01c-74cd-11e4-bd1b-03009 bd3e984_story.html

Oksanen, A., Hawdon, J., & Räsänen, P. (2014). Glamorizing rampage online: School shooting fan communities on YouTube. *Technology in Society, 39*, 55–67.

Omero, M., Bocian, M., Carpenter, B., DiVall, L., Feldman, D.T., Lake, C., Schoen, D.E., Quinlan, A., Ulbarri, J., & Gerney, A. (2013, March 27). What the public really thinks about guns. *Center for American Progress*. Retrieved from https:// www.americanprogress.org/issues/civil-liberties/report/2013/03/27/58092/ what-the-public-really-thinks-about-guns/

O'Neal, G.S. (1997). Clothes to kill for: An analysis of primary and secondary claims-making in print media. *Sociological Inquiry, 67*(3), 336–349.

O'Neill, A. (2015, April 8). Tsarnaev guilty of all 30 counts in Boston bombing. *CNN*. Retrieved from http://www.cnn.com/2015/04/08/us/boston-marathon -bombing-trial/

Osborne, M., & Dredze, M. (2014). *Facebook, Twitter and Google Plus for breaking news: Is there a winner?* Paper presented at the International AAAI Conference on Weblogs and Social Media, Ann Arbor, MI. Retrieved from http://home pages.inf.ed.ac.uk/miles/papers/icwsm14.pdf

O'Toole, M.E. (2000). *The school shooter: A threat assessment perspective*. Quantico, VA: Critical Incident Response Group, FBI Academy, National Center for the Analysis of Violent Crime.

Outlaws slay judge in court; Also kill the prosecutor and sheriff at Hillsville, VA. (1912, March 15). *New York Times*. pp. 1, 2. Retrieved from http://query .nytimes.com/mem/archive-free/pdf? res=9A02E1DB143CE633A25756C1A9659C946396D6CF

Page, S. (2014, September 28). Gabby Giffords' comeback: Word by word, step by step. *USA Today*. Retrieved from http://www.usatoday.com/story/news/politics/ 2014/09/28/day-in-the-life-of-gabby-giffords/16281013/

Pankratz, H. (2003, February 7). Lawsuit is settled in school shootings; Case blamed drug in Columbine attack. *Denver Post*. p. B-01. Retrieved from http://go.gale group.com.ezproxy.oswego.edu:2048/ps/i.do?id=GALE%7CA97353745&v=2 .1&u=oswego&it=r&p=ITOF&sw=w&asid=a754603430e2a8e0a9e9ffeb5af9f6c6

Park, A. (2014, March 11). Don't blame Adam Lanza's violence on Asperger's. *Time*. Retrieved from http://time.com/19957/adam-lanzas-violence-wasnt-typical-of-aspergers/

Parker, R.J. (2012). *Rampage: Spree killers and mass murderers*. Toronto: R.J. Parker Publication, Inc.

Parker, R. (2014, September 30). Colorado theater massacre trial can be televised, judge rules. *Los Angeles Times*. Retrieved from http://www.latimes.com/nation/nationnow/la-na-nn-aurora-theater-trial-televised-20140930-story.html

Patient Protection and Affordable Care Act, 42 U.S.C. § 18001 (2010).

Paton, N.E. (2012). Media participation of school shooters and their fans. In G.W. Muschert & J. Sumiala (Eds.), *School shootings: Mediatized violence in a global age* (pp. 203–230). Bingley, United Kingdom: Emerald Publishing Group Limited.

Patten, D. (2014, August 17). Cinemark again denied attempt to toss Colorado theater shooting lawsuits. *Deadline.com*. Retrieved from http://deadline.com/2014/08/cinemark-aurora-theater-shooting-lawsuit-jury-dark-knight-rises-820639/

Patton, D.U., Hong, J.S., Ranney, M., Patel, S., Kelley, C., Eschmann, R., & Washington, T. (2014). Social media as a vector for youth violence: A review of the literature. *Computers in Human Behavior, 35*, 548–553.

Paulsen, D. (2003). Murder in black and white: The newspaper coverage of homicide in Houston. *Homicide Studies, 7*(3), 289–317.

Payne, A. (2014, December 10). New school administrators receive active shooter training. *MetroNews*. Retrieved from http://wvmetronews.com/2014/12/10/new-school-administrators-receive-active-shooter-training/

PC kills eight in shooting spree. (1992, August 26). *New Straits Times*. Retrieved from https://news.google.com/newspapers?id=ArFUAAAAIBAJ&sjid=YJADAAAAIBAJ&pg=6868,2599671&dq=&hl=en

Pearson, M. (2012, July 27). Court appearance fuels theories about Colorado shooting suspect. *CNN*. Retrieved from http://www.cnn.com/2012/07/24/justice/colorado-shooting-holmes/

Peasant kills seven. (1937, February 12). *The Pittsburgh Press*. p. 14. Retrieved from https://news.google.com/newspapers?id=KOUdAAAAIBAJ&sjid=JEwEAAAAIBAJ&pg=6472,6535156&hl=en

Pérez-Peña, R. (2007, April 21). Media outlets ease off video of killer, but not because of complaints, they say. Retrieved from http://www.nytimes.com/2007/04/21/us/21backlash.html?adxnnl=1&pagewanted=print&adxnnlx=1311093612-RkaNZtlO++0Uw9QKPE606A

Petee, T.A., Padgett, K.G., & York, T.S. (1997). Debunking the stereotype: An examination of mass murder in public places. *Homicide Studies, 1*(4), 317–337.

Peterson, B. (2014, November 30). 'Lockdown' vs. 'silent safety drill': The school security language debate. *Boston Globe*. Retrieved from http://www.bostonglobe.com/ideas/2014/11/30/lockdown-silent-safety-drill-the-school-security-language-debate/v30JvvEZR8T2R8dARoGG2H/story.html#

Peterson, S. (2014, November 10). At Sandy Hook's new school, striving for invisible security. *Curbed*. Retrieved from http://curbed.com/archives/2014/11/10/svigals-partners-safety-sandy-hook-design.php

Petrosino, A.J., Fellow, S., & Brensilber, D. (1997). Convenient victims: A research note. *Criminal Justice Policy Review, 8*(4), 405–420.

Pew Research Center for the People & the Press. (1999, December 28). *Columbine shooting biggest news draw of 1999*. Retrieved from http://people-press.org/report/48/columbine-shooting-biggest-news-draw-of-1999

Pew Research Center for the People & the Press. (2000, April 19). *A year after Columbine public looks to parents more than schools to prevent violence*. Retrieved from http://www.people-press.org/2000/04/19/a-year-after-columbine-public-looks-to-parents-more-than-schools-to-prevent-violence/

Pew Research Center for the People & the Press. (2007, April 25). *Widespread interest in Virginia Tech shootings, but public paid closer attention to Columbine*. Retrieved from http://people-press.org/report/322/widespread-interest-in-virginia-tech-shootings

Pew Research Center for the People & the Press. (2011, January 19). *No shift toward gun control after Tucson shootings*. Retrieved from http://www.people-press.org/2011/01/19/no-shift-toward-gun-control-after-tucson-shootings/.

Pew Research Center for the People & the Press. (2012a, July 23). *Colorado shootings capture public's interest*. Retrieved from http://www.people-press.org/2012/07/23/colorado-shootings-capture-publics-interest/.

Pew Research Center for the People & the Press. (2012b, December 17). *Public divided over what Newtown signifies*. Retrieved from http://www.people-press.org/2012/12/17/public-divided-over-what-newtown-signifies/.

Pew Research Center for the People & the Press. (2012c, December 20). *After Newtown, modest change in opinion about gun control*. Retrieved from http://www.people-press.org/2012/12/20/after-newtown-modest-change-in-opinion-about-gun-control/.

Pew Research Center for the People & the Press. (2013, April 23). *Most expect 'occasional acts of terrorism' in the future*. Retrieved from http://www.people-press.org/2013/04/23/most-expect-occasional-acts-of-terrorism-in-the-future/

Pew Research Center for the People & the Press. (2014, December 10). *Growing public support for gun rights*. Retrieved from http://www.people-press.org/2014/12/10/growing-public-support-for-gun-rights/.

Pew Research Center's Project for Excellence in Journalism. (2006, March 13). *Cable TV audience: 2006 annual report, Fox News vs. CNN*. Retrieved from http://www.journalism.org/node/507

Philippine hospital orderly kills 8 with rifle in rampage. (1995, October 22). *The Orlando Sentinel*. Retrieved from http://articles.orlandosentinel.com/1995-10-22/news/9510220278_1_private-hospital-philippine-hospital-child-hospital

Phone system, 'panic buttons' failed during deadly LAX shooting. (2014, February 27). *RT*. Retrieved from http://rt.com/usa/phone-panic-systems-failed-lax-092/

Pickert, K., & Cloud, J. (2011, January 11). If you think someone is mentally ill: Loughner's six warning signs. *Time*. Retrieved from http://content.time.com/time/nation/article/0,8599,2041733,00.html

Pigee, J. (2014, December 9). Dixon parents learn about school safety procedures. *Sauk Valley.com*. Retrieved from http://m.saukvalley.com/2014/12/08/dixon-parents-learn-about-school-safety-procedures/akr2km7/

Pinckard, C. (2014, November 24). Ohio school district considers putting guns in buildings for teachers, staff (poll). *Daily News*. Retrieved from http://www.cleveland.com/nation/index.ssf/2014/11/ohio_school_district_considers.html

Piquero, A.R., MacDonald, J., Dobrin, A., Daigle, L.E., & Cullen, F.T. (2005). Self-control, violent offending, and homicide victimization: Assessing the general theory of crime. *Journal of Quantitative Criminology, 21*(1), 55–71.

Plotts, A. (2014, December 5). Local law enforcement develops plan for safer schools. *Circleville Herald*. Retrieved from http://www.circlevilleherald.com/news/local-law-enforment-develops-plan-for-safer-schools/article_65bb390b-30ba-5c61-aaa7-0a06fd44b036.html

Plumer, B. (2012, December 14). Why are mass shootings becoming more common? *Washington Post*. Retrieved from http://www.washingtonpost.com/blogs/wonkblog/wp/2012/12/14/why-are-mass-shootings-becoming-more-frequent/

Pohjanpalo, K. (2008, September 23). Finnish student kills 10 at college, commits suicide. *Bloomberg News*. Retrieved from http://www.bloomberg.com/apps/news?pid=newsarchive&sid=aQMA6H5DksD0&refer=home

Policeman massacres 12. (1994, December 30). *Moscow Times*. Retrieved from http://www.themoscowtimes.com/news/article/policeman-massacres-12/344566.html

Police named officer who shot to death twelve people in Bahir Dar. (2013, May 14). *Addis Standard*. Retrieved from http://addisstandard.com/an-unnamed-police-officer-shot-to-death-twelve-people-in-bahir-dar/

Pollak, J.M., & Kubrin, C.E. (2007). Crime in the news: How crimes, offenders and victims Are portrayed in the media. *Journal of Criminal Justice and Popular Culture, 14*(1), 59–83.

The Port Arthur massacre. (n.d.). Retrieved from http://www.abc.net.au/archives/80days/stories/2012/01/19/3412072.htm

Port Arthur massacre in Australia. (n.d.). Retrieved from http://www.history.com/this-day-in-history/port-arthur-massacre-in-australia

Post-ABC poll: Gun control politics. (2013, April 12). *Washington Post*. Retrieved from http://www.washingtonpost.com/page/2010-2019/WashingtonPost/2013/03/12/National-Politics/Polling/release_217.xml?uuid=Ehn7LIsBEeKbGt6yWKJPLQ

Postmasburg killings stun quiet town. (2002, July 3). *IOL News*. Retrieved from http://www.iol.co.za/news/south-africa/postmasburg-killings-stun-quiet-town-1.89096#.VYxcnPlVhBc

Powers, A. (1999, April 25). The nation; the stresses of youth, the strains of its music. *New York Times*. Retrieved from http://www.nytimes.com/1999/04/25/weekinreview/the-nation-the-stresses-of-youth-the-strains-of-its-music.html

Prendergast, A. (2015, February 2). Columbine killers' basement tapes destroyed. *Westword*. Retrieved from http://www.westword.com/news/columbine-killers-basement-tapes-destroyed-6283043

Presuitti, C. (2013, April 26). Multi, social media play huge role in solving Boston bombing. *Voice of America News*. Retrieved from http://www.voanews.com/content/multi-social-media-play-huge-role-in-solving-boston-bombing/1649774.html

Price, J., & Sandelson, M. (2011, August 19). Police reveal Breivik called twice, broke communication. *The Foreigner*. Retrieved from http://theforeigner.no/pages/news/police-reveal-breivik-called-twice-broke-communication/

Pridemore, W.A. (2005). A cautionary note on using county-level crime and homicide data. *Homicide Studies, 9*(3), 256–268.

Primorye rampage. (2002, August 30). News in brief. *Moscow Times*. Retrieved from http://www.themoscowtimes.com/news/article/news-in-brief/243956.html

Prince, R. (2014, July 27). 9/11 death toll rises as cancer cases soar among emergency workers. *Telegraph*. Retrieved from http://www.telegraph.co.uk/news/world news/northamerica/usa/10994227/911-death-toll-rises-as-cancer-cases-soar-among-emergency-workers.html

Pritchard, D., & Hughes, K. (1997). Patterns of deviance in crime news. *Journal of Communication, 47*(3), 49–67.

'Pumped Up Kicks' & Newtown: Foster the People's song pulled from radio after school shootings. (2012, December 19). *Huffington Post*. Retrieved from http://www.huffingtonpost.com/2012/12/19/pumped-up-kicks-newtown-foster-the-people-school-shooting_n_2329503.html

Purdum, T.S. (2001a, March 6). Shooting at school leaves 2 dead and 13 hurt. *New York Times*. Retrieved from http://www.nytimes.com/2001/03/06/us/shooting-at-school-leaves-2-dead-and-13-hurt.html

Purdum, T.S. (2001b, March 23). Gunman fires on school near site of earlier shooting. *New York Times*. Retrieved from http://www.nytimes.com/2001/03/23/us/gunman-fires-on-school-near-site-of-earlier-shooting.html

Quan, D. (2012, December 21). Band talks 'Pumped Up Kicks' post school shooting. *CNN*. Retrieved from http://marquee.blogs.cnn.com/2012/12/21/foster-the-people-school-shooting/

Quijano, E. (2013, November 27). Sandy Hook victims' loved ones say shooter's mother shares blame. *CBS News*. Retrieved from http://www.cbsnews.com/news/sandy-hook-victims-loved-ones-say-shooter-needed-help/

Quinn, B. (2011, April 9). Gunman kills six and wounds 16 at Dutch shopping centre. *Guardian*. Retrieved from http://www.theguardian.com/world/2011/apr/09/gunman-kills-five-dutch-shopping-centre

Rahman, J. (2015, January 13). School security forum highlights need for armed security guards, metal detectors. *Paterson Times*. Retrieved from http://patersontimes.com/2015/01/13/school-security-forum-highlights-need-for-armed-security-guards-metal-detectors/

Raittila, P., Koljonen, K., Valiverronen, J., Pentti, R., Kari, K., & Jari, V. (2010). *Journalism and school shootings in Finland 2007–2008*. Tampere: Tampere University Press.

Rasmussen, C., & Johnson, G. (2008). The ripple effect of Virginia Tech: Assessing the nationwide impact on campus safety and security policy and practice. *Midwestern Higher Education Compact*. Retrieved from http://files.eric.ed.gov/fulltext/ED502232.pdf

Raurimu killer let out on leave. (2000, June 30). *New Zealand Herald*. Retrieved from http://www.nzherald.co.nz/nz/news/article.cfm?c_id=1&objectid=15231

Rawdon, S. (2014, December 1). Parent group to donate 3007 door barricades. *Licking County News*. Retrieved from http://www.thisweeknews.com/content/stories/lickingcounty/news/2014/12/01/southwest-licking-parent-group-to-donate-307-door-barricades.html

Rayner, G. (2011, July 27). Norway shootings: Anders Behring Breivik surrendered with his hands above his head. *Telegraph*. Retrieved from http://www.telegraph.co.uk/news/worldnews/europe/norway/8666351/Norway-shootings-Anders-Behring-Breivik-surrendered-with-his-hands-above-his-head.html

Reese, S.D. (2007). The framing project: A bridging model for media research revisited. *Journal of Communication, 57*(1), 148–154.

Reid, N. (2009, July 26). Schizophrenic gunman who killed six is released. *Stuff*. Retrieved from http://www.stuff.co.nz/national/crime/2674389/Schizophrenic-gunman-who-killed-six-is-released

Reinhold, R. (1989, January 19). After shooting, horror but few answers. *New York Times*. Retrieved from http://www.nytimes.com/1989/01/19/us/after-shooting-horror-but-few-answers.html

Reinwald, C. (2014, June 10). Muscatine teachers' invention could save your child's life. *WQAD 8*. Retrieved from http://wqad.com/2014/06/10/muscatine-teachers-invention-could-save-your-childs-life/

Renfrew, B. (1992, January 21). Mass killing caused by dispute over price of cattle. *Associated Press*. Retrieved from http://www.apnewsarchive.com/1992/Mass-Killing-Caused-by-Dispute-Over-Price-of-Cattle/id-b0bcf68e215390aea2692b442744d53e

Reuters. (1998, May 13). Rwandan soldier kills seven before being shot. *Daily News*. Retrieved from https://news.google.com/newspapers?id=hEEPAAAAIBAJ&sjid=L4YDAAAAIBAJ&pg=6583,536909&dq=&hl=en

Reuters. (2009, March 11). Teenage gunman takes own life after German school shooting. *DW Akademie*. Retrieved from http://www.dw.com/en/teenage-gunman-takes-own-life-after-german-school-shooting/a-4088804

Reuters. (2013, April 23). Boston Marathon bombing injury total climbs to 264, officials say. *Huffington Post*. Retrieved from http://www.huffingtonpost.com/2013/04/23/boston-marathon-bombing-injury-total_n_3138159.html

Reynolds, J. (2014, October 24). Safety glass in future for county schools. *Times Gazette*. Retrieved from http://www.t-g.com/story/2131390.html

Riccardi, N., & Elliott, D. (2012, October 24). James Holmes, Aurora shooting suspect, made threats months before 'Dark Knight' massacre, prosecutors say. *Huffington Post*. Retrieved from http://www.huffingtonpost.com/2012/08/24/james-holmes-threats-aurora-colorado_n_1828616.html

Richinick, M. (2015a, January 22). Gun manufacturer moves Sandy Hook lawsuit to federal court. *MSNBC*. Retrieved from http://www.msnbc.com/msnbc/gun-manufacturer-moves-sandy-hook-lawsuit-federal-court

Richinick, M. (2015b, June 18). President Obama: 'This type of mass violence does not happen in other advanced countries.' *Newsweek*. Retrieved from http://www.newsweek.com/attorney-general-loretta-lynch-reacts-south-carolina-shooting-344362

Rivera, R., & Robbins, L. (2010, August 3). Troubles preceded Connecticut workplace killing. *New York Times*. Retrieved from http://www.nytimes.com/2010/08/04/nyregion/04shooting.html

Robbins, L. (2010, January 7). Gunman kills 3 co-workers in St. Louis factor and then himself. *New York Times*. Retrieved from http://www.nytimes.com/2010/01/08/us/08gunman.html

Roberts, J. (2003, August 28). 7 dead in Chicago rampage. *CBS News*. Retrieved from http://www.cbsnews.com/news/7-dead-in-chicago-rampage/

Robertson, T. (2006, January 30). Prosecutor: Dozens knew school shooter's plan. *Minnesota Public Radio*. Retrieved from http://news.minnesota.publicradio.org/features/2006/01/30_robertsont_redlake/?refid=0

Robinson, M.B. (2011). *Media coverage of crime and criminal justice*. Durham, NC: Carolina Academic Press.

Rochman, B. (2012, December 19). Guilt by association: Troubling legacy of Sandy Hook may be backlash against children with autism. *Time*. Retrieved from http://healthland.time.com/2012/12/19/guilt-by-associationtroubling-legacy-of-sandy-hook-may-be-backlash-against-children-with-autism/

Rocque, M. (2012). Exploring school rampage shootings: Research, theory, and policy. *The Social Science Journal, 49*(3), 304–313.

Rodger, E. (2014a, May 13). *Being lonely on Spring Break sucks* [video file]. Retrieved from https://www.youtube.com/watch?v=sOAX59sk9nY

Rodger, E. (2014b, May 23). *Why do girls hate me so much?* [video file]. Retrieved from https://www.youtube.com/watch?v=zBvaVWdJRQM

Rodger, E. (2014c, May 23). *Life is so unfair because girls dont want me* [video file]. Retrieved from https://www.youtube.com/watch?v=7KP62TE1prs

Rodger, E. (2014d, May 23). *My reaction to seeing a young couple at the beach, envy* [video file]. Retrieved from https://www.youtube.com/watch?v=9qe7ikxzqe0

Rodger, E. (2014e, May 23). *Elliot Rodger, lonely vlog, life is so unfair* [video file]. Retrieved from https://www.youtube.com/watch?v=-4CressiIo

Rodger, E. (2014f, May 24). *Elliot Rodger's retribution* [video file]. Retrieved from http://www.nytimes.com/video/us/100000002900707/youtube-video-retribution.html

Rodger, E. (n.d.). *My twisted world: The story of Elliot Rodger*. Retrieved from http://www.nytimes.com/interactive/2014/05/25/us/shooting-document.html?_r=1

Rogers, A. (2012, December 28). Why do gunmen kill themselves after committing mass shootings? *Business Insider*. Retrieved from http://www.businessinsider.com/suicide-and-mass-shootings-2012-12

Rohrbough v. Stone, 189 F.Supp.2d 1088 (2001).

Rohrbough v. Stone, 189 F.Supp.2d 1144 (2002).

Romano, A. (2013, March 20). Tumblr's creepy fascination with Ohio school shooter T.J. Lane. *Daily Dot*. Retrieved from http://www.dailydot.com/society/tumblr-tj-lane-ohio-school-shooter-fandom/

Roughan, J. (2012, September 13). NZ memories: Thirteen killed in Aramoana massacre. *New Zealand Herald*. Retrieved from http://www.nzherald.co.nz/nz/news/article.cfm?c_id=1&objectid=10831910

Roy, L. (2009). *No right to remain silent: What we've learned from the tragedy at Virginia Tech*. New York: Three Rivers Press.

Ruegsegger v. Jefferson County Board of County Commissioners, 197 F.Supp.2d 1247 (2001).

Ruegsegger v. Jefferson County School District R-1, 187 F.Supp.2d 1284 (2001).

Russia Today. (2012, November 8). 'Russian Breivik' releases hate manifesto, kills 6 over relationship breakup. *Russia Today*. Retrieved from http://rt.com/news/rigla-killer-five-dead-161/

Russia Today. (2013, September 9). Humanity hating 'Russian Breivik' sentenced to life in jail. *Russia Today*. Retrieved from http://rt.com/news/russian-breivik-massacre-life-609/

Ryan, S. (2014, September 27). Reading, Stoneham and Wakefield seek 'more nimble' school safety protocols. *The Stoneham Sun*. Retrieved from http://stoneham.wickedlocal.com/article/20140927/NEWS/140928763

Saad, L. (1999, April 23). Public views Littleton tragedy as sign of deeper problems in country. *Gallup News*. Retrieved from http://www.gallup.com/poll/3898/public-views-littleton-tragedy-sign-deeper-problems-country.aspx

Saad, L. (2012a, December 27). Americans want stricter gun laws, still oppose bans. *Gallup*. Retrieved from http://www.gallup.com/poll/159569/americans-stricter-gun-laws-oppose-bans.aspx.

Saad, L. (2012b, December 28). Parents' fear for children's safety at school rises slightly. *Gallup*. Retrieved from http://www.gallup.com/poll/159584/parents-fear-children-safety-school-rises-slightly.aspx

Sacco, V.F. (1995). Media constructions of crime. *Annals of the American Academy of Political and Social Science, 539*, 141–154.

Sack, K. (1999, July 30). Shootings in Atlanta: The overview; Gunman in Atlanta slays 9, then himself. *New York Times*. Retrieved from http://www.nytimes .com/1999/07/30/us/shootings-in-atlanta-the-overview-gunman-in-atlanta-slays -9-then-himself.html

Safe & Sound. (n.d.a). *Our model*. Retrieved from http://www.safeandsoundschools .org/our-model-2/

Safe & Sound. (n.d.b). *The straight 'A' safety toolkits: Assess, act, audit*. Retrieved from http://www.safeandsoundschools.org/straight-a-security2/

Salt Lake City Police Department. (2008). *Trolley Square shooting incident investigative summary*. Salt Lake City, UT: Salt Lake City Police Department. Retrieved from http://extras.mnginteractive.com/live/media/site297/2008/0129/ 20080129_023518_trolleyreport.pdf

Sampson, R.J., & Laub, J.H. (2003). Life-course disasters? Trajectories of crime among delinquent boys followed to age 70. *Criminology, 41*(3), 555–592.

Sanburn, J. (2014, September 26). Why the FBI report that mass shootings are up can be misleading. *TIME*. Retrieved from http://time.com/3432950/fbi-mass -shooting-report-misleading/

Sanchez, R. (1998, May 23). Educators pursue solutions to violence crisis; as deadly sprees increase, schools struggle for ways to deal with student anger. *Washington Post*. Retrieved from http://pqasb.pqarchiver.com/washingtonpost/

Sandell, C., McKinley, C., & Ng, C. (2013, June 4). James Holmes' insanity plea accepted by court in Colorado theater massacre. *ABC News*. Retrieved from http://abcnews.go.com/US/james-holmes-insanity-plea-accepted-court-colorado -theater/story?id=19320525

Sanders v. Acclaim Entertainment, Inc., 188 F. Supp. 2d 1264 (2002).

Sanders v. The Board of County Commissioners of the County of Jefferson, Colorado, 192 F.Supp.2d 1094 (2001).

San Diego girl slays 2 with rifle and wounds 9 on school grounds. (1979, January 30). *New York Times*. p. 10. Retrieved from http://query.nytimes.com/mem/archive -free/pdf?res=9B05E5D81639E732A25753C3A9679C946890D6CF

Sandy Hook Advisory Commission. (2015). *Final report of the Sandy Hook Advisory Committee*. Hartford, CT: Sandy Hook Advisory Committee. Retrieved from http://www.shac.ct.gov/SHAC_Final_Report_3-6-2015.pdf

Santa Barbara County Sheriff's Office. (2015). *Isla Vista mass murder, May 23, 2014: Investigative summary*. Santa Barbara, CA: Santa Barbara County Sheriff's Office. Retrieved from http://www.sbsheriff.us/documents/ISLAVISTA INVESTIGATIVESUMMARY.pdf

Santos, F. (2012, August 7). Life term for gunman after guilty plea in Tucson killings. *New York Times*. Retrieved from http://www.nytimes.com/2012/08/08/ us/loughner-pleads-guilty-in-2011-tucson-shootings.html

Sargent, J. (2012, December 15). Connection between Nancy Lanza, mother of Newtown shooter, and Sandy Hook Elementary still in question. *Gawker*. Retrieved from http://gawker.com/5968684/connection-between-nancy-lanza -mother-of-newtown-shooter-and-sandy-hook-elementary-still-in-question

Satterfield, J. (2009, February 10). Church shooter pleads guilty; letter released. *Knoxville News Sentinel.* Retrieved from http://www.knoxnews.com/news/local-news/church-shooter-pleads-guilty-letter-released

Scheufele, D.A., & Tewksbury, D. (2007). Framing, agenda setting, and priming: The evolution of three media effects models. *Journal of Communication, 57*(1), 9–20.

Schildkraut, J. (2012a). Media and massacre: A comparative analysis of the reporting of the 2007 Virginia Tech shootings. *Fast Capitalism, 9*(1). Retrieved from http://www.uta.edu/huma/agger/fastcapitalism/9_1/schildkraut9_1.html.

Schildkraut, J. (2012b). The remote is controlled by the monster: Issues of mediatized violence and school shootings. In G.W. Muschert & J. Sumiala (Eds.), *School shootings: Mediatized violence in a global age* (pp. 231–254). Bingley, United Kingdom: Emerald Publishing Group Limited.

Schildkraut, J. (2014). Mass murder and the mass media: An examination of the media discourse on U.S. rampage shootings, 2000–2012. (Unpublished doctoral dissertation). Texas State University, San Marcos, TX.

Schildkraut, J., & Donley, A.M. (2012). Murder in black: A media distortion analysis of homicides in Baltimore in 2010. *Homicide Studies, 16*(2), 175–196.

Schildkraut, J., & Elsass, H.J. (In press). The influence of media on public attitudes. In L. Wilson (Ed.), *The Wiley handbook of the psychology of mass shootings.* Oxford, UK: Wiley.

Schildkraut, J., Elsass, H.J., and Meredith, K. (2015). *Mass shootings and the media: Why all events are not created equal.* Manuscript submitted for publication (copy on file with authors).

Schildkraut, J., Elsass, H.J., and Muschert, G.W. (In press). Satirizing mass murder: What many think, yet few will say. In L. Eargle (Ed.), *Gun violence in American life.* Lanham, MD: University Press of America.

Schildkraut, J., Elsass, H.J., and Stafford, M.C. (2015). Could it happen here? Moral panics, school shootings, and fear of crime among college students. *Crime, Law and Social Change, 63*(1–2), 91–110.

Schildkraut, J., & Hernandez, T.C. (2014). Laws that bit the bullet: A review of legislative responses to school shootings. *American Journal of Criminal Justice, 39*(2), 358–374.

Schildkraut, J., McKenna, J.M., and Elsass, H.J. (2015). Understanding crisis communications: Examining students' perceptions about campus notification systems. *Security Journal.* doi: 10.1057/sj.2015.9

Schildkraut, J., & Muschert, G.W. (2013). Violent media, guns, and mental illness: The three ring circus of causal factors for school massacres, as related in media discourse. *Fast Capitalism, 10*(1). Retrieved from http://www.uta.edu/huma/agger/fastcapitalism/10_1/schildkraut10_1.html.

Schildkraut, J., & Muschert, G.W. (2014). Media salience and the framing of mass murder in schools: A comparison of the Columbine and Sandy Hook school massacres. *Homicide Studies, 18*(1), 23–43.

Schlott, R. (2013, June 20). Century of massacres: Remembering Bremen, the first-ever school shooting. *Spiegel Online International*. Retrieved from http://www.spiegel.de/international/zeitgeist/a-century-after-the-first-school-shooting-in-bremen-a-906996.html

Schneider, T. (2001). New technologies for school security. *National Clearinghouse for Educational Facilities*. Retrieved from https://scholarsbank.uoregon.edu/xmlui/bitstream/handle/1794/3368/digest145.pdf?sequence=1

Schneider, T. (2007). Crime prevention through environmental design and security technology for schools. *Proceedings of Persistently Safe Schools: The 2007 National Conference on Safe Schools and Communities*. Retrieved from https://www.ncjrs.gov/pdffiles1/ojjdp/grants/226233.pdf?q=student-reports-of-bullying-results-from-the-2001-school#page=235

Schneider, T. (2010a). Mass notification for higher education. *National Clearinghouse for Educational Facilities*. Retrieved from http://files.eric.ed.gov/fulltext/ED508002.pdf

Schneider, T. (2010b). School securities technologies. *National Clearinghouse for Educational Facilities*. Retrieved from http://files.eric.ed.gov/fulltext/ED507917.pdf

Schnurr v. Board of County Commissioners of Jefferson County, 189 F.Supp.2d 1105 (2001).

School gunman stole police pistol, vest. (2005, March 23). *CNN*. Retrieved from http://www.cnn.com/2005/US/03/22/school.shooting/

School shootings trend toward rural, suburban schools. (1999, April 22). *CNN*. Retrieved from http://www.cnn.com/HEALTH/9904/22/suburban.urban/

School teacher's crime: Kills a young woman and then drowns himself. (1902, February 27). *Los Angeles Herald*. p. 8. Retrieved from http://cdnc.ucr.edu/cgi-bin/cdnc?a=d&cl=search&d=LAH19020227.2.123&srpos=1&e=25-02-1902-28-02-1902--en--20-LAH-1--txt-IN-barnett------#

Schoolyard killings: Second student dies, security beefed up. (n.d.). *Nation*. Retrieved from http://www.nationmultimedia.com/home/SCHOOLYARD-KILLINGS-Second-student-dies;-security-80057.html

Schrank, A. (2014, October 31). School safety improvements a statewide priority. *Wyoming Public Radio*. Retrieved from http://wyomingpublicmedia.org/post/school-safety-improvements-statewide-priority

Schreck, C.J., & Miller, J.M. (2003). Sources of fear of crime at school: What is the relative contribution of disorder, individual characteristics, and school security? *Journal of School Violence*, 2(4), 57–79.

Schudson, M. (1989). The sociology of news production. *Media Culture Society*, 11(4), 263–282.

Schulman, A.N. (2013, November 8). What mass killers want – and how to stop them. *Wall Street Journal*. Retrieved from http://www.wsj.com/articles/SB10001424052702303309504579181702252120052

Schwirtz, M. (2012, December 12). 3 dead, including gunman, in shooting at Oregon mall. *New York Times*. Retrieved from http://www.nytimes.com/2012/12/12/us/fatal-shooting-in-oregon-shopping-mall.html

Sedensky, S.J. (2013). *Report of the State's Attorney for the judicial district of Danbury on the shootings at Sandy Hook Elementary School and 36 Yogananda Street, Newtown, Connecticut on December 14, 2012.* Danbury, CT: Office of the State's Attorney, Judicial District of Danbury.

Seelye, K.Q. (1999, May 20). Campaigns find all talk turns to Littleton. *New York Times.* Retrieved from http://www.nytimes.com/1999/05/20/us/campaigns -find-all-talk-turns-to-littleton.html

Sekularac, I. (2011, April 10). Dutch town in shock after shooting rampage. *Reuters.* Retrieved from http://www.reuters.com/article/2011/04/10/us-dutch-shooting -idUSTRE7381P920110410

Seo, D.C., Torabi, M.R., Sa, J., & Blair, E.H. (2012). Campus violence preparedness of U.S. college campuses. *Security Journal, 25*(3), 199–211.

Serazio, M. (2010). Shooting for fame: Spectacular youth, web 2.0 dystopia, and the celebrity anarchy of generation mash-up. *Communication, Culture & Critique, 3* (3), 416–434.

Seynor, E. (2013, June 5). Police arrest 3 suspects in gay youth center shooting. *YNet News.* Retrieved from http://www.ynetnews.com/articles/0,7340,L-438 8862,00.html

Sgueglia, K., & Sanchez, R. (2015, March 15). Sandy Hook families sue estate of shooter's mother. *CNN.* Retrieved from http://www.cnn.com/2015/03/14/us/ connecticut-sandy-hook-lawsuits/

Shelley, L.I. (1981). *Crime and modernization: The impact of industrialization and urbanization on crime.* Carbondale: Southern Illinois University Press.

Sherman, E. (2014, September 26). With school safety, Waltham promotes proactive response. *Waltham News Tribune.* Retrieved from http://waltham.wickedlocal .com/article/20140926/NEWS/140927786/12423/NEWS

Sherring, S. (2012, December 17). St. Pius X shooting survivor reflects on Newtown killings. *Ottawa Sun.* Retrieved from http://www.ottawasun.com/2012/12/17/ st-pius-x-shooting-survivor-reflects-on-newtown-killings

Shocked & sleepless in killer home – Shootout jawan was 'nicest guy.' (2004, November 30). *Telegraph India.* Retrieved from http://www.telegraphindia .com/1041130/asp/nation/story_4067218.asp

Shoels v. Klebold, 375 F.3d 1054 (2004).

Shoels v. Stone, Nos. Civ. 00-B-1614, Civ. 00-B-718, Civ. 01-B-969, 2003 WL 25509224 (D. Col. June 23, 2003).

Shoemaker, P.J. (2006). News and newsworthiness: A commentary. *Communications, 31*(1), 105–111.

Shontell, A. (2012, December 17). What it was like being Ryan Lanza's Facebook friend when the world thought he was a killer. *Business Insider.* Retrieved from http://www.businessinsider.com/what-it-was-like-to-be-ryan-lanzas-facebook -friend-when-the-world-thought-he-was-a-killer-2012-12

Shootings in Atlanta; Cable coverage. (1999, July 30). *New York Times.* Retrieved from http://www.nytimes.com/1999/07/30/us/shootings-in-atlanta-cable -coverage.html

Shot to death at a dance: Fatal affray at a Negro entertainment in the South. (1893, March 27). *San Francisco Call.* p. 1. Retrieved from http://cdnc.ucr.edu/cgi-bin/cdnc?a=d&d=SFC18930327.2.11&e=————————en–20–1–txt-txIN————————

The sickening tweets of internet users with 'crushes' on Batman killer James Holmes. (2012, July 26). *Daily Mail.* Retrieved from http://www.dailymail.co.uk/news/article-2179107/James-Holmes-Sickening-tweets-girls-crushes-cute-Denver-Batman-killer.html

Simmons, J.L. (1965). Public stereotypes of deviants. *Social Problems, 13*(2), 223–232.

Simon, M., and Spellman, J. (2009, November 7). 'Tough woman' cop hailed Fort Hood hero. *CNN.* Retrieved from http://www.cnn.com/2009/CRIME/11/06/fort.hood.munley/index.html?iref=nextin

Simon, S. (2013, December 1). Sandy Hook spurs states' mental health push. *Politico Pro.* Retrieved from http://www.politico.com/story/2013/12/sandy-hook-mental-health-spending-100453.html

Simone Pianetti. (n.d.). Retrieved from http://www.worldlibrary.org/article/whebn0008646201/simone%20pianetti

Simpson, K., & Blevins, J. (1999, May 4). Did Harris preview massacre on 'Doom?' *Denver Post.* Retrieved from http://extras.denverpost.com/news/shot0504f.htm

Singh, R. (1999). Gun politics in America: Continuity and change. *Parliamentary Affairs, 52*(1), 1–18.

Skogan, W.G. (1977). Dimensions of the dark figure of unreported crime. *Crime & Delinquency, 23*(1), 41–50.

Slinger, A. (2014, December 5). Southwest Licking schools order firefighter-designed safety device for every classroom. *WSYX-ABC 6.* Retrieved from http://www.abc6onyourside.com/news/features/top-stories/stories/Southwest-Licking-Schools-Order-Firefighter-Designed-Safety-Device-for-Every-Classroom-61749.shtml#.VYMqIPlVikp

Smith, J.F., and Fitzsimmons, E.G. (2014, January 25). Three dead in shooting at Maryland mall; police call the episode isolated. *New York Times.* Retrieved from http://www.nytimes.com/2014/01/26/us/3-reported-dead-in-maryland-mall-shooting.html

Smith, J.P. (2014, October 27). Delsea to run security drill next week. *The Daily Journal.* Retrieved from http://www.thedailyjournal.com/story/news/local/2014/10/27/delsea-run-security-drill-next-week/18016753/

Smith, P.J. (2013, July 17). School slayings – NZ's place in history of horror crime. *New Zealand Herald.* Retrieved from http://www.nzherald.co.nz/nz/news/article.cfm?c_id=1&objectid=10899013

Smith, Q. (2013, December 9). Clackamas shooting: A year later, impact of the tragedy still being felt at the mall. *Oregonian.* Retrieved from http://www.oregonlive.com/business/index.ssf/2013/12/clackamas_shooting_a_year_late.html

Smith, T.W. (2002). Public opinion about gun policies. *The Future of Children, 12*(2), 154–163.

Snowdon, Q. (2015, July 2). Aurora theater shooting trial day 42: Doctor describes "abnormal" drop in Holmes' IQ. *Aurora Sentinel.* Retrieved from http://www

.aurorasentinel.com/news/aurora-theater-shooting-trial-day-42-doctor-describes
-abnormal-drop-holmes-iq/

Soliwon, D., & Nelson, S. (2012, December 14). Was an innocent person wrongly identified as the Ryan Lanza responsible for the Connecticut elementary school shooting? *U.S. News & World Report.* Retrieved from http://www.usnews.com/news/articles/2012/12/14/was-an-innocent-person-wrongly-identified-as-ryan-lanza-responsible-for-connecticut-elementary-school-shooting

Sollid, S., Rimstad, R., Rehn, M., Nakstad, A.R., Tomlinson, A., Strand, T., Heimdal, H., Nilson, H., & Sandberg, M. (2012). Oslo government district bombing and Utøya island shooting July 22, 2011: The immediate prehospital emergency medical service response. *Scandinavian Journal of Trauma, Resuscitation and Emergency Medicine, 20*(3). doi: 10.1186/1757-7241-20-3

Solochek, J.S. (2014, November 24). Florida school districts may hire armed guards, AG office determines. *Tampa Bay Times.* Retrieved from http://www.tampabay.com/blogs/gradebook/florida-school-districts-may-hire-armed-guards-ag-office-determines/2207702

Solomon, A. (2014, March 17). The reckoning. *New Yorker.* Retrieved from http://www.newyorker.com/magazine/2014/03/17/the-reckoning

Soothill, K., & Grover, C. (1997). A note on computer searches of newspapers. *Sociology, 31*(3), 591–596.

Soraghan, M. (2000). Colorado after Columbine: The gun debate. *State Legislatures, 26*(6), 14–21.

Sorenson, S.B., Manz, J.G., & Berk, R.A. (1998). News media coverage and the epidemiology of homicide. *American Journal of Public Health, 88*(10), 1510–1514.

Soto et al v. Bushmaster Firearms International, LLC et al, No. 3:15-CV-00068-RNC (D. Conn., filed Jan. 14, 2015).

Spector, M., & Kitsuse, J.I. (1977). *Constructing social problems.* Menlo Park, CA: Cummings.

Springhall, J. (1999). Violent media, guns, and moral panics: The Columbine High School massacre, 20 April 1999. *Paedagogica Historica, 35*(3), 621–641.

SST. (n.d.). *SecureCampus.* Retrieved from http://www.shotspotter.com/secure-campus

Stableford, D. (2014, June 13). What is a 'school shooting'? It depends who you ask. *Yahoo News.* Retrieved from http://news.yahoo.com/how-many-school-shootings-since-sandy-hook-150152463.html

Stankiewicz, J.M. (2014, December 19). Enfield officials begin discussion on possibly renewing armed security guards program. *Journal Inquirer.* Retrieved from http://www.journalinquirer.com/page_one/enfield-officials-begin-discussions-on-possibly-renewing-armed-security-guards/article_7654f53c-8790-11e4-b47c-873592329f45.html

States restore, add to mental health spending as Sandy Hook anniversary nears. (2013, December 8). *Fox News.* Retrieved from http://www.foxnews.com/politics/2013/12/08/report-states-restore-add-to-mental-health-spending-as-sandy-hook-anniversary/

The Stationery Office. (1996). *The public inquiry into the shootings at Dunblane Primary School on 13 March 1996.* London: The Stationery Office. Retrieved from https://www.gov.uk/government/uploads/system/uploads/attachment _data/file/276631/3386.pdf

Stebner, B. (2014, January 26). Three people confirmed dead in shooting at suburban Baltimore mall in Columbia, including suspected gunman. *New York Daily News.* Retrieved from http://www.nydailynews.com/news/national/shooting -suburban-baltimore-mall-report-article-1.1591124

Stein, S., & Cherkis, J. (2014, June 16). With school shootings routine, parents turn to bulletproof backpacks, child clothing. *Huffington Post.* Retrieved from http:// www.huffingtonpost.com/2014/06/16/school-shootings_n_5497428.html

Stephens, K.K., Barrett, A.K., & Mahometa, M.J. (2013). Organizational communication in emergencies: Using multiple channels and sources to combat noise and capture attention. *Human Communication Research, 39*(2), 230–251.

Stephens, K.K., Ford, J., Barrett, A.K., & Mahometa, M.J. (2014). *Alert networks of ICT and sources in campus emergencies.* Paper presented at the 11th International ISCRAM Conference, University Park, PA. Retrieved from http://iscram 2014.ist.psu.edu/sites/default/files/misc/proceedings/p30.pdf

Stern, G. (2015, April 13). 10 domestic terrorist attacks since the Oklahoma City bombing. *Knoxville News Sentinel.* Retrieved from http://www.knoxnews.com/ news/domestic-terrorism-since-the-oklahoma-city-bombing-1

Stern, J. (2013, April 16). Boston Marathon bombing: The waves of social media reaction. *ABC News.* Retrieved from http://abcnews.go.com/blogs/technology/ 2013/04/boston-marathon-bombing-the-waves-of-social-media-reaction/

Stevens, A. (2014, October 27). Bond denied for alleged high school game shooter. *The Atlanta Journal-Constitution.* Retrieved from http://www.ajc.com/news/ news/suspect-in-high-school-game-shooting-booked-into-j/nhsNt/

Stevenson, J. (2014, October 27). Safety measures to prepare for school shooter. *Upper Michigan's Source.* Retrieved from http://www.uppermichigansource .com/news/story.aspx?id=1115232#.VZLflflVikq

Stewart, D. (2015, February 17). Sandy Hook families push to move Bushmaster lawsuit back to state court. *Fox CT.* Retrieved from http://foxct.com/2015/02/ 17/sandy-hook-families-push-to-move-bushmaster-lawsuit-back-to-state-court/

Stewart, W. (2012, November 8). Pictured: Gunman seconds before embarking on shooting spree in his office in rampage that has now claimed six lives. *Daily Mail.* Retrieved from http://www.dailymail.co.uk/news/article-2229919/ Dmitry-Vinogradov-Gunman-seconds-embarking-shooting-spree-office-rampage -claimed-lives.html

Stoklasa, R., & Vodstrcilova, P. (2015, February 24). Gunman kills eight in Czech restaurant then kills himself. *Reuters.* Retrieved from http://www.reuters.com/ article/2015/02/24/us-czech-shooting-idUSKBN0LS1OJ20150224

Stoller, G., & Strauss, G. (2013, December 4). Chilling 911 tapes of Sandy Hook massacre released. *USA Today.* Retrieved from http://www.usatoday.com/story/

news/nation/2013/12/04/sandy-hook-school-shooting-911-recordings-to-be
-released-today/3868249/

Stolzenberg, L., & D'Alessio, S.J. (2008). Co-offending and the age-crime curve. *Journal of Research in Crime & Delinquency, 45*(1), 65–86.

Strait, M. (2010). *Enoch Brown: A massacre unmatched.* Retrieved from http://pabook.libraries.psu.edu/palitmap/Enoch.html

Strasburger, V.C., & Donnerstein, E. (2014). The new media of violent video games: Yet same old media problems? *Clinical Pediatrics, 53*(8), 721–725.

Struck, D. (2006, September 14). Montreal massacre: 1 killed, 19 injured by gunman who is slain by police. *San Francisco Gate.* Retrieved from http://www.sfgate.com/news/article/MONTREAL-RAMPAGE-1-killed-19-injured-by-gunman-2469739.php

Student shoots two others, one fatally. (2003, September 25). *New York Times.* Retrieved from http://www.nytimes.com/2003/09/25/us/student-shoots-two-others-one-fatally.html

Suder, J. (2014, December 17). Lawmakers draft school security bill. *Jackson Hole News.* Retrieved from http://www.jhnewsandguide.com/news/legislature/lawmakers-draft-school-security-bill/article_fda76723-f3f3-55fa-9710-b721683e24c3.html

Sullivan, E., Barr, M., & Zezima, K. (2013, April 19). Tamerlan Tsarnaev dead: Boston Marathon bombing suspect one dies in shootout. *Huffington Post.* Retrieved from http://www.huffingtonpost.com/2013/04/19/tamerlan-tsarnaev-dead-boston-bombing-suspect-dies_n_3116056.html

Sumiala, J., & Tikka, M. (2010). "Web first" to death: The media logic of the school shootings in the era of uncertainty. *Nordicom Review: Nordic Research on Media & Communication, 31*(2), 17–29.

Sumiala, J., & Tikka, M. (2011a). Imagining globalized fears: School shooting videos and circulation of violence on YouTube. *Social Anthropology/Anthropologie Sociale, 19*(3), 254–267.

Sumiala, J., & Tikka, M. (2011b). Reality on circulation: School shootings, ritualised communication, and the dark side of the sacred. *ESSACHESS: Journal for Communication Studies, 4*(8), 145–159.

Surette, R. (1992). *Media, crime, & criminal justice: Images and reality.* Pacific Grove, CA: Brooks/Cole Publishing Company.

Surico, J. (2015, July 29). What we know about mass shootings in America in 2015. *Vice.* Retrieved from http://www.vice.com/read/what-we-know-about-mass-shootings-in-america-in-2015-729

Sutter, J.D. (2012, July 20). Theater shooting unfolds in real time on social media. *CNN News.* Retrieved from http://www.cnn.com/2012/07/20/tech/social-media/colorado-shooting-social-media

Swedish mass murderer to walk free after 20 years. (2014, June 11). *The Local.* Retrieved from http://www.thelocal.se/20140611/swedish-mass-murderer-to-walk-free

Sweeten, G., Piquero, A.R., & Steinberg, L. (2013). Age and the explanation of crime, revisited. *Journal of Youth & Adolescence, 42*(6), 921–938.

Swift, A. (2014, October 31). Less than half of Americans support stricter gun laws. *Gallup.* Retrieved from http://www.gallup.com/poll/179045/less-half -americans-support-stricter-gun-laws.aspx.

Tam, D. (2013, January 30). Facebook by the numbers: 1.06 billion monthly active users. *CNET News.* Retrieved from http://news.cnet.com/8301-1023_3 -57566550-93/facebook-by-the-numbers-1.06-billion-monthly-active-users/

Tammen, K. (2015, February 14). Securing schools: Walton beefs up school entrances. *Northwest Florida Daily News.* Retrieved from http://www.nwfdailynews .com/local/securing-schools-walton-beefs-up-school-entrances-1.438192

Tapper, J. (2014). *Transcript from the Lead (12/13/13).* Retrieved from http://www .cnn.com/TRANSCRIPTS/1312/13/cg.02.html (Original work broadcast December 13, 2013).

Tavernise, S., & Preston, J. (2012, February 28). Ohio shooting suspect confesses, prosecutor says. *New York Times.* Retrieved from http://www.nytimes.com/ 2012/02/29/us/ohio-school-shooting-suspect-confesses-prosecutor-says.html? pagewanted=all&_r=0

Taxi gunman Derrick Bird goes on killing rampage in Cumbria in the Lake District of England, killing 12 and injuring 25. (2010, June 4). *Herald Sun.* Retrieved from http://www.heraldsun.com.au/archive/news/gunman-goes-on-killing -rampage-in-lakes-district-of-britain/story-e6frf7lf-1225874762500

Taylor v. Solvay Pharmaceuticals, Inc., 223 F.R.D. 544 (2004).

Teacher who slew 7 denied wish to see pupil perform. (1962, July 25). *Toledo Blade.* Retrieved from https://news.google.com/newspapers?id=H2gUAAAAIB AJ&sjid=KQEEAAAAIBAJ&pg=7282,775520&dq=&hl=en

Tepfer, D. (2015, March 15). Victims' families sue Lanza estate. *Connecticut News.* Retrieved from http://blog.ctnews.com/newsdesk/2015/03/13/victims -families-sue-lanza-estate/

Terkel, A. (2012, December 21). Columbine High School had armed guard during massacre in 1999. *Huffington Post.* Retrieved from http://www.huffingtonpost .com/2012/12/21/columbine-armed-guards_n_2347096.html

Texas training school employees to be undercover, armed marshals. (2014, November 15). *CBS Houston.* Retrieved from http://houston.cbslocal.com/2014/11/ 15/texas-training-school-employees-to-be-undercover-armed-marshals/

Thibeault, M. (2014, December 18). Security measures 'always improving' say school officials. *The Valley Breeze.* Retrieved from http://www.valleybreeze .com/2014-12-10/observer-smithfield-west/security-measures-always-improving -say-school-officials#.VZOCVPlVikp

Thomas, S. (2012, March 3). School districts tough on bullying. *Observer.* Retrieved from http://www.yourhoustonnews.com/lake_houston/news/school -districts-tough-on-bullying/article_ef77db91-9372-52d5-ac2b-503951b 5c1b4.html

Thompson, J.F. (2005, April 7). Texas father charged with assault in football coach's shooting. *USA Today*. Retrieved from http://usatoday30.usatoday.com/news/nation/2005-04-07-coach-shot_x.htm

Thompson, M. (2011, March 4). *How the Virginia Tech shooting changed the Washington Post's reporting and online publishing*. Retrieved from http://www.poynter.org/uncategorized/103954/how-the-virginia-tech-shooting-changed-the-washington-posts-reporting-and-online-publishing/

Thorsen, T. (2005, October 7). Schwarzenegger signs game-restriction bill. *Gamespot*. Retrieved from http://www.gamespot.com/articles/schwarzenegger-signs-game-restriction-bill/1100-6135332/

3 days in hell: Russia mourns Beslan school siege victims 10 years on. (2014, September 1). *Russia Today*. Retrieved from https://www.rt.com/news/183964-beslan-school-hostage-crisis/

Tofani, L. (1994, September 24). Details surface in Chinese officer's shooting spree. *Philadelphia Inquirer*. p. A3. Retrieved from http://search.proquest.com.ezproxy.oswego.edu:2048/docview/286615298/CB6614B1D07E40C9PQ/1?accountid=13025

Tonso, K.L. (2009). Violent masculinities as tropes for school shooters: The Montréal massacre, the Columbine attack, and rethinking schools. *American Behavioral Scientist, 52*(9), 1266–1285.

Traynom v. Cinemark USA, Inc., 940 F.Supp.2d 1339 (2013).

Trifunov, D. (2012, December 14). *Obama, politicians react to Sandy Hook shooting with sadness, questions*. Retrieved from http://www.globalpost.com/dispatch/news/regions/americas/united-states/121214/politicians-react-sandy-hook-shooting-sadness-qu

Tuchman, G. (1978). *Making news: A study in the construction of reality*. New York: Free Press.

Tuoti, G. (2014, September 29). School security experts stress preparation. *Winchester Star*. Retrieved from http://winchester.wickedlocal.com/article/20140929/NEWS/140926520/12423/NEWS

2 convicted in club shooting. (1995, May 13). *Star-News*. p. 7A. Retrieved from https://news.google.com/newspapers?nid=1454&dat=19950513&id=S3paAAAAIBAJ&sjid=gRUEAAAAIBAJ&pg=3261,4979223&hl=en

2 dead in school tragedy; Miss Weed, mentally deranged, shoots her friend Miss Hardee, and herself. (1908, March 12). *New York Times*. p. 3. Retrieved from http://timesmachine.nytimes.com/timesmachine/1908/03/12/104719437.html?pageNumber=3

2 doctors slain in medical center; killer ends life. (1935, December 13). *New York Times*. pp. 1, 3. Retrieved from http://query.nytimes.com/mem/archive/pdf?res=980CEFD61238E13ABC4B52DFB467838E629EDE

Uhlmann, E., & Swanson, J. (2004). Exposure to violent video games increases automatic aggressiveness. *Journal of Adolescence, 27*(1), 41–52.

United Press International. (1966, August 2). Sniper in Texas U. tower kills 12, hits 33; Wife, mother also slain; police kill him. *New York Times.* pp. 1, 14. Retrieved from http://timesmachine.nytimes.com/timesmachine/1966/08/02/issue.html

United Press International. (1972a, August 30). Gunman kills six in shooting spree. *Ellensburg Daily Record.* p. 3. Retrieved from https://news.google.com/newspapers?id=e_UPAAAAIBAJ&sjid=144DAAAAIBAJ&pg=6895,3461989&dq=&hl=en

United Press International. (1972b, August 31). Mental patient charged with B.C. slayings. *Bulletin.* p. 9. Retrieved from https://news.google.com/newspapers?id=2agSAAAAIBAJ&sjid=g_cDAAAAIBAJ&pg=3519,4203016&dq=&hl=en

United Press International. (1977). Berserk policeman kills 13. *Reading Eagle.* Retrieved from https://news.google.com/newspapers?id=2N0hAAAAIBAJ&sjid=4qAFAAAAIBAJ&pg=5174,3423173&dq=&hl=en

United Press International. (1979, November 19). Belgian soldier fires into crowd, kills two persons. *The Eugene Register-Guard.* p. 4A. Retrieved from https://news.google.de/newspapers?id=h4cRAAAAIBAJ&sjid=EeIDAAAAIBAJ&pg=4063,5796818&dq=&hl=de

United Press International. (1983a, June 4). Around the world: Classroom gun rampage leaves 6 Germans dead. *New York Times.* Retrieved from http://www.nytimes.com/1983/06/04/world/around-the-world-classroom-gun-rampage-leaves-6-germans-dead.html

United Press International. (1983b, July 25). Policeman goes berserk, kills 13 people. *Ottawa Citizen.* Retrieved from https://news.google.de/newspapers?id=gtEyAAAAIBAJ&sjid=B-8FAAAAIBAJ&pg=1916,1778591&dq=&hl=de

United Press International. (1989, July 15). French farmer charged in 14 slayings. *Deseret News.* p. 2. Retrieved from https://news.google.com/newspapers?id=PvhSAAAAIBAJ&sjid=8IMDAAAAIBAJ&pg=4443,5614569&dq=&hl=en

Upstate youth in sniper trial a suicide. (1975, November 2). *New York Times.* p. 34. Retrieved from http://query.nytimes.com/mem/archive-free/pdf?res=9906E3DD1431E33ABC4A53DFB767838E669EDE

U.S. Census Bureau. (2011). *Overview of race and Hispanic origin: 2010.* Washington, DC: US Department of Commerce. Retrieved from http://www.census.gov/prod/cen2010/briefs/c2010br-02.pdf

U.S. Department of Defense. (2013). *Internal review of the Washington Navy Yard shooting: A report to the Secretary of Defense.* Washington, DC: Secretary of Defense for Intelligence. Retrieved from http://www.defense.gov/pubs/DoD-Internal-Review-of-the-WNY-Shooting-20-Nov-2013.pdf

U.S. Department of Education. (2007). *Issue brief: Public school practices for violence prevention and reduction: 2003–04.* Washington, DC: National Center for Education Statistics. Retrieved from http://nces.ed.gov/pubs2007/2007010.pdf

U.S. Department of Education. (2013). *Guide for developing high-quality school emergency operations plans.* Washington, DC: U.S. Department of Education. Retrieved from http://www2.ed.gov/about/offices/list/oese/oshs/rems-k-12-guide.pdf

U.S. Department of Homeland Security (DHS). (2008). *Active shooter: How to respond.* Washington, DC: DHS. Retrieved from http://www.dhs.gov/xlibrary/assets/active_shooter_booklet.pdf

U.S. Department of Justice. (2002). *Reporting school violence.* Washington, DC: Office of Justice Programs. Retrieved from https://www.ncjrs.gov/ovc _archives/bulletins/legalseries/bulletin2/ncj189191.pdf

U.S. Department of State. Office of the Historian. (n.d.). *U.S. involvement in the Vietnam War: The Tet Offensive, 1968.* Retrieved from https://history.state.gov/milestones/1961-1968/tet

U.S. Secret Service, National Threat Assessment Center. (2002). Preventing school shootings: A summary of a U.S. Secret Service Safe School Initiative report. *NIJ Journal, 248,* 10–15. Retrieved from https://www.illinois.gov/ready/plan/Documents/PreventingSchoolShootingsSecretService.pdf

Valencia, M.J. (2015, May 15). Dzhokar Tsarnaev gets death penalty for placing Marathon bomb. *Boston Globe.* Retrieved from http://www.bostonglobe.com/metro/2015/05/15/dzhokhar-tsarnaev-death-penalty-sentencing-jury-boston -marathon-bombing/canMEfLmeQJxQ4rFU0sERJ/story.html

van den Heuvel, J., & Houses, B. (2009, August 25). Slachter jaren op verlof [Slaughterer years on leave]. *De Telegraaf.* Retrieved from http://www.telegraaf .nl/binnenland/article20494609.ece

Vann, D. (2013). *Last day on Earth: Portrait of the NIU school shooter.* Athens: University of Georgia Press.

Villapaz, L. (2015, April 27). James Holmes found sane after two mental health evaluations: Prosecutor. *International Business Times.* Retrieved from http://www .ibtimes.com/james-holmes-found-sane-after-two-mental-health-evaluations -prosecutor-1898732

Virginia hoodlums. (1898, December 13). *Los Angeles Herald.* p. 3. Retrieved from http://cdnc.ucr.edu/cgi-bin/cdnc?a=d&d=LAH18981213.2.48&e=——————— en–20–1—txIN————————#

Virginia Tech Review Panel. (2007). *Mass shootings at Virginia Tech April 16, 2007: Report of the review panel.* Arlington, VA: Governor's Office of the Commonwealth of Virginia. Retrieved from http://www.governor.virginia.gov/TempContent/techpanelreport.cfm

Volsky, G. (1982, August 21). Gunman in Miami kills 8 in rampage. *New York Times.* Retrieved from http://www.nytimes.com/1982/08/21/us/gunman-in -miami-kills-8-in-rampage.html

Vossekuil, B., Fein, R.A., Reddy, M., Borum, R., & Modzeleski, W. (2002). *The final report and findings of the Safe School Initiative: Implications for the prevention of school attacks in the United States.* Washington, DC: United States Secret Service and United States Department of Education

Waldron, M. (1966, September 9). Texas sniper's tumor is found 'highly malignant.' *New York Times.* p. 32. Retrieved from http://query.nytimes.com/mem/archive -free/pdf?res=9805E1DC1630E43BBC4153DFBF66838D679EDE

Walker, I. (2015, March 20). Strathfield massacre: How Wade Frankum killed seven and injured six before turning the gun on himself on August 17, 1991. *Daily Telegraph.* Retrieved from http://www.dailytelegraph.com.au/news/strathfield -massacre-how-wade-frankum-killed-seven-and-injured-six-before-turning-gun -on-himself-on-august-17-1991/story-fni0cx4q-1227244405889

Walker, M. (2014, January 29). Social media helps experts understand, prevent school shooters. *USA Today.* Retrieved from http://college.usatoday.com/2014/ 01/29/for-experts-social-media-a-tool-in-understanding-preventing-school -shooters/

Wallace, L. (2015). Responding to violence with guns: Mass shootings and gun acquisition. *The Social Science Journal, 52*(2), 156–167.

Walsh, S., & Mazza, E. (2001, June 21). Protests in Denver over Marilyn Manson gig. *ABC News.* Retrieved from http://abcnews.go.com/Entertainment/story? id=104105&page=1&singlePage=true

Warnick, B.R., Johnson, B.A., & Rocha, S. (2010). Tragedy and the meaning of school shootings. *Educational Theory, 60*(3), 371–390.

Warr, M. (2000). Fear of crime in the United States: Avenues for research and policy. In D. Duffee (Ed.), *Measurement and analysis of crime: Criminal justice 2000.* Washington, DC: U.S. Department of Justice, Office of Justice Programs.

Warr, M., & Stafford, M.C. (1983). Fear of victimization: A look at the proximate causes. *Social Forces, 61*(4), 1033–1043.

Warren, L., & Stebner, B. (2012, December 15). 'It was my brother. I think my mother is dead. Oh my God': Moment accountant sibling of school shooter saw himself named as killer on TV in case of mistaken identity. *The Daily Mail.* Retrieved from http://www.dailymail.co.uk/news/article-2248327/Ryan-Lanza -Moment-brother-Adam-Lanza-saw-CNN-mistakenly-report-Sandy-Hook -shooter.html

Washington Post-ABC News poll. (n.d.). *Washington Post Politics.* Retrieved September 4, 2013 from http://www.washingtonpost.com/wp-srv/politics/polls/ postabcpoll_20121216.html

Weaver, D.H. (2007). Thoughts on agenda setting, framing, and priming. *Journal of Communication, 57*(1), 142–147.

Weaver, D., & Elliott, S.N. (1985). Who sets the agenda for the media? A study of local agenda-building. *Journalism Quarterly, 62*(1), 87–94.

TheWebStats.com. (2011). MSNBC.com. Retrieved from http://www.thewebstats .com/msnbc.com

Webster, R. (2005). *At the fireside: True South African stories, Volume 3.* Claremont, South Africa: Spearhead.

Weiner, J. (2013, December 6). West Orange High shooter a "documented gang member," cops say. *Orlando Sentinel.* Retrieved from http://articles.orlandosentinel .com/2013-12-06/news/os-west-orange-high-shooting-gang-20131206_1_gang -member-gang-affiliation-west-orange-high-school

Weiss, A., & Chermak, S.M. (1998). The news value of African-American victims: An examination of the media's presentation of homicide. *Journal of Crime and Justice, 21*(2), 71–88.

Welsh-Huggins, A. (2015, July 25). School safety: Experts disapprove of new classroom locks. *Columbus Dispatch*. Retrieved from http://www.dispatch.com/content/stories/local/2015/07/25/experts-disapprove-of-new-classroom-locks.html

Why the Sikh temple shooting got less coverage than the Aurora massacre. (2012, August 8). *Week*. Retrieved from http://theweek.com/article/index/231650/why-the-sikh-temple-shooting-got-less-coverage-than-the-aurora-massacre

Wigley, S., & Fontenot, M. (2009). Where media turn during crises: A look at information subsidies and the Virginia Tech Shootings. *Electronic News, 3*(2), 94–108.

Wike, T.L., and Fraser, M.W. (2009). School shootings: Making sense of the senseless. *Aggression and Violent Behavior, 14*(3), 162–169.

Wilgoren, J. (2003, August 28). Man fired by warehouse kills 6 of its 9 employees. *New York Times*. Retrieved from http://www.nytimes.com/2003/08/28/us/man-fired-by-warehouse-kills-6-of-its-9-employees.html

Wilgoren, J. (2005a, March 14). After shootings in Wisconsin, a community asks 'why'? *New York Times*. Retrieved from http://www.nytimes.com/2005/03/14/national/14milwaukee.html

Wilgoren, J. (2005b, March 22). Shooting rampage by student leaves 10 dead on reservation. *New York Times*. Retrieved from http://query.nytimes.com/gst/fullpage.html?res=9C0CE4DA1F3CF931A15750C0A9639C8B63

Willis, J. (2015, June 24). Marilyn Manson says Columbine school shooting 'shut down my career.' *Entertainment Tonight*. Retrieved from http://www.etonline.com/news/166762_marilyn_manson_says_columbine_shootings_ruined_his_career/

Willox, I., & Darby, A. (1987, December 11). Killer had Clifton Hill news clippings. *Age*. Retrieved from https://news.google.com/newspapers?id=FXxVAAAAIBAJ&sjid=BpcDAAAAIBAJ&pg=1404,6649&hl=en

Wilson, M. (2012, February 3). During an ill-fated trip, taking a bullet to the head and beating the odds. *New York Times*. Retrieved from http://www.nytimes.com/2012/02/04/nyregion/taking-a-bullet-to-the-head-and-beating-the-odds.html?_r=0

Wind, A. (2014, October 19). Waterloo schools prepare to provide dangerous intruder training to students. *WCF Courier*. Retrieved from http://wcfcourier.com/news/local/education/waterloo-schools-prepare-to-provide-dangerous-intruder-training-to-students/article_de9185a2-6691-53d6-8b0c-7822e0f58094.html

Wing, N., & Stein, S. (2014, June 10). If it's a school week in America, odds are there will be a school shooting. *Huffington Post*. Retrieved from http://www.huffingtonpost.com/2014/06/10/school-shootings-since-newtown_n_5480209.html

Wintemute, G.J. (2013). Comprehensive background checks for firearm sales: Evidence from gun shows. In D.W. Webster & J.S. Vernick (Eds.), *Reducing gun violence in America: Informing policy with evidence and analysis* (pp. 95–108). Baltimore, MD: The Johns Hopkins University Press.

Wise, T. (2001). School shootings and white denial. *Multicultural Perspectives, 3*(4), 3–4.

Withnall, A., & Lichfield, J. (2015, January 7). Charlie Hebdo shootings: At least 12 killed as shots fired at satirical magazine's Paris office. *Independent*. Retrieved from http://www.independent.co.uk/news/world/europe/charlie-hebdo -shooting-10-killed-as-shots-fired-at-satirical-magazine-headquarters-according-to -reports-9962337.html

Witkin, G. (2012, April 16). On anniversary of Virginia Tech shooting, law to close loophole hasn't accomplished much. *The Center for Public Integrity*. Retrieved from http://www.publicintegrity.org/2012/04/16/8660/anniversary-virginia -tech-shooting-law-close-loophole-hasnt-accomplished-much

Wozniak, K.H. (2015). Public opinion about gun control post-Sandy Hook. *Criminal Justice Policy Review*. doi: 10.1177/0887403415577192.

Wright, M., Levine, R., & Herron, C.R. (1984, July 22). The nation; Day of killing in California. *New York Times*. Retrieved from http://www.nytimes.com/1984/ 07/22/weekinreview/the-nation-day-of-killing-in-california.html

Xie, T. (2014, June 19). Mass shooters have a gender and a race. *Political Research Associates*. Retrieved from http://www.politicalresearch.org/2014/06/19/mass -shooters-have-a-gender-and-a-race/#sthash.bHg5mJqG.dpbs

Yaccino, S., & Davey, M. (2012, October 21). Three killed in shooting at spa in Wisconsin. *New York Times*. Retrieved from http://www.nytimes.com/2012/ 10/22/us/three-killed-in-shooting-at-spa-in-brookfield-wis.html

Yaccino, S., Schwirtz, M., & Santora, M. (2012, August 5). Gunman kills 6 at a Sikh temple near Milwaukee. *New York Times*. Retrieved from http://www.nytimes .com/2012/08/06/us/shooting-reported-at-temple-in-wisconsin.html

Yates, J. (2013, July 31). First U.S. school massacre was in 1764. *Examiner.com*. Retrieved from http://www.examiner.com/article/first-us-school-massacre-was -1764

Yemen executes killer of six. (1997, April 6). *Washington Post*. p. A24. Retrieved from http://go.galegroup.com.ezproxy.oswego.edu:2048/ps/i.do?id=GALE%7CA578 63340&tv=2.1&u=oswego&it=r&p=ITOF&sw=w&asid=966a267c0f172054c 501f63f2221945e

Yemen Post Staff. (2011, June 12). Man on shooting spree kills six in northern Yemen. *Yemen Post*. Retrieved from http://yemenpost.net/Detail123456789 .aspx?ID=3&SubID=3688&MainCat=3

Yemen soldier kills 8 at polling station. (1997, April 28). *Washington Post*. p. A16. Retrieved from http://go.galegroup.com/ps/i.do?id=GALE%7CA5786728 3&v=2.1&u=oswego&it=r&p=ITOF&sw=w&asid=ba46422dd2e387e432c21e 127f2d7147

Young Allen bandit gives up to posse; Claude, worn to exhaustion, throws up pistols when seen in mountain thicket. (1912, March 28). *New York Times*. p. 1. Retrieved from http://query.nytimes.com/mem/archive-free/pdf?res=9A04EFD 8133AE633A2575AC2A9659C946396D6CF

Young, J.R. (2008). For emergency alerts, some colleges try sirens. *The Chronicle of Higher Education, 54*(31), 22.

Zelikow, P. (2005). *The 9/11 Commission report: Final report of the national commission of the terrorist attacks upon the United States.* Washington, DC: Government Printing Office.

Zimmer, B. (2013, May 12). "Boston Strong," the phrase that rallied a city. *Boston Globe*. Retrieved from http://www.bostonglobe.com/ideas/2013/05/11/boston -strong-phrase-that-rallied-city/uNPFaI8Mv4QxsWqpjXBOQO/story.html#

Zino, A. (2008, March 7). 8 killed in Jerusalem terror attack. *YNet News*. Retrieved from http://www.ynetnews.com/articles/0,7340,L-3515985,00.html

Ziv, S. (2014, December 15). Sandy Hook victims' families sue gunmaker. *Newsweek*. Retrieved from http://www.newsweek.com/sandy-hook-victims -families-sue-gunmaker-292000

Zurawik, D. (2014, January 29). Reports claiming to know motive complicate, confuse Columbia mall coverage. *Baltimore Sun*. Retrieved from http://articles .baltimoresun.com/2014-01-29/entertainment/bal-tweets-wbal-nbc-columbia -mall-coverage-20140127_1_nbc-news-tweet-domestic-situation

Index

About the Authors

JACLYN SCHILDKRAUT, PhD, is an assistant professor of public justice at the State University of New York (SUNY) at Oswego. Her research interests include school/mass shootings, homicide trends, mediatization effects, moral panics, and crime theories. She has published in *Homicide Studies, American Journal of Criminal Justice, Fast Capitalism, Security Journal*, and *Crime, Law and Social Change*, as well as other journals and several edited volumes.

H. JAYMI ELSASS, PhD, is a lecturer in the School of Criminal Justice at Texas State University. Her primary research interests include episodic violent crime, moral panics, fear of crime, and juvenile delinquency. She has published in *Criminology; Criminal Justice; Law & Society; Crime, Law, & Social Change; American Journal of Criminal Justice; Security Journal;* and edited volumes.